Spirit Speaks - The Transformation Connection

By Johan Adkins

Bon Nuit Publishing

The names and human characters in this book are fictional and are amorphous amalgams, and only some of them bear some resemblance to real friends and family of Johan Adkins.

©Text Copyright 2010 by author. All rights reserved. Material contained herein may not be reproduced or copied without express permission of the author, Johan Adkins. Permission was granted for the poems and articles previously published in the Transformation Connection Newsletter under the name of Prism Metaphysical Center by DeJon and Marvin "Marvine" Syferd, who are considered contributing authors of this work.

Wyoming sunset photograph by Johan Adkins.

No part of this publication may be reproduced in whole or in part, or stored in a retrieval system, or transmitted in any form by any means, electronic, mechanical, photocopying, recording, or otherwise without written permission from the publisher Bon Nuit Publishing and/or author, Johan Adkins.

See the author's web page at http://www.johanadkins.com

ISBN: 0982758928
ISBN-13: 9780982758922

Library of Congress #1-489346591

Body Mind and Soul/Channeled

Bon Nuit Publishing
1740 H Dell Range Blvd. #142
Cheyenne, WY 82009

Printed in USA, First Printing 2010.

Preface

Practical tools are given in "Spirit Speaks-The Transformation Connection" to help mankind in their individual journeys toward their next transformational evolution. Learn Rock language, called the Pen'l Leina, and how to work in a protected environment in Medicine Wheel Meditations, and how to work with pendulums and divining rods. Hand charts for a Threefold Reading cross the Physical, Emotional and Spiritual aspects to help a person understand where they are on their transformational path. This information has only been available in the past to a very few.

For years, the author Johan Adkins, experienced a virtual "downpour" of information streaming through her fingers as fast as she could type. As she was typing, she was reading the information for the first time. The energy surrounding the direct transmissions was angelic, and intensely full of white light and spiritual protection. It is by that experience, that she understood that a precious gift was being given. This book belongs to everyone and is a message to us all.

It is controversial...it stands conventional understanding of the energies in the universe, the nature of existence and concepts of the divine on its head.

It also comes with a caveat...not one word can be altered so that the message from Spirit is clear. And it is being gifted to you with a request from the author, "Read it with an open heart... and don't kill the messenger."

Dedication

This book is dedicated to the Fleur d'leis who work together to save us all.
To Spirit - who has truly written this book, thank you for your blessed teaching and patient guidance.
Bless you all.
May you receive our love, and wishes for healing, strength wholeness and joy!
I wish this in the perfect way, the perfect number of times.

Johan Adkins

OUTLINE OF SPIRIT SPEAKS

Chapter 1. Spring – Beginnings

    A. Creative Force of Story Teaching and Non-Verbal Teaching
    B. Poetry and Short Stories by Johan Adkins, DeJon and Marvine

Chapter 2. Summer – Awareness

    A. Aromatherapy

    B. Energy Network

Chapter 3. Fall - Change/Ascention

    A. Spirit Speaks

Chapter 4. Winter - Death/Rebirth

    A. Message from Prime

    B. Message from the Creator

CHAPTER 1 SPRING - BEGINNINGS

Creative Force of Story Teaching and Non-Verbal Teaching
By Johan Adkins

Before the written word, "story-telling" was the means to teach some universal truths to all the generations. As anyone who has ever played the game of passing a whispered "secret" down a line of people know, spoken words are often distorted in the telling. That is why many societies and cultures made a very marked point of teaching and learning the creation myths and stories "verbatim." No deviation from the story was allowed. Some cultures took this a step further - even the gestures and intonation had to be recreated and learned <u>exactly</u> as taught. It assured many things; not only were the stories legitimately passed in true form from generation to generation, but the universal tonalities and movements "sang" along with the telling.

Much of the "value" of the spoken word is not so much the words, as setting up universal vibrations and patterns in the telling (and the hearing.) There is more healing and power to the spoken word than many could accept. A word spoken with love behind it - the songs of a young mother to her baby, for example, set up whole ripples and tickles throughout the universe - sending love to all. A word spoken in anger does the same thing unfortunately. The same word with different tonalities sends that emotional/spiritual vibration along the tonality "scale." It is the tone that Spirit and the universe "hear."

Words are very important and very powerful, but they are not as pivotal as the tones and vibrations that "send" them along. That is one reason that the dolphin's "language" is adapted to tones and subtle variations of vibrations and <u>not</u> words. They provide words in their "Song of Universal Healing" (see Water Beings message) for the benefit of humans and not because a word represented a tone.

Poetry has, for centuries, been a very "sound" example of people's ability to tap into something besides the spoken word. The words or strings of words elicit an emotional/spiritual response - a music in the spoken word, or patterns of words. Words that can strike an emotion carry with them the benefit of healing and calming. Many children cannot go to sleep until a parent "reads" a story or sings a lullaby.

Story telling, especially when spoken aloud (with feeling and love behind it, as an actor or parent would read the story,) is not only universally instructive but it also sets up vibrations of healing to all.

The following stories have been "selected" for the vibrational and tonal response that speaking them aloud gives to the reader. They were also pieces gifted to Johan Adkins as creation myths or stories that have a legitimate place in very old cultures and histories. The specific tribes did not go by the names given, but the general, overall stories are stories retold and retold in many cultures.

The poetry by DeJon in the body of the book is meant to be read aloud. DeJon is walking Spirit on Earth. He is beloved of the entire spiritual realm, not only because God/Prime is his active "higher self," but DeJon, the man, has evolved into a wonderful, warm, loving, funny and totally delightful person. He was once a preacher, turned atheist, turned agnostic. He whimsically said that he believes in the energy and the concept of Spirit, he just had problems with the metaphors. He was in his fifties (in 1994 when this was written) and was told several years ago by doctors to quit his high pressure, high paying, high rolling job and go home and tell his family goodby. The doctors did not expect him to live six months. He was grossly overweight and his heart was a piece of "hamburger." DeJon quit his high pressure executive job, moved closer to his family and proceeded to get on a bicycle. He worked as a janitor and did not drive a car unless absolutely necessary. He lost over seventy-five pounds and in the 1990's, he had the metabolism of a 40 year old.

His heart was vastly improved. He coached ten and twelve-year-olds in basketball and played basketball with the best of them.

He lived far beyond his death sentence of six months and totally "rethought" his emotional/physical and spiritual place in life. He lived each day in complete awareness of the moment, for the most part, and found delight in everything. He is a good example for people to follow as he operates in a "mindfulness" that few entities can achieve. He headed a local writer's group, the Wordsmiths, and belonged to another and was working on his own book which he intends to call, "The Ethereal Gem." He doesn't like punctuation or capitalization, as a general rule, because it interrupts the flow of the spoken word. Speak his work aloud and feel the healing. His method of healing has saved and prolonged his life and he offers it to you.

Marvin "Marvine" Syferd is another "precious" Spirit on earth. He began his spiritual journey early in life when his entire family embraced the "I am Activity" in the 1930's. Marvin is from Wyoming and Colorado, and as a young man he joined the Army as a pilot and left as a Lt. Colonel in the Air Guard as a pilot. He has traveled the world in his "movement to the Spiritual" at the feet of the world's healers, the metaphysical, spiritual. and philosophical school, teachers and masters who presented themselves to his attention in his long life. His journeys have taken him to England, Cairo, Rome, and France and all over the globe, and many metaphysical and spiritual disciplines have been explored by him. His interest is in healing, moving and working with energy, listening to the choir of the universe and learning how to work with music and tones and to "really hear." He listens and learns through meditation and rises most days at 4:00 a.m. to sit in meditation...even at 90 years young. He has always seen himself as the student. Yet, he is the Master to those of us priviliaged enough to have been in his presence and listened closely to his wisdom. He does his work quietly and in the background. He is walking Spirit, an Archangel on Earth, and is the physical incarnation and embodiment of the Lord of Hosts. He is also the physical embodiment of an ascended master that so many have spoken to. This ascended master's name is "Serapis Bey." Speak his "work" aloud and feel the healing.

Those of you who read this section aloud will benefit not only yourselves, but the universe. <u>Any</u> writing that has a generally positive and life-affirming message works its magic on those who read it!

Spirit encourages writers to join together in writing or reading groups in order to have the opportunity to read their work aloud and watch the response of the audience. See the wonder on their faces when you have created a work that "heals." The universe appreciates the "creative" effort of those who write to "bring up" the masses!

Spirit works through many writers as it has worked through Johan Adkins in the writing of this book. But Spirit would like to say this to those who experience "divine" help...never, never underestimate your own ability. Spirit chooses "writers" who have chosen to be life-affirming and healing in their overall message. Spirit also chooses writers who would speak the truth despite the consequences.

If you are one of those people who write their thoughts and feelings down in order to "sort" through them, Spirit knows that this practice is very good "psychology" and is cleansing, BUT be sure to, in actual or perceptual fact, burn the papers afterward. Do not "hold," in power, words and tones that are harmful to anything or anyone - even you!

If you do not belong to a writer's group, but love to write, know this. Spirit loves to read and listen to your work! Read it to them and you heal them too!!

Blessings to you all.

*Spring is
A time of doing!
What?
I never know,
but I want to do it so <u>badly</u>
my body can barely contain my heart!*

Johan Adkins

The Garden
By Johan Adkins

*I dance by midnight upon the soft
mother
who, dampened with evening mist is
Tired and waiting for slumber.
Smiling, she watches and lends a
spongy tread.
As fog rises from the earthly bed,
She dances around me!*

Lysette stepped off the porch barefooted and lightly tread on the soft earth which she had worked so diligently all afternoon. The sun was dipping below the horizon. It was the golden time - those few moments in late afternoon when the sun stretched his rays to bathe the earth in his most spellbound glory! Always these few moments of golden lights were too short - just long enough to utter praise and scan every nook and cranny to delight in the subtle golden changes! Lysette tilted her head back and stretched with the sun - soaking in as much golden wonder as time would share with her! Life. What a joy! How lucky she was to be kissed by the sun!

She sat on the newly tilled earth, still warm from the day and watched her toes dig under the darkness. How wonderful the earth felt! So soft. She could hardly wait to plant the wildflower seeds she had so carefully gathered last fall. Death and rebirth - the cycle of time. Plants were somehow a reaffirmation that all that returns to mother earth is reborn in another form - shining and new and so beautiful! Isn't there another word to describe the new shoots bending from the earth to stand tall and blossom into the delicate colors and intricate patterns of flowers? Beautiful, yes, but so much more! Regal? Spiritual? A word is needed beyond beautiful.

    Lysette carefully mixed the seeds in the compost and peat moss mixture and cast them lightly on the bed she had prepared. She laughed as she danced around the ground - using toes and hands to press the seeds into the soil. What a miracle that they find a nesting place on their own in nature's wilderness. She giggled as she imagined that rabbits, ground squirrels, deer and certainly fairies, must gather in the forest and plains to do what she is doing now.

    The new shoots showed their shining greens in just a few weeks. Every day was a day to dance with the water! Just enough water to moisten, but not puddle. Lysette could never resist the temptation to spray the water directly overhead and wait as the cold drops fell upon her - tickling, cold and utterly delightful! It must feel that way to plants as well! The sun glinted off the droplets and rainbows formed in the mist. "See, babies?? Magic!"

Every morning she would awaken to a new life springing from the soft earth. Each afternoon a smiling face would delight her. Cosmos, Baby's Breath, Pansies, Eyebright, Baby Blue Eyes, Flax; what wonderful names for the newborn! Some newborn faces she didn't have a name for so she followed a many generation tradition of making up names! Muddy Bledsoe, Pennywinkle, Starlight O'Hara! Maybe words are not what we need at all. Lysette felt humble in the presence of the delicate pink folds of the four o'clocks. All senses alive, she sensed a gift from each new face as it blessed her with an intimate sharing of scents; each one unique, each a delight! Silently she thanked the flowers for sharing with her, and told each "baby" how "beautiful" they were.

A summer full of new faces as the newborn matured into the adults that die to make the seeds for next summer's babies!

Isn't life a miracle??

Ashtanuga Creation Myth - The Dream Makers
By Johan Adkins

In dreams we return to the Dream Makers who weave the threads of truth and wisdom in our minds. We seek to unravel these threads in the world of the awakened ones. The dream is the reality and speaks the truth. Life is illusion. It is full of strife and chaos. We know this to be true, because we must strive to survive the delusion, but return nightly to the Dream Makers to learn new truths.

My mother, Sheaha of the Snake Clan, told me the story of how the Dream Makers came to be. My brothers and sister of my mother, Sheranah, will join me in our talk together.

In the beginning there was only forces of good and evil. Good was incarnate in an energy form known as the Great One and evil dwelled in the putrefying form of "Yazatn." Our solar system began as a sliver in the eye of the Great One. Because the sliver was annoying, the Great One plucked it from his eye and cast it away into the universe.

Inside the sliver lived a very tiny, wise spider. The spider began to grow and had to eat the wood around him to accommodate his size. At last he grew too large for the sliver, and indeed, had almost consumed his former home! He perched precariously on the sliver and began to spin a silky thread. He threw the thread to surrounding stars to anchor his web. The spider began to weave an intricate pattern.

The weaving was so beautiful that it attracted the attention of an evil sprite. The sprite decided to make it his home, and approached the spider for permission to live within the web. The spider refused, of course! The sprite devised a devious plan and craftily lured the spider away with a false illusion of a beautiful female spider in the distance. The clever sprite concocted the illusion to entice the spider into getting further and further from the web; the closer the spider would come to reaching his "mate," the further away the mate would be. The spider was lonely and followed the lovely illusion.

The sprite quickly moved into the web and began fouling it with evil. Because the sliver at the center of the web was originally a part of the Great One, it held the energy of the Great One which was good and pure. The web vibrated against the foulness that was inhabiting it and created a slight "ping!" that rang in the ears of the Great One like a bell. The Great One followed the sound and came upon the lovely web. He donned a mask of the sprite's evil master, Yazatn, and demanded that the sprite vacate the web. Quickly, the sprite rushed to comply.

Unknown to the Great One, Yazatn was watching the transaction with great interest. He confronted the Great One, and demanded that he justify using a false means to accomplish his own wish. Did not the falseness make a mockery of the Great One's goodness? The Great One reluctantly agreed that this was so and abandoned the web because he considered himself unworthy.

After much time had passed, the spider, who was much wiser to evil sprites, finally returned to his web. He learned of the story that had transpired and felt sadness that the Great One felt such shame. He began to weave more starstuff into the web, avoiding the areas that had been befouled by evil. He worked diligently to weave all the goodness, love and light that he could find into intricate patterns in the web. He wove planets around the center of the web and added moons around the planets. He concentrated on the third planet which he dedicated to his lovely illusive mate and wove mountains, deserts and plains, seas, grand lakes, rivers and streams. So that the land would not be lonely, he wove helpmates in the form of human beings, trees, plants and animals. He built intricacies upon intricacies. The last thing he wove was a lovely mate - a web creation of the illusion he fell in love with.

The Great One heard of the grand feat and visited the web. Its beauty overwhelmed him and he began to cry. His tears caught in the web and where they pooled, the web illusions began to live! He cried until he had brought the entire web to life! The last thing he brought to life was the lovely mate for the lonely spider. The Great One cried so hard it cleansed the shame in his heart and he began to forgive himself.

Suddenly he realized that he had given substance to the entire web world and was now responsible for the new life he had created. The spider and his mate were overjoyed with each other and the lovely world that the Great One had bought to life. They offered their help. The Great One carefully considered the new lives. He decided that he must protect these fragile creatures and the fragile structures they lived upon from the evil one and his minions. He was at a disadvantage, because now, due to his shame, he could only fight the evil one in symbolic terms and in an indirect manner. He could rally his forces for good, but only if the spider and his mate would intervene directly with the new world. The spider and his mate agreed and became the Dream Weavers.

The Dream Weavers concentrated most heavily on the People, the Ashtanuga, because they could teach the others how to dream. The Great One had looked long upon the beauty in the land of the

Astanuga, and his tears had overflowed and filled many Great Lakes that stretched as far as the eye could see. The Great One bought life to the fish people that help to sustain us. The tears were concentrated in us and the life energy runs strong in the Ashtanuga. He gave us "our life" and assured the health of future generations with maize, squash and beans. He gave us tobacco so that we may pay homage to the unseen wise ones who guide us. He gave us the trees that shelter and hide us. We used these bodies, so full of his tears, to structure a society that was fair and complex. The energy of the Great One runs deep in our veins. All life is imbued with this goodness. It is for these reasons and more that the people became the special emissaries of the Dream Weavers.

We are not like the other people we have met. They do not know reality and do not seek answers from their dreams. We have witches that have learned to work with the fouled section of the web and cause great trouble. Witches are crafty, they can hide as any object - human, animal or even objects which are not alive. We have members in our society that fight the evil. We can all fight it within ourselves. The Dream Makers teach us the way.

The Bones of Naruk
By Johan Adkins

"Hey Ben, take a look at this!"

    Ben Greaves jumped down from the tractor and wiped a grimy hand across his forehead, he shifted the baseball cap on his head and bent down beside his brother, George.

"What d'ya suppose this is - animal or something?"

"Looks human, George - real old." Ben suddenly felt a chill up his spine. "Ya, well, let's just leave it in the crevice or the dogs'll have it spread all over." Funny place to find a body - wedged in the rocks like that."

    The brothers placed the femur bone back where they found it and went back to clearing the ground around the rocky outkeep. Ben stopped and said a gentle prayer asking forgiveness of the spirit whose bones they had disturbed. He wished the owner peace. He was thankful George couldn't read minds - he'd never understand such "superstitious nonsense."

    Ben had always said these strange things to himself. He often found himself speaking to creatures, the elements, plants and trees. Heck, he'd even talked to rocks and heard them talk back. He giggled out loud at that one. George just looked at him like he was crazy. It was a familiar look Ben received often, not just from George but from the other members in their family as well. None of them could understand Ben's dreamy ways or how he could always find game where it was scarce. If George knew the secret of Ben's success he would probably have him committed! Ben had always treated the animals they hunted for food with respect and thankfulness. With grace and humility they offered themselves for sacrifice. Ben always made sure his shots were clean and that the animals didn't suffer. He always blessed the animal and sent them a wave of light and thankfulness to see them upon their way.

Ben glanced back at the rocky outkeep which housed the human skeleton and silently asked, "Who were you? What happened to you ? Were you alone? Did you have family that wondered whatever became of you?" On a deeper level he wondered if the spiritual aspects of burial had been met in any way - honored, or consecrated in whatever fashion was his or her people's way. Suddenly, Ben felt an overwhelming sadness - from a male, yep, it definitely felt male.

That night Ben couldn't sleep. A nagging sense of unease kept him tossing and looking at the ceiling. Finally, he drifted off into fitful sleep. His dream was strange - more vivid than usual.

It was dark and there was a sense of terror all around him. He was hiding in a small enclosed space. He could hear his heart beating through throbbing eardrums. The sound was deafening! Could the enemies hear his heart beat? He tried not to breathe and the resultant shudders of breath seemed to echo around him, as if the rocks were breathing him and would scream his position away any moment. The warriors were still all around and searching for him. Pain, overwhelming loss and indescribable fear mixed in the center of his stomach. All of his family - all of his friends - dead. He almost cried out. His eyes filled with tears and he bit his lip until it bled. Quiet, quiet - he tried to melt into the stones. "Grandfather Owl," he silently prayed, "please hide the moon, please hide your son." He wedged himself deeper into the stones and watched in awe as a cloud slid over the moon.

Silently, he thanked Grandfather Owl and strained to hear the warriors outside. What was that? - a slight sliding noise. There it was again - and it was closer. Suddenly a scream emitted from flying hair and the form of a warrior filled the gap in the stones. The warrior thrust a spear deep into the crevice. Ben felt a deep pressure thrusting him against his prison and then came piercing, overwhelming pain. He looked into the warriors eyes for pity, but saw only a flash of triumph! He felt his life blood, warm and oozing, and realized he would never see another sunrise. Weakly, he looked to the skies now clear of clouds and saw Grandfather Owl silhouetted in the *face of Sister Moon. He heard himself saying, "Thank you, Grandfather, for trying."*

Ben woke up and discovered he was crying in his sleep. He got up and pulled on his jeans and grabbed his rucksack. He quietly slipped out of the house and walked across the field they had cleared that morning. He stood in front of the rock outcropping. He could feel a sense of anticipation in the air around him. He pulled the bones out - piece by piece and placed them carefully in the rucksack. He carried them to the old oak by the stream that ran through their property and dug a hole in the soft earth. He placed the bones in the hole and gathered sufficient "squaw" wood to build a small fire in the pit he had just dug. His face was highlighted against the night with the sudden flash of the match. He lit the fire and sat watching the smoke and flames play. He looked to the sky and saw the smoke dancing to the moon. As the flames died down - he heard the sound of giant wings. A smile played across his lips, and a tear escaped from the corner of his eye. An overwhelming sense of peace and thankfulness surrounded him.

Sequoia - A Christmas Gift (A True Story)
By Johan Adkins

Christmas is a hard time for me. It has some happy childhood memories but my father's death in recent years has created a sadness around the season that I have been unable to transcend. Now that my little ones are adults and my daughter and son-in-law are far away, it is a season that only intensifies the loneliness I feel for my family.

Last Christmas season I was unusually despondent. The weather was frigidly cold and it was snowing again. The wind chill factor had dipped an already miserable cold snap to sub-zero temperatures. I was getting ready to close my metaphysical store, Prism, after a long day and noticed a man struggling with his wheelchair at the front of the store. His younger friend who was supposed to be "pushing" was quite drunk and not much help. Finally, they managed to make it into the store. Sequoia, a Lakota gentleman in the wheelchair, announced quietly that he had come to sing me a song to brighten my day. Both men asked to borrow a hand-hewn Native drum that was sitting in the window on display. They proceeded to beat the drum and sing a loud and energetic "joy" song. The drunken Navaho man reeled, stamped and danced for his friend in the wheelchair who could not dance.

    I poured hot coffee and pushed snacks at them, knowing that they must be sober to have a place for the night at Comea Shelter.
    Over the next couple of hours my friend Stew and I learned quite a bit about the man who could dance. He had been injured in Vietnam. He and a number of Navaho brothers had been placed in very dangerous positions. The Navaho communication network was one that the Vietnamese could not break. His group had served faithfully during the war. Many of his friends did not return (and we heard songs to them!) The man who could dance said over and over, "We risked our lives for this country and when we returned, they didn't appreciate what we had done. The people didn't welcome us and they sang us no song - we had no song!"

    Sequoia watched me intently for some time and quietly gestured me to him. He pulled a battered cork and plastic necklace from his pocket and blessed it to the four directions and sang a song of blessing over it. With tears in his eyes he told me quietly that this necklace was blessed with the love of Christ and the blessings of his people and he wanted me to have it as a gift from him. It was all he had - he had no luggage, no extra clothing or blankets to warm him. Something told me to accept it. With humility and thanks and tears in my eyes and more gratitude than I could express, I told him I would keep it with me always.

They had sobered up sufficiently to sleep at Comea Shelter for the night.

The next night, however, Sequoia was found in front of a downtown hotel. he died from exposure to the frigid temperatures.

My adopted sisters and I met in a pipe ceremony and sang his spirit a song...and privately, I danced a dance.

Yantuk Creation Myth - The Worm Hole
by Johan Adkins

    Our people understand that the earth must have a hole for the birds to escape to the other world, for it is through this hole that the worm father, Samhanna, created the heart of the world. We build our canoes of redwood and keep them alive with a small hole for their heart. All things are living and have a spirit; thus it has been taught by my people for generations. This is the story my father and the men of the village told to me in the bathhouse.

    At one time Samhanna lived alone in a hot dry place, and burrowed beneath the desert sands. One day he noticed a beautiful, great bird soaring through the sky. He watched the graceful movements and envied the bird the freedom of the skies. One day the bird landed on Samhanna who was sleeping peacefully under the sand. Samhanna jumped up quickly and the quick rolling movement pinned the beautiful bird to the ground, crushing her wing. Samhanna grieved for the hurt bird and nursed her to health. They spent many hours talking to one another and soon became fast friends.

    Samhanna told her of his envy of her ability to fly. He flattered the bird greatly by telling her how lovely and breathtaking she was when she soared along the currents of air with the reflection of the blue and red suns shining on her wings. In appreciation of all that Samhanna had done for her, the bird promised to teach Samhanna to fly as soon as her wing was fully healed. So great was his desire to soar in the clouds, Samhanna did not doubt for one moment that he could learn.

The day finally came when the bird's wing was strong and well mended. She tested the wing with a few great hops and then lifted her great weight into the sky. "Follow me, Samhanna!" Samhanna mimicked her every movement, and he too hurled his body into the air with a few great hops. Without even thinking about it, Samhanna followed the bird into the air. It felt free, clean and wonderful. It took merely a wish to go here, or go there, to move through the sky. He giggled with joy and even managed a few mid-air rotations to show off.

Turning and turning, he lost his sense of time and direction. He soon parted from his friend. In his joy, he continued to rotate his body as he flew. He flew higher and higher, until suddenly, the rotation of his body created a hole in the dome above his world. What beauty and adventure lay beyond? He knew he must find out and left through the hole. The bird looked around and barely caught a glimpse of her friend leaving the world through the great hole. The bird followed and cavorted among the stars in space with the worm.

They flew and flew and encountered wonders each more magnificent than the last. Both of them finally grew tired, but had lost their way to their home. The worm noticed land below which was surrounded by great pools of blackened pitch. The land was warmed by a yellow sun and was rich in trees; Douglas fir and giant redwoods. A body of blue water surrounded the land and many streams emptied into the water. A fish jumped and the bird became excited for she was now tired <u>and</u> hungry. The worm began his slow rotation, but soon was whirling faster and faster. He created a hole in the dome of the land and they entered it to rest and eat. They were very happy on the land and the land responded beautifully, for it had needed a hole for a heart. In thankful return, the land invited the worm and the bird to stay. The worm was content to swim in the ocean, which was much like flying, only with plenty of salmon to eat!

The bird stayed for a time, but soon began to miss her home. She bid good-bye to the worm and promised to return at the same time next year. Before she left she laid hundreds of small eggs that curved into themselves. She dropped the eggs in the sea and instructed Samhanna to take good care of her children. She left the land through the heart of the world and traveled back home.

Samhanna swam around the eggs and fertilized them. He protected the shells in a house beneath the sea until they were ready to hatch, and then gently pushed them to the beach. When the shells hatched, the Yantuk people emerged with the spirit of the bird and the worm inside of them, but in the form you see here today.

Through the years we have forgotten how to fly, but honor the worm father Samhanna and bird mother by wearing the tiny shells from which our ancestors came. They have great value to us.

Mother bird sends her other children through the heart of the world to revisit their home of the yellow sun. They still try to teach us to fly. Each year they return through the heart to their other world of the blue and red sun; but they always come back to the land of the Yantuk.

Tsiscat Origin Myth - Father Bear
Johan Adkins

My mother's brother told me this tale. It is for me to tell my sister's children and for my sister's sons to tell their sister's children and so on and so on; this has been so for all remembered time of the people.

For seasons upon seasons, we lived in the white, cold lands. Our life was very different then and we followed caribou, fished, and even learned to hunt the great whale! Life is much better now because many kinds of game and plants are more plentiful for us than they were to our old ones. We sometimes hunt the great whale to honor our ancestors, and of course, to honor the whale. The people were led to this rich, warm land by Father Bear who followed the warm winds and currents. It is a blessed place that we were led to by Father Bear and the people have grown fat from the land.

Father Bear once lived in the sky and hunted along the river of white stars. He looked deep into the river and saw faint colors which magically appeared and disappeared. The colors were far away and the star river was very, very deep. The colors danced so beautifully that they drew Father Bear to them, and he jumped into the river. He swam down and down until he reached a world of color and light. This world was filled with curious forms that appeared to be naked animals. They would open their mouths wide and show their teeth, and strange noises came from their mouths. The noises made him happy. The naked animals were not afraid of him, but pulled his hair and playfully tried to ride his back.

The noises coming from their mouths began to make sense and he found he could speak to the hairless ones. They asked again and again, "Take us for a ride, we wish to go down there!" They pointed to a flat expanse of white beneath the dome of colors.

Father Bear replied, "I cannot carry all of you, you must make yourself small and ride in my stomach." The hairless ones climbed into his mouth and he swallowed them. A great black bird appeared in the sky. She flew to Father Bear and landed in front of him.

"Where do you take the light children?" she inquired.

"They have asked me to take them below, to the white land," he replied.

"Come," she said, "Climb upon my back. I will take you there with great speed."

Father Bear climbed upon her great back. As she left the lights of colors, her feathers grew whiter and whiter. When she landed upon the earth, she quickly flew to the north and could not be seen against the white of the snow.

Father Bear was surprised to find that the white expanse was cold and wet, but his coat kept him warm. Father Bear regurgitated the light children. Their forms had mixed with the contents of his stomach and they became solid beings. These were the first humans to live on the flat, white land.

"We are cold! Take us back!" they cried, but Father Bear could not return and this saddened him. He called to the white bird, but if she was there, he could not see her and she did not answer. Many of the light children died and followed the rainbows to the upper world.

Father Bear found that they were not alone, the earth was bountiful in caribou and animals in the sea. He taught the cold, naked ones, the Tsiscat People, as he called them now, by example. They watched him and learned to hunt the caribou and sea animals. Soon, they became quite self-sufficient. This allowed Father Bear to wander further and further away to satisfy his curiosity about the vast land he had come to. The Tsiscat taught themselves to make shoes of wood and the hide from the caribou to walk more easily upon the snow. They began to follow Father Bear further and further. The white expanses opened up into forest and mountains.

Father Bear wandered on and on until he came to the great inlet at the edge of the sea where we live now. It was a paradise away from the harsher climates they had come from and the Tsiscat were very happy there. Father Bear's friend, the sea otter, showed the Tsiscat how to catch the salmon and how to eat clams and mussels. The streams were full of trout. Many more animals were willing to sacrifice themselves for food; the mountain goat and sheep, hare, muskrat, squirrel and beaver. The plants were plentiful and berries dripped from the bushes.

The Tsiscat expressed their joy and appreciation to the spirits of the animals and plants by carving images in wood to honor those who nourished them. They named their families after the animals and carved tall poles to honor the spirits of their dead and those who would take their place.

Father Bear was weary and missed his home. He journeyed far to the white world. The white bird appeared to him once again to return him to the great river of white stars in the sky. He was never seen again, but his children come to visit sometimes.

Spirituality
By Johan Adkins

Nalani shifted her weight and stepped quietly from behind the tree. She crouched behind a cropping of stones framing the beach. She was safe, she could not be seen. She knew it was forbidden to trespass upon the sacred meeting of the Huani Wise Ones. With each moment her heart beat faster and beads of sweat formed on her forehead. Her hands were wet and she could smell fear in her body odor...fear, and something else. There was something in the pit of her stomach that made her senses alive. She could see more clearly in the dark night and her hearing was so acute she was aware of all of the sounds around her -the rhythmic ocean tides, the rustling of the trade winds, the speech of the Wise Ones and the sound of the beetles feet as they dashed into the foliage. She noticed a throbbing in the stone beneath her hand and she could feel a tingle growing from her feet against the sand. The tingle began to warm and spread throughout her entire body. This sensation was like no other she had ever experienced before and she knew the Gods were touching her and making her welcome.

The Wise Ones were meeting to cast the sacred stones in order to learn from the Gods what they must do about the hairy, white ones who had landed in boats of sticks which were belched from the belly of a great vessel. The tribe had initially welcomed them with trust, love and open homes as was the Huani way. They had to double the hunting and gathering to feed the seemingless bottomless appetites of the thirty men and indeed had even had to ask the forgiveness of the Gods when they were forced to give the sacred foodstuffs and gifts meant for offerings.

The guests did not return the hospitality and made no gifts to the Gods. Contrary to tribal etiquette, they did not leave at an appropriate time in order not to cause hardship on their hosts. The People did not understand and could not begin to communicate with the hairy ones. The strange tongue spoken by the hairy, white ones was unintelligible and sounded harsh to the Huani ears. The white language did not sing as the Huani's did. Worst of all, the hairy white ones had broken taboo when they did not allow the women, who had offered their warmth and companionship for a time, to leave when the women had fulfilled their tribal custom and wished to leave. These women were daughters, mothers and cousins. Something had to be done. One of the women had become ill and her body broke out in sores, swelled and burned until she crossed over. No such death had even been seen.

Nalani forced her attention back to the group of Wise Ones and blessed the Gods for allowing her to witness the sacred ceremony. This council represented all aspects of the Huani life. Akunu-ani spoke to the stones and interpreted all signs of nature. Mawa-laua was the spiritual link between the worlds of the ancestors. He often spoke to the ancestors and the ancestors and Gods spoke through him. Tanai-lani was the healer who knew the secrets of the body and practiced the arts that enticed the body to heal itself. All were here and the Gods were here.

Akunu-ani spread the sacred spiral cloth and cast the seven stones. Nalani knew that he was studying the picture created by the stones, the colors in relation to one another and the position of each stone in the casting. All was quiet until Akunu-ani softly spoke.

"The white ones come from a place of great corruption to test the patience and faith of the Huani. They are not real, but we have given them shape and form by believing they are real and have power over us. We must gather together and ask the powers of the earth and sky and water to help them to see the wisdom of returning to their own home. We must return them to the land of dreams and make them more and more invisible to our eyes. We must pay no heed to their ravings and protestations. We must smile and show love in all ways and bid them safe journey. Four men and three women are to attend to the packing and well-wishing of each man. We must remember that for a time, although they are becoming invisible, they may try to hurt us. Move in closely so that they may not, but do not hurt them. Smile and keep them walking back to the stick boats that will guide them to their great vessel. Assure them that the vessel may swallow them, but will regurgitate them when they arrive home. We will give ample food and water for their journey so that they will not need to return."

The Wise Ones nodded their agreement and all blessed the stones and thanked the Gods for such wise council. After the white ones slept, the tribe was gathered and the Mawa-laua explained. All marveled at the wisdom and recognized the truth of it. The white ones were surrounded by their group of well-wishers and awoke to find themselves being carefully escorted to the stick boats. Initial protestations and rantings quickly turned to looks of confusion and fear. In addition, something like shame haunted each of their faces.

It has been many moons since the white ones left and more Huani die daily of the disease they left behind. Each day, the raft builders build more death rafts and the small ones gather more flowers to make the leis that drift beside the raft to lead it to the Great Brightness. Mawa-laua, says that we die because we gave our power away to the evil ghosts who so ungraciously took the gifts meant for the Gods. They did not honor tribal custom and the gifts the Gods had given to the Huani and therefore, the Gods were angry. We vow not to ever give our power away and pray for forgiveness, but the Gods' anger takes more sacrifices daily.

We must learn to love more and keep our power for good.

Ah! Youth!!
By Johan Adkins

Getting out of bed isn't as easy as it used to be. I have to do it in stages. During the hazy time of half sleep, I watch to see if the images are there - images from dreams that tell the inner secrets. I try to remember my nightly escapades and seek to recreate each frame for instant re-run. Sometimes it works, sometimes it doesn't. I lie in bed and gradually become aware of my physical body. The covers are warm and the soft breathing of my husband beside me is vaguely reassuring that life goes on.

As I become more aware of my body in its physical form, I remind it that it is time to move - when I move it reminds me that it doesn't want to. Aches and pains - must be morning. I get out of bed and slug into the bathroom. I look in the mirror and wonder who that is looking at me. It is vaguely that same face that has greeted me with each morning of my life, but it is definitely aging - saggy eyes and double chins and paper thin-lizard skin texture has taken the place of the great elastic skin I used to have and a sensual blush of youth - the tight little body replaced by a bad joke. I look deeper into my eyes - oh there I am, and there I'll always be. So I stick my tongue at the mirror and begin my day.

The Beggar's Bag
By Johan Adkins

The way was familiar.
Right hand extended,
passing cold flat plain, rough/smooth
to the place of smells sharp/pungent
whose bins of nourishment and treasures
often contained masses which separated into
Pasty/cool tendrils with an occasional ball so tasty.

Vibrations
Passion/busy/happy.

Hunger fed, passing to the empty space of
warm/strength/sweetness.

God lives here.
Bow/worship/thankful.

All things warmer, and the body feels
love/renewal.
Aches melt when God visits here.

Time passes slowly,
lazy/bliss, until God leaves
or hands hurt
or thirst drives on to
Edge/cold flat,broken/rough to
the pipe from above,

cool/smooth,
ending in a place for the hand to twist.
Blessed Water/cold/happy.

Body renewed.
Prayers/thankfulness.

A sudden drop in temperature and the place of rest ahead
past the cold flat plain smooth/rough to
down/steps five
Around a corner, under the down/steps.
Secure by walls on all sides.
Smooth/ dry and sheltered against the wind and cold/stillness/damp.

Home/thankful/peace/rest.

Tomorrow, the crossing!
Right hand extended for breakfast!

No hands hurt or pushed today!

A whole day of worship!

Sleep, welcome/warm/safe.

Life is good!

NON-ETHNIC SPIRITUAL ENHANCEMENT

by DeJon

(Printed originally in the Transformation Connection newsletter)

Becoming more spiritual simply means understanding more about yourself. Using that understanding as a source of compassion and spreading that compassion on others like blackberry jam on an English muffin.

To gain and keep the perspective on how incredibly precious we are, we need to get out into nature. We need to interact with nature's splendor, nature's goodness, nature's power and nature's wrath. When we listen to mother earth as she groans and strains to do her work, when we see, hear, touch and delight in nature's bounty, we get a glimpse of our own grand value. We also can't help but notice how precious our acquaintances are.

Listen as children to the whistle of the wind. Listen to the trees rustle and grow. Listen to the grass as it reaches for the sun. Listen to the birds bustling, hooting and chirping. Listen to every animal you can find. Why you can even hear a bug scurry across our mother earth. Listen children, listen.

Outside clean fresh air reaches down into my lungs giving me energy and a fresh sense of value. The sights and sounds of nature enlighten my soul. The wondrous variation of textures flood me with joy! True understanding of nature comes only from exposure to it. Understanding how and where we each fit into nature's glory gives us our sense of worth.

Begin now, as a child would to entreat every thing you hear, and everything you see and everything you touch with eager anticipation. Clear your mind of present expectations and prejudice. Hope and pursue a new each moment, like a child lurching into the remainder of the day - For this is spiritual. Is not this eternally turning globe with its eternally changing weather, terrain and ocean currents only completed by the millions of especially beautiful living species? Is not this earth set in a heaven full of twinkling stars the most marvelous, the most awe inspiring and the most just plain gorgeous spectacle thus far beholdable.

Say now to yourself (as hopeful fledglings) with a loud voice - I am not culturally white, black, yellow or red, I am of earth. I am not Moslem or Christian or Jew or Buddhist or Wiccan - I am of mother earth. I am not a Russian or American or Japanese - I am of this beautiful planet.

When you meet another person, plant, animal or any entity - first, know yourself and how good you are. Know how deserving you are and how beautiful you are. Know that your heritage is of mother earth and you are beautiful and could not be otherwise. Knowing how valuable you are will allow you to see the beauty of whomever you encounter.

If we understand how valuable another person is, we can take time to listen to that soul. For to listen is greater than to teach. Listening is a gift un giveable. Listening to a soul reaching out will allow that soul to acquire by inference the gift of self-esteem.

Listen to his wit, listen for his wisdom, for he has it, I assure you. Listen for her hopes, listen to her dreams - For to hear another soul is to love another soul.

Oh! Loving Ones! Go now and know how beautiful you are and how deserving. If you know a thing to be helpful, endeavor to do that thing and if you know a thing is harmful to any entity on mother earth (or as yet undiscovered entity) resist you the doing of it. For that is spreading compassion like blackberry jam on a hot English muffin.

If they come up against you - -

Just dance with them!!

DeJon

DANCE

By DeJon

(Printed originally from Transformation Connection Newsletter)

Years have gone since I fought my fight
but fight I did
Against the establishment with all my might
against religion, monogamy and the family unit

Yes, I fought and I argued
I attacked their minds and beat on their heads
I presented a case for rational society
open relationships and just exchange

I fought for freedom from religion
for the right to think for myself
and for children to be free from the brainwash

For twenty years I held the bandage for the bleeding youth

Suddenly I saw a better way
Beating on heads seldom changes the mind inside
attacking a point strengthens the position
the presentations all fell on deaf ears

Ah, but dance can work

Choreograph two opposite thoughts and watch them dance
they often dance till a concept is formed
the dance gives reward to both sides

By giving credit to an opponent
he feels good about himself and credits me
When I attack him he feels bad about himself and blames me

Here then is the answer

Identify your point
Find a source of opposition
approach each argument as if it were dance
and we will choreograph our way to a better world

BELOVED

by Marvin "Marvine" Syferd
(Printed as written originally in the Transformation Connection Newsletter)

(In my use of the term "beloved," I address the God within. This (writing) is my prayer - my thoughts - my awareness at this time)
Beloved,

I call upon you to manifest now my conscious awareness and realization of my oneness with thee. That is the divine inspiration and the driving force controlling my experience on every level of my being.

We know (whether we know we know or not) with the gift of conscious awareness, there comes a mighty given. The freedom of choice and its inevitable co-creator, responsibility.

There is in this concept (of freedom and responsibility) our infinite potential. This then, is the River upon which our entire experience of life floats.

There can be a gradual (or perhaps a sudden) realization that there is an absence of apprehension - a sense of security and protection. (A sense) that it

really and truly is an infinite God that is having this unique experience of life at my level of awareness.
> All experience is valid
> There are no mistakes
> There is only EXPERIENCE.

(It is) that (which) moves us in an infinite number of speeds and directions along our unique pathway of realization of our oneness with God.

And the journey!! The marvelous journey is our destination.

We are now - as much as we will ever be - in the very centre of our eternity.

Marvine

CHAPTER 2 - SUMMER/AWARENESS AROMATHERAPY ENERGY NETWORKING

AROMATHERAPY

Aromatherapy is a very important tool for healing. The following "recipes" were given to me for the most part by Spirit during a period of time that I was involved with Prism Metaphysical Center in Cheyenne, Wyoming. In some cases, others presented them to me as gifts. "Smell" is another "vibration" that we respond to and Spirit responds to as healing, cleansing and purifying. A proper "combination" of smells can elicit needed "therapy" as surely as a body responds to a warm, tingly shower after a hard day. Our cells and brain respond to smell in very specific ways to heal.

Incense has the added direct benefits of fire, earth, air and water and combination elements respond to the elemental affiliations of the individual.

You are very welcome to "use" the recipes for personal use or gifts. Any combination of ingredients that you feel comfortable with is correct.

One last thing! Please invite your guardians and Spirit to enjoy the scents with you! Incense is very energizing and revitalizing to them!

PRISM'S CUSTOM INCENSE BLENDS

Prism's Custom Blend Receipes

Prism's Custom Blend recipes were put together by Prism Aromatherapists and checked by the pendulum for specific properties that the blend represents. This is "divine" or "astral" therapy, in that combinations of smells should help to enhance meditation and general "atmosphere." Burning incense designed in this fashion should help the individual manifest the qualities and things they desire.

Spiritual Smudge

To be used for spiritual cleansing. The Native American tradition has long used "smudging" to purify the body of negative energies and to "cleanse" an area of negative energies. The purification readies the body for meditation and protects the individual from negative harm around him. The spiritual smudge is very helpful to calm fears and feelings of unease.

The "Spiritual Smudge" package may contain: Sweetgrass, Sage, Mesquite, Juniper, Cedar or Lavender.

Friends

The "Friend" blend was put together as a wonderful gift that can be given to our dear friends to let them know how precious they are to us and how much we value their friendship. These blends used here are ancient "representations" of love and friendship and the bond we feel for each other. They are "gifts" from the Earth as well.

The "Friends" package may contain: Rose, Sweetgrass, Lavender, Frankincense or Spice.

Sweet Success

The "Sweet Success" mix was designed to celebrate life's joy and our moments of success. These blends represent pure love and their combinations enhance the joy that "success" brings! If the person meditates upon successful completion of their desires with the "Sweet Success" mixture - the pure scents help the individual to manifest that success!

The "Sweet Success" package may contain: Rose, Vanilla and Jasmine.

Cosmic Wanderer

This is an interesting package in that the pendulum solely chose certain incense which would aid an individual in astral and/or dream work. This is the wonder of the universe which is open to the individual if the desire is stated and love is the impetus.

The "Cosmic Wonder" or "Cosmic Wanderer" package may contain: Rose, Lavender, Ylang-Ylang, Sandalwood and Vetivert.

Magi's Gift

The three kings presented baby Jesus with Frankincense and Myrrh - the most precious scents and perfumes available in their time. Treasured as is their wont. To this package has been added cedar - another precious gift from Earth.

Garden Diva Meditation

Plant lovers and garden enthusiasts, have a special bond with plants and growing things. These "earth children" often speak to them. The plant energy is pure and joyful, and again, the pendulum chose this combination to aid the individuals in speaking to their plants or opening a door to hear them speak.

This combination is for the plants of the day (of the sun) and contains: Lavender, Rose and Jasmine.

Moonshadow

This combination is primarily for the evening blossoms that bloom with the moon. The plants of the day enjoy it too! The "Moonshadow" blend helps us to understand the plants and the creatures of the evening - those old, wise ones who help the dreamwalkers.

This combination contains: Lavender, Rose, Jasmine, Vetivert and Lotus.

Bedlam Calmer

Sometimes the stress of the day turns from stressful to bedlam and we need something to help ground the negative energies. The negative energies manifest an energy in a room as well and that energy needs to be calmed in order for the individuals to calm!

This combination may contain: Lavender, Sweetgrass, Bergamot, Geranium, Sandalwood and Vetivert.

Gram's Kitchen

This combination of smells is to evoke memories of childhood visits to Grandma's house which was always a wonderful, magical combination of aromas! I can't help but remember my grandmother when I smell this combination. I remember her stories and her joy of living!
Ths combination contains: Lavender, Rose, Vanilla and Spice.

Passion Power

The name speaks for itself! These are ancient combinations that help the individual create or sustain an atmosphere conducive to the passionate and vibrant sides to our lives!

"Passion Power" may contain: Patchouli, Bergamot, Ylang-Ylang, Frankincense and Myrrh.

Healing Meditation

This is for self-healing of emotional battering; jobs, family and just overall stress that takes its toll on our peace seeking souls! This was designed also by the pendulum to aid us in defining the areas within ourselves (and for others if they ask) that need healing energies directed to them. Green is earth healing and it is wonderfully indulgent to just "bathe" in the healing "ko" or incense and surround ourselves with healing green.

"Healing Meditation" may contain: Rosemary, Thyme, Eucalyptus, Sandalwood, Lavender, Geranium, Bergamot and Ylang-Ylang.

Indra's Web

This combination was chosen to help us meditate upon our place in the universe in relation to all things. To the one - the common thread that runs through all belief systems and cultures across time and space. Meditation with this combinaion should help us to define our place within and bathe in the peace that resides there.

This combination, again, was chosen by the pendulum: Sandalwood, Patchouli and Ylang-Ylang.

WOOD ELEMENTAL

Oriental astrology adds the element of Wood (and Metal) to the Western Elements of Fire, Air, Water and Earth. If we could maintain elemental energy balance; we would greatly aid our body in utilizing all elemental energies to remain healthy and balanced in our energies.

If you are the type of person who <u>needs</u> (not only likes, but <u>needs</u>) to get out in the woods - near trees and nature to feel a sense of the world's problems and stresses releasing - you are probably lacking wood in your elemental balance! This wood elemental package was put together to give you a "hit" until you can get out into nature for a time! Nature meditation while burning this "ko" or incense should help. Having plants around, natural wood products and wearing wood is vital to you.

This "Wood Elemental" package was put together by the pendulum and may contain: Juniper, Cedar, Sandalwood, Mesquite, Sage, Pine, Cypress, Amber, Frankincense and Myrrh.

METAL ELEMENTAL

If you are a metal sign or lack metal in your elemental chart, this combination will greatly help you to persevere in your earthly tasks and learn how to become more disciplined.

If you are a metal person, the below isn't a problem for you and lighting the metal "ko" will help you to focus and direct your healing energy.

If you lack metal element, which most of us do, you will have difficulty calming the constant "clatter" in your mind in order to direct your thoughts toward a specific meditation, prayer or endeavor. If you have difficulty concentrating on one task at a time, burning the metal elemental package will help to clarify your thinking. Metal is a difficult energy and element to "master" or understand, but once you discipline your mind to seek its teaching, life will become much more serene and ordered.

The Metal Elemental package should contain: Bergamot, Llang-llang, sweetgrass and rose.

EARTH ELEMENTAL

If you are an earth sign or lack the earth element or just love to play in the dirt, this is something you will greatly enjoy!

If you are an "Earth Element" person the below isn't a problem for you and you can just enjoy your element and ground and center yourself!

Astrologically, if you lack the earth element, you may feel constantly "spaced out." It is like you don't quite have your feet on the ground, or you are walking around in your body, but don't feel you have any "roots" anywhere. You have difficulty feeling that you belong anywhere or with anyone. Sometimes you need help functioning in the physical world.

This "Earth Elemental" package was put together by the pendulum and may contain: Patchouli, Lavender, Bergamot, Llang-Llang, Cactus Flower or Vetivert.

FIRE ELEMENTAL

If you are a fire sign, lack the fire element or need energy, the Fire Elemental package may just be the thing to help! If you are normally a person who is easy going, but you need to assert yourself more, this can be <u>really</u> helpful (just look out!)

If you are primarily a Fire Elemental person, the below isn't a problem for you and you can just enjoy your element.

A lack of fire in life brings these sets of challenges to bear: lack of energy, feelings of despondency or low self-worth, lack of passion and motivation, problems with digestion (and darn!) the joy of living just isn't there anymore. If this describes you, this incense grouping will help greatly. When energy is depleted, wear the colors of fire; oranges, reds, brilliant or electric blues. Go on a camping trip and watch the campfire burning. Light candles and meditate upon the flames! See the fire around you and imagine that it is a ball in your abdomen!

This "Fire Elemental" package was put together by the pendulum and may contain: Bergamot, Sage, Peppermint, Sweet Pea, Eucalyptus, Juniper, Orange (Neroli), Carnation, Spearmint, Rosemary or Lemongrass.

WATER ELEMENTAL

If you are a water sign, lack the water element, need to "go with the flow" more, (or just love to play in the water,) you will enjoy this package.

If you are primarily a water person - the below isn't a problem for you and you can just enjoy your element!

A lack of water results in these challenges to bear: difficulty in understanding or expressing "feelings," difficulty in getting in touch with the feeling behind the scenes which affects what is happening now. Understanding your own emotions is elusive and you are often misunderstood because of this problem. It is difficult to get in touch with the true feelings and needs of others. This doesn't mean that you don't have deep feelings or that you are cold and aloof (although people may see you that way,) it just means that feelings confuse you - and you have difficulty trusting your inner voices or intuition. Perhaps you were frightened away from trusting your intuition and would like to get more in touch with this gift again.

This "Water Elemental" package was put together by the pendulum and may contain: Apple, Gardenia, Geranium, Magnolia, Lemon, Thyme, Water Lily, White Ginger, Yarrow, Vanilla, Spice or Rose.

AIR ELEMENTAL

If you are an Air sign, lack the air element, love the wind or need to be able to dream or do astral work - you will enjoy this combination!

If you are primarily an Air person - the below isn't a problem for you and you can just enjoy your element!

If you have difficulty adjusting to new people, changes and are getting "bogged" down in the day to day world, you may enjoy a break from that by courting the element "Air." If you find yourself getting physically ill or emotionally upset with material problems - that is a sign of someone who <u>needs</u> the element "Air" to help lift the burdens. Air helps introspection and spiritual development. Air helps one to seek an objective viewpoint. It would also be helpful if you find yourself in this paragraph to wear colors of blue and white, watch clouds and bathe in gentle breezes. Meditate upon the colors blue and purple.

This "Air Elemental" package was put together by the pendulum and may contain: Honeysuckle, Lilac, Lemongrass, Sweet Pea, Glacier Lily, Jasmine or Llang-Llang.

Energy Network
By Johan Adkins

We are such powerful beings, a thought is energy; loving, healing thoughts directed towards others helps to surround them with additional energy needs, love and healing when they need it. All we have to do is visualize/think about, meditate/pray for someone, and that person receives the benefit of our positive and loving energy. When that energy is directed by many, many people, it is a powerful, positive wave of healing. We don't even have to know them or be in close proximity, just visualize what we perceive the person to look like (explanations help) and visualize the parts of the body that need our healing energy and see the organs and the person whole and healed. Visualize the person healthy and happy and free of pain.

When someone <u>needs</u> our energy (ie. they <u>ask</u> for it and we <u>consent</u> to give energy - that is vitally important) we may direct it with a loving thought, prayer, mantras (waves, water, fire - whatever you have to do to visualize the energy you are sending going to them!)

When a person asks for help, they must also be open to receive what is being given.

When a need is expressed to you, please call your friends and ask them to include these people in your thoughts and ask your friends to ask their friends! These "networks" can work miracles.

If you have serious needs that you would like help with, an energy network can help you feel that you are not alone in your times of trouble.

Remember though, you have to <u>ask</u> for help from your friends, angels, spirit guides, etc. and be willing to receive it. We shouldn't take energy from others without asking or assume that it is being given (or should be given) without asking for it. We need to be aware of our energy levels and spend them wisely. We also need to be able to accept a "no" from ourselves and our friends if reserves are to low to "share." We all need to learn to say "no" to each other without fear of loss. Everyone has low energy periods when they must regroup and recuperate their energies. Sometimes, it seems to take everything we have to exist. However, if that is the position you find yourself, ask your friends and family for help. Even if they really don't understand what you want from them - it is a subconscious message not to "take" from you.

It is also very helpful to write out all of our troubles and woes and bad feelings. After writing out our negativity, burn the sheets and let what was written go with the burning. Say goodbye to the trouble and inform it that you do not need it anymore and please just go away! Beat it! Ciao! This is very helpful when you don't wish to burden your friends and family with every little thing, but really need to get it off your chest!! Or write letters to someone telling them everything you ever wanted to say and then burn the letters!!

Perhaps it is time to send a letter and close a relationship - but wait for a time and try to rework your reasons into positives. It is probable that time will take the edge off a potentially biting and needlessly hurtful letter.

Sometimes we are aware (or vaguely suspect) that negative feelings, emotions or thoughts of harm are being directed toward us. When you feel you need protection from the negative energies of others there are a number of things you can do.

Visualize a safe-place, or place yourself in a protective pyramid and fill the pyramid with color. Ask your angels/spirit guides or the elemental or cosmic energy around you to protect you from harm and negative influences (even our own negativity toward ourselves can manifest harm!)

It may be helpful to "smudge" yourself (and your family and friends if they'll let you!) and your home. As the incense, sweetgrass, sage -candle (whatever) burns, ask that negative or harmful energy be dissipated with the smoke. Ask that love and harmony fill the area and that no bad things or negative feelings remain. Talk to the negativity. Let it know it is not welcome and to leave your home and your life!

The black stones are protective stones that help keep negative or draining energy away from you. Carry or wear onyx, obsidian, or jet and ask the stone energy to protect you.

Remember, to respect the people, stones, incense, angels/spirit guides, by asking for their help as friends. Treat them as you would a dear friend and thank them for helping you.

We are <u>not</u> alone.
We are surrounded by love and Spirit.

CHAPTER 3 - FALL/CHANGE - ASCENTION SPIRIT SPEAKS

SPIRIT SPEAKS

The next section of the book is information "channeled" by Johan Adkins from a number of sources. When I receive this information, I hear it as I am typing. It feels to me that my fingers move of their own accord and I do not know from one second to the next what will be written. I hear those who are dictating their articles and feel their presence surrounding me and sometimes within me. I am fully aware of my surroundings when this is happening. I do not relinquish any control of my mind or body, but hear them like one would "hear" a memory.

Just as if I were conversing with a friend beside me, I can feel their presence to be "good" and pure of heart - or I do not listen to them and reject their presence. Those who hear, can hear both good and "evil" and that is the problem with a lot of channeled work. Many cannot tell the difference and write what "evil" speaks. "Evil" often speaks in the guise of good - but the energy and feeling when it speaks is markedly different.

I have agreed with the spiritual pool to write what they speak VERBATIM. I do not edit or allow editing without their permission. This is done because they have spoken to many who cannot resist the opportunity to embellish or change in some way what is being "heard." This happened largely in the Bible and other sacred texts.

The intention of the articles is to teach us that we are, indeed, very different "beings" than we may have originally thought. We have abilities far beyond that which is accepted as "normal." We communicate with each other psychically all of the time. Some are more aware and tuned in to this constant prattle, and can sift through it enough to label themselves "psychics." However, all human beings on earth can do what legitimate psychics do if they unlearn the barriers that filter out information that is given.

Spirit speaks constantly to mankind and attempts to teach that which is given here. If you are receiving this instruction, the following articles will seem familiar. The word "Spirit" is very broad and the spiritual "pool" from which these articles are derived includes every living thing alive or "dead" across all time and space. As a fleur d'leis, I am gifted with teaching from all Spirit. Fleur d'leis may request communication and instruction from whomever they wish. In a neutral and responsible universe - instruction will come when the student is ready and that is determined by your higher self who is a part of the soulforce pool.

I have spoken to many religious figures such as: the Creator (Holy Spirit, Great Sun, Great Spirit,

Wellspring Father/Mother), God, the Father of Jesus who is referred to in the spiritual pool as "Prime," The Lord God, the white light leader of the Angelic Realm who is referred to in the spiritual pool as "Lord." All are one in the spiritual meld, but they can also separate themselves sufficiently so that when you speak to them, you are speaking directly to them.

Communication is open from other major spiritual figures as well; Rainbow Lady who is the heavy energy inner sun, Earth Mother and the Caretaker Council, the Elementals (Metal, Wood, Earth, Air, Water and Fire) and Vortex beings who are the living chakras.

If you are fleur d'leis (blessed healers), there are no barriers to speaking to anyone or anything that wishes to speak to you, including "extraterrestrial" lifeforms or the planets themselves. I was agnostic before this work began and as I have spoken and worked with God Prime, Wellspring Father and Mother, the Lord and Jesus himself, I am not agnostic any longer. However, do not misunderstand this work. It is not "religious" or cultish in the sense of established religion either. These religious "leaders" would like to dispel the old concepts almost entirely. Their message has always been simple: Love and cherish each other and treat all life as sacred. These are friends and teachers who, among other friends and teachers have given me the gifts of their words. I impart them wholly and happily along with the messages of other "holy" speakers; the plants, the animals, the stones, assorted angels, saints, guides and teachers.

When a healer achieves "fleur d'leis" communication, all aspects of Spirit are open and it is rather like receiving phone calls that instruct and teach and have messages to impart to humankind. We are all interconnected with all of life on earth and indeed, the whole universe. Everything is alive and everything has responsibilities in the universe. They offer us the gifts of themselves. A door to secrets long kept and an opportunity to work with them to heal ourselves and others. Along with the opportunity to heal others comes the commitment to heal Spirit and to work with them to heal the universe.

We are microcosms of a whole universal system. We have within us, great healing and visualization skills that enable us to direct energy to heal anything.

Among the following work, you will find articles written by:
The Great Spirit or Great Father (Wellspring Father- the Creator of all)
The Elementals: Astangas People or Fire People, Water Beings -Dolphins, Whales and Sea Spirits, Gas and Air Beings and Minervan Wind Beings, Earth

Beings (represented by Earth Mother and the Caretaker Council,) Metal Beings and Wood/Tree Beings.

Rainbow Lady

God Prime

Lord God

The Great Vortex

Lemp Beings - from Sirus Minor who have lived with us as universal historians and friends.

Spirit speaks 4-19-94

A Message from the Great Father regarding the nature of life and healing

Your body has layers of energy known as "aura" and within each aura are 18 primary chakras, or living vortex that concentrate energy and move energy from point to point. There are literally thousands of smaller and secondary chakras. All are in various degrees of openness or closedness depending on the health of the body, the health of the organ systems and various perameters of a healthful state.

1st auric field is etheric 3/4"

2nd--is a wider field, etheric field 2 usually measures up to 36" off hand

3rd--auric field is etheric field 3. usually measures about 6' from body

4th--is etheric field 4. usually measures about 30' from body

5th--is etheric field 5. usually measures about 60' from body

6th--is etheric field 6. usually measures about 120' from body

7th--is etheric field 7. usually measures about 280' from body

8th--is etheric field 8. usually measures about 360' from body

In truth there are thousands of fields. The fields above encompass the etheric "bodies." The earthly and planetary incarnations however, deal with at least these eight physical/material etheric fields which for convenience sake are referred to in this book as dimensions negative 1, 1 and 2. The angelic realm or spiritual realm encompasses all dimensional fields after etheric field eight (which is dimensional field 2) which would be considered the beginning of the soulforce "pool."

All fields have thousands of chakras that are widely spaced in the longer fields. They are in the general vicinity of high to low (sensory high to low). From great heights looking down the chakras appear lined up-just as linear as a DNA strand would appear to a physicist.

This pattern allows Spirit to instantly view all chakras and analyze pattern strength and uniformity to aid in discovering blockages or severed chakras or compromised areas. Each person has a unique pattern and basic color arrangement--the color varies slightly with mood and condition--but basic patterns are easily discernable as individuals. This is how we see you...this is all we see of you unless we adopt your form and join you on earth.

You are indescribably beautiful to all the beings that perceive energy forms. When you are grouped in great groups, your energies merge and the individual is impossible to discern. Your energies do meld with one another and the interplay of lights dancing and colors moving is breathtaking to behold. If you could only see yourselves as we see you--no ugliness, no separation, really--one beautiful rainbow spectrum with dancing, twinkling lights that are your chakras.

When love is prevalent among your people, the colors are bright, radiantly luminescent like no colors your eyes have seen. This clarity cannot be reproduced for you to see how beautiful love is. Imbalance and discord muddy the colors and foulness or evil behavior blackens vast areas. Imbalance in one radiates to others and very often one person's imbalance can muddy an entire area.

You are all exquisitely sensitive to the moods or imbalance of others and a bright, happy aura will immediately muddy when exposed to blackness. This is one reason you need to "build" visually manifested pyramids around yourselves; to protect a shining clear aura from being compromised by others and to give others who may also be compromised by negativity or blackness a brighter, shinier aspect to emulate.

If you build a pyramid of energy around yourselves, practice balance, healing and clarifying your auras within, you become bright beacons in the seas of mud. All systems strive for balance and if you exhibit balance, clarity, healing, and love--those around you will try to "rise" to your vibrational level.

Construct for yourself and teach others to construct visual pyramids and teach them how to keep it pure and loving. It is very simple--find a quite, restful place (outside is preferable), or just a nook or privacy in your homes. Sit on the ground or floor and close your eyes. Place your hands open on your knees. Build the floor of your pyramid about 6' on every side. Build the walls of the pyramid one wall at a time--visualize yourself as; in the very center of your pyramid.

After all four walls are built, visualize your etheric auric layers contracting to fit within the walls. Seal your pyramid--perhaps turn the stones into solid sheets or the bricks into glass--no seams.

Breathe in and slowly let your breath out to a count of ten. As you let your breath out, let your vocal chords naturally vibrate the sound. (a rounded or oval "huhhh" helps). If you wish to say ahoem or om--try to make the sound come from your solar plexus instead of your voice box. As you let your breath out, see the negativity in your body coming out with the breath and let the negativity fill the pyramid. It will find a home with other negative or muddy thoughts already clouding your auric fields.

After you have calmed the mind, and calmed and relaxed the physical body, begin a meditation prayer or mantra that states the intent of dispelling all negativity from the body and the auric fields within the pyramid. Ask all auric fields to seek serenity, peace, brotherhood, love, healing, balance and to radiate that condition to all you meet or touch.

Ask your spirit guides/angels/plant, rock, animal guides to assist you in radiating serenity, peace, brotherhood, love, healing, bliss ask them to assist you in keeping negativity and imbalance out of the pyramid structure and to assist in building a strong defensive wall of protection from imbalance/negativity. Visualize each auric field as a rainbow of colors with dancing, twinkling lights and see all negativity "turn off" or dissolve aura field by aura field.

The infinity sign is a figure of balance and this movement will help you to balance the field.

The six petal flower sign is a figure of healing and this will help you to heal an injured or compromised field.

The three rotation clockwise spiral that rolls into a three rotation counterclockwise spiral is thee healthy chakra sign. This sign is a figure of a perfect, healthy chakra and will help you to visualize all healthiness in all your fields.

Ask any injured area to present itself for examination, contemplation and healing. Close your eyes and use the movements of balance, healing and perfection as a heavy area presents itself. Ask the heaviness to identify its problem or malady. Be prepared for the answer. It may be an injustice you have done to another or a possible past problem you have tried to keep at arms length away from you. Look at the problem; see it for what it is and let it go in love.

If it is a problem you cannot resolve and let go of, ask it to go to the furthest corner of your aura for future healing, and come no closer and take on no further energy until you are ready to deal with it.

Unless forgiven and released in love, the energy you have manifested in hate or bitterness or imbalance does not go away. It lurks and moves and continues to contaminate the auric field in which you have placed it.

You bring "problems" closer and give them more weight and substance to imbalance or you darken them and place them in the corners of the outer layers. You create your own monsters when you do not face your problems and deal with them directly.

If too much energy is spent either dwelling on or attempting to keep the problems at arms length, they will eventually compromise the aura you keep them in and will move closer, aura by aura to contaminate those auras as well. When the contamination has reached the physical body - and cannot be moved away any longer, it will manifesting illness or disease in the body. You choose your diseases by not dealing with imbalance and allowing it a home in the physical body.

To us, the physical body is one more auric level--the center one and is discernable by more brightness (or darkness if imbalanced).

You are dual-unisex beings. You are born one sex, but are reborn many times as male or female. You have to realize that being dual in nature, you can destroy part of your duality by disease or maltreatment or denial. If you destroy or reject your present incarnation sex, you doom your soul-force to ultimate death or disassembly.

To Spirit, when your physical form "dies", in your view, there is no change in energy. You "death" is "transformation" to us. You return to Spirit and are reborn when you choose the parents you choose as teachers of the lessons you wish to learn.

All souls are seeking one-ness or "meld" in the soulforce pool. The primary goal of the higher self is for the earthly or planetary incarnation to become aware of their spiritual paths and directives on earth, to transform into living/material Spirit. This transformation is known as the fleur d'leis process. In order to rejoin the soulforce pool, the physical being must meet their own higher self "scripts" and furthermore be tested greatly by Spirit. In other words, they must accomplish on earth the goals they have set for themselves. Furthermore, there is testing in the physical/material body by Spirit. One-ness is accomplished when the physical being has fulfilled the ultimate balance of love and lifeforce healing that allows you to stop the incarnations and join Spirit. If you do not kill or destroy by pernicious disease the sex you are currently residing in, you have innumerable lives and a great wealth of learning and growing spiritually.

You only die to Spirit if you kill one-half of yourself and when you cannot be reborn because you have "maxed" out the balance of male and female incarnations. There must be a balance of male and female lives ultimately and your soul (or higher self) decides what form it will return in and what goals must be accomplished in that incarnation.

Each aura is you. You really don't "fool" yourself by burying problems "away." There is truly no "away" and all you really do is bring imbalance and disease closer to the physical form. Only when it reaches the physical form can you manage to "kill" one half of yourself. When you do that, to us, you are dead (disssembled) and you may only have a few lives before you are no longer reborn. You may never reach Spirit, and we grieve you greatly. You are quintessential imbalance if you do not heal yourself.

There is no "hell," there is only balance and imbalance. Know that when you "die" naturally in your physical form, you are not dead but transforming. Do not panic that all disease will kill one half of you. You may have "scripted" for yourself to suffer a certain illness or disability. HOWEVER, you have within you the ability to heal yourself. There are teachers who can help you if you desire to be helped, just ask. Seek and ye shall find, knock and the door shall be opened. (we did say that!)

No disease need be fatal to the body or half the body if you truly believe you can heal yourself. Remember, however, that you do have an established life cycle that requires "death" at the end of it. Remember also, that <u>you</u> determined, in the script for yourself, when you would end your earthly existance. Sometimes, a specific time and date are chosen, but more often, it is a matter of leaving the physical/material body when certain script goals are accomplished or not accomplished. If you practice balance and healing you will have a disease-free lifespan and may find that you can join Spirit if you heal others and your universe along with yourselves.

We see you as beautiful. You need to see yourselves as beautiful and graced by Spirit who deeply loves each one of you! Love and heal yourselves. Love and heal each other and your universe. Love and heal Spirit! We're all one!!

Elemental Spirit Speaks

Elemental Spirit is separate from the Ethereal Spirit and we like to be recognized for ourselves. We help to balance fire, air, water, earth, wood, metal and like elements of those combinations. That means the atmosphere, gases and elements of life. Life is ethereal and elemental. Balance also requires elemental balance. Without elemental balance there is no substance to the life the ethereal form manifests as reality.

Lifeforce (a balance of earth energy with other elemental energies) is just that--the force that holds life in a form that fits your reality. You manifest your own reality and elemental energy provides the stage with props and backdrops (so to speak) for you to play out your manifestation.

Life is a complex stage and the reality is that you are an actor on that stage--acting out the script you wrote for yourself in order to learn the lessons you desire in your path to one-ness. Elements and elemental energies are like absent-minded stage managers who serve to set up the stage, but leave out props and scenery your script requires to throw in variables and tests of your acting ability. The result is a test of the meddle of the actor to complete the play (incarnation) within a state of confusion and uncertainty. The actor has to think on his feet, keep the intent and plot line clear despite efforts of the stage managers to confuse them. The audience is the Ethereal Spirit and the Elemental Spirits in joint cahoots.

Additionally, we are acting out a complex play (of our own) in moving earth energies toward (for) balance and toward the love aspect in the universe. That means doing what we have to, to relieve pressures of imbalance within and on the earth. Earth is a living, breathing organism, we are to help her maintain life/health/balance. That might mean an earthquake to ease an aching "back" or a tidal wave to relieve stress.

Some of the elemental work is directed to remind actors in their smug plays not to be so content with a boring script. Life is dynamic change and man must change dynamically to survive. He has, in a short time, done a great deal of damage to a living organism and like a bacteria, he will have to change to survive on earth or die because he has so polluted his own environment, it is now unhealthy and imbalanced to his lifeform. The earth will ultimately heal provided all of us survive the great judgment...man may or may not be written into the script.

We appreciate each life in our care. Ethereal Spirit trusts us with the incarnations and to move the energy back to them at transformation.

We are not malicious in our teaching. We may be task masters in order to teach you to be strong (if that is your script). We are to provide challenge to balance without creating imbalance. We are powers of balance, remember, so challenges in your path are to help you grow. If you do not grow, that is a challenge you must address in another incarnation.

SELF HEALING
by Dejon

IDENTIFICATION OF PROBLEMS

(Printed originally from the Transformation Connection Newsletter)

if you will tighten up an area
you can know how the feeling differs from relaxed

try it with your toes
force them into the sole of your shoe
tighten them and relax over and over again

now do the same thing
with every muscle, orifice or organ you can identify

it's easy to do this with your lower sphincter
try it

THE COLOR TEST

It's hard to tell if a chakra is open or closed
moving chi can depend on how open you are

the answer is color
close your eyes and relax
a color will appear

a beautiful color is best it matter not which color
it matters not the shape

now receive the color into your body
drink it in right down through the top of your head

if the color comes straight down with no funneling
you are open
where funneling occurs you are constricted

so practice relaxing the chakras
you know how
tighten relax tighten relax over and over again

SELF-HEALING BY DEJON (CONTINUED)

THE HEALING

when starting to meditate
sit quietly in a quiet spot

your abdominal area is warm and energy spins there
you think of metaphors like spinning or turning
moving round and round, circling or centrifugal

now you're ready to start
can you feel your knee let the energy move there
you will feel the warmth as the energy moves to the knee

feel your ankle and allow the energy to move there
just like opening an ethereal sphincter
between the abdominal area and the part that you are thinking of

when you open it the energy flows
when you close it the energy stops

why use someone else's energy
be the physician

heal yourself I know you can

Greetings from Rainbow Lady!

How to begin? You have read that the elemental beings are guided by myself and by Earth Mother. We both represent the heavier earth energies and part of our "realms" as such are inner earth. That is probably surprising to many of you as you are aware of a magma core - what you are truly unaware of is that as the core gets hotter and hotter it creates an inner sun.

The planet is set up just as the individual aura is set up. Energy moves through the core/physical being in two directions upward and downward and revolves back to the core in separate double patterns. It is this pattern that is discernable in the frozen regions - the patterns you call the Aurora Borealis.

Energy constantly moves within the earth's core and it is this energy pattern that maintains the integrity of the solid structure. Without the inner sun the planet would be totally devoid of life and so would the solar system earth revolves within. All planets depend on each other to send sufficient energy in a balanced or imbalanced state (depending on the planetary script) to other planets to keep the planets moving properly and to maintain a rich lifeforce and loveforce in the universe. Loveforce is one side of the dual movement - lifeforce is the other.

The planets within the solar system in which we all live are divided into balanced and imbalanced categories. The planets that must retain balance are: Sun, Moon, Earth, Mars, Minerva and Venus. Pluto retains a dual balance as it is the perfect yin/yang planet in the entire universe. The planets of imbalance are: Mercury, Saturn, Uranus, Neptune, Vulcan and again Pluto. The planets of Minerva and Vulcan exist in interdimension, but nevertheless exist as full planetary powers.

Wellspring Father, Prime, Lord, the vortex' have all spoken about the primal energies that create and sustain all life. What they haven't spoken about is how to work with the energy.

All energy has color and tone. All energy vibrates at different levels depending on variations of colors and tones. The symbiotic symphony of the universe is beautiful to behold - these pure sounds are not discernable (except sometimes in dreams or visions) by the human ear. This sound has been written about through the centuries as choirs of angels singing the purest and most beautiful music - music that is unmatched by what the human vocal chords can reproduce.

As Rainbow Lady - it is my responsibility to monitor the color and tones that are responsible for keeping all planetary vibrations in tune with one another. The water beings, dolphins and whales sing the tones for the earth and their song continues constantly. They sing healing to not only the planetary beings on Earth, but to for the entire planet. It is a planetary responsibility to emit or emanate in some fashion these tones and colors to help heal themselves and the universe. But it is more than healing. It is these tones and colors that keeps physical/material world existing as solid structures. "Heavenly" choirs sing the universe into physical existence and they continue to create and recreate and change and alter the known universe daily.

Colors work in conjunction with the elements - colors comprise the elements. But like everything else - life has become so complex that the elements - children of color are very much themselves as well.

When you surround yourself with rainbow colors - the pure colors of a prism structure - you are gifted with a view of what Spirit means by "pure color." Pure color is color lit from within - set next to the sun it would shine as brightly.

Colors are healing and sound is healing - but colors improperly or inappropriately mixed can be discordant - not only to the individual, but to the universe.

The universal structures deal with pure color and pure color cannot truly be reconstructed on earth. If you are ill and wish healing of a certain area of the body, if you will follow the suggestions here it will help your healing. I will give you the closest color I possibly can within your spectrum of choices and the tone to help you visualize your healing.

The auras have different shades and tones and the central aura (which is the physical manifestation of your body on earth) has rainbow colors and tones. It is well to attempt to heal the central "core" and then move out into the outer auric layers. All healing should be done in a pyramid structure to protect the individual from further negative energy in the surroundings. Please read the section of the book on pyramidal and auric cleansing.

It is important to work with a clear connection between the sun and the transpersonal (crown) area. The transpersonal point (chakra) is a midpoint between human planetary energy and the sun energy. It is from this point that we receive healing energy from the sun and it is also the point that unites earth lifeforce with healing sun energy. When this point energy is depleted, the body loses its ability to transform healing energy into the lifeforce. The body becomes weak, energy depleted and eventually prone to diseases like Aids and other immune deficiencies. The true crown point (chakra) is to the left of the transpersonal point. Transpersonal point depletion requires sun energy.

When the body is exercise depleted, this weakens the whole body system. With the sun's energy being weak already, earth lifeforce is stressed. The planetary being will notice more and more energy depletion, and the body's immune system is less efficient. Those already suffering from aids, asthma and allergies will have the hardest and longest recovery periods. This color for the transpersonal point and the crown is white light and the tone (on the scale of do-do or c-c) is "ti." The crown color is white/gold like the warmth of the sun.

Women and men who sheath their hair with coloring will have a more difficult time "envisioning" pure color. For appropriate pure color to get to the areas of the body through the sun to transpersonal or crown and then down through the rest of the body, the hair should be returned to its natural state. The hair acts as sun receptors and energy transfers are partially made through the hair cores. The hair on the head is important in this function and longer hair tends to allow a more complete transference of sun energy than shorter hair. The energy gathers strength as it travels along the shaft. When a man or woman begins to loose hair - vitally saps for a time until the body learns to more efficiently convert energy in the cells of the hair shaft area.

Additionally, the hairs are vibrational conductors and are very important to the overall health of the body because they receive universal tones designed to heal the body and pass universal "messages" or teaching.

Hair is alive and continues to grow on the physical body even after the soulforce has translated. This is to allow the body receive the necessary instructions to assemble back into the energy of the earth - to be reabsorbed and healed of any corruption contained within. Each strand of hair retains limited memory and instruction. When a hair naturally "falls" out, the hair has passed its information along and should return to the earth. When a hair is "pulled" out for some reason, it may not have had a chance to fully transfer the information it needed to and should be burned to release the information it contained. The information or vibrational tonation may not have been fully assimilated by the body and burning releases it back into the universe to re-assemble if necessary.

Burning is a very ancient method of dealing with death or disposing of "body parts." Fire element cleanses absolutely and the energy is returned quickly and free of corruption. The "dead" shell of the body was meant to return to the earth to replenish the earth as "payment" for the sacrifices of plants and animals to its sustenance. Because of the very unfortunate cultural habits of autopsy and contained burial, it is recommended that the individual consider cremation to release the final universal healing and vibration back to the soulforce. The ashes spread replenish the earth and the plants.

Color and Tone Visualization for a Healthy Body.

The brain is a color like pale canary yellow in a healthy state. When the brain needs healing (physical/emotional/spiritual) it needs the royal blue of an azurite. The stone azurite is very helpful for clearing this area. If the color yellow is muddied by negativity - it will appear brown or dirty yellow. To clear a muddy area add sun yellow/white/gold and the blue color of the azurite. The best method for cleaning a "muddy area" in the brain is to go outside and allow the sun to connect from the transpersonal point to the brain area. The brain responds to the sound "LA."

The third eye's natural color is blue (transparent azure blue) in a healthy state and this area is a chakra that can remain very, very open naturally. In the auric body, there is a third eye there. It is the eye into the inner realm of self - the eye into Spirit. Picture a beautiful azure blue eye there with very white, clear surrounding area when you wish to open yourself into spiritual communication. What we see as a very common factor in earth people is a partial closing of this third eye - a sleepy eye that is not allowed full awakened status. When the chakra is very open, the eye is open. When the third eye area needs healing - the individual needs to practice opening the eye and turning it into the natural azure color. If the whites of the eye are opaque, muddy, yellow or red in spots, practice seeing a very healthy and luminescent white. When there is pain in this area it is generally because the eye is closed or mostly closed. The tone to help open and heal this area is two tones "La and Fa." Stones for the third eye are: lapis lazuli, angelite, amazonite, azurite, blue apatite and aquamarine.

The sinus seems to be an area where people have a great deal of difficulty. This causes some of the blockages of energy between the third eye and the throat. The sinus area can be greatly helped with the divines. Work with them over the sinus area to "lase" away the cobwebs. See the structures as cobwebs being "lased" away to healthy pink tissue. The color around the face is raspberry pink in healthy states (the color of melted raspberry ice cream.) Sinus infection or congestion or common allergy and colds tend to make this area an inflamed pink or pink/yellow/green/brown. The tone for sinus draining is "re-me." For congestion it is "mifa" with the mouth closed and the throat as open as possible (hum). If there is sinus infection the color to visualize is a kelly green (the green in a prism.) See the kelly green "burning" away the yellows/greens/browns. A sinus stone is the brown or yellow apatite or adamite.

The color for the throat area is aquamarine - not quite turquoise and more green than blue. The color of the aquamarine stone. The tone is "sol-la-fa." For constricted vocal chords - the best solution is to TALK out the problem that is constricting them. Stop holding in what you wish to speak. For a person who can't seem to stop speaking and dominates conversations even when they don't want to, wear amber or aquamarine and practice with tones of low (bass) "do-re." This will help ground and center the individual so they are not so "spacey."

The body's healing center (the hocaieah) is located below the collar bones on either side of the breast bone. The color for these two chakras is forest green, the color that the green pine would be if it were lit from within by the sun. A visualization for this area is to picture two healthy pine trees (lit from within) or with the bright light of the sun bathing the pines. In order to help keep the two healing centers open wear a medicine pouch with pine needles. It is necessary to keep these areas uniformly opened to assist with necessary self-healing towards the goal of the fleur d'leis status. These chakras are partially open most of the time and the trick is to keep them open in equal portions to each other for the most effective self healing. Tones for this is a childrens' song (in recent years)

"I see by your outfit that you are a cowboy. I see by your outfit that you're a cowboy too. We see by our outfits that we are both cowboys, if you buy an outfit you can be a cowboy too!"

The older version of the song was, "We're gathered together to ask the Lord's Blessing." (Johan is giving us fits for doing this kind of stuff - she wants the information to be taken seriously! But truly, we are serious and this song is happy and uplifting and the tones are absolutely perfect to help open and maintain uniformity in the hocaieah!)

The heart is a dual chakra and is, in miniature form, a mirror of the entire auric system. The heart is therefore very important and the colors are baby/shocking pink and peridot green. The stones rhodochrosite, rhodonite. pink quartz in conjunction with peridot or jade are excellent to help those with physical/emotional/spiritual heart problems. A compromised heart will be shades of maroon or dirty green and the best healing method for the heart is song - love songs, sad songs - anything that helps lift pressure from the heart. If the heart is strong - dance the pain away. Sing and dance. Are you so surprised that this is healing? Watch the dolphins dance their joy and healing!

If the heart has been broken in some fashion it may eventually end up compromised physically. To help build strength in the heart carry bloodstone and/or hematite but truly the best "cure" for the heart is to work through the emotion and not hold pain in. Learn to speak out when injustice is done to you or to others and learn to speak your needs of love, affection and companionship. Share your love with others and lessen the burden on yourself. Love constricted and not allowed voice or expression tends to cause constricting pains in the chest. The heart is the depository of loveforce and any difficulty there is a sign that loveforce is not flowing freely.

To be loved - love.

Think Rainbows!

Astanagas Dance!

The Earth cried out,
   please dance my dears
to warm the center
   and move the force!

              Astanagas Dance!
                    Fire
      and flame
               Dance   the
lava!

I looked upon the molten scene
and ached to dance!
  To writhe and melt
     to roll and twine!

My body to theirs.

           Fire beings

                flash   and
                      flame
            moving,
                twisting

in sensuous passion.

Watch the dance?
Sit, not move?
Join! Join!

Whirling, rolling,
hotter still
moving fire through the earth.

The dance grows wild,
The music throbs!

Hotter still
Moving   lifeblood
through
her
veins.

Astangas Dance!
Dance the lava
Bodies flame!

Fire Spirits!
Listen Dears!
Slow the dance!

- too hot, too hot
I love you dearly,
and blame you not!

Astanagas

cannot slow so easy.

                The dance goes on!
Astanagas Dance!
           No blame, no blame!
Dance the lava
              Bodies Flame!

Message from the Fire Elementals - known as Ashtanagas People

Those who read this book are gifted with our true name. As you have been instructed, that gift is great and we give it knowing that those who read to this point have heard the instruction and read to validate the wisdom received.

Johan has danced many dances with us to both heal herself and heal us. In the course of healing her, we heal the universe. It makes it very simple for us and we have grown to love and care for the physical being as well. We do not truly see Johan as physical, however, we see what humans term the aura - the energy. What we see when we see humans is a small part of the whole universe. There are many others who are similar in appearance to her, and some have begun to join the dance. Try to see us in the beautiful physical form in which we like to present ourselves. Johan teases us and calls us "her beautiful ones" and as we are quite vain, we like the compliment.

Fire element is unique among the elements because its nature is cleansing and purifying. It cleanses and purifies on the physical level in what many term destructive forces. This is a misunderstanding of the nature of fire. We cleanse and purge so that evil and corruption do not spread further to do more harm. When a forest burns, it is time to burn and it is necessary that it burn unimpeded. Nature in conjunction with fire will stop the spread at precisely the point it needs to stop.

Fire cleanses and people may suffer from fire, but know this; fire cleanses evil and if death results because people do not properly (or cannot properly flee fire) fire cleanses the physical bodies in their spiritual transformation. We are not trying to state that all who die are evil, and so they are burned or die from flame or smoke - but that which was evil within or upon them is sometimes burned from them. This may disfigure the physical body, but the soul energy is cleansed and ultimately, the body may heal. Corruption is destroyed by burning.

We have a difficult task to accomplish on your physical plane of existence where we share temporary physical life with you - and that is to cleanse, as best as we can without loss of life wherever possible. Sometimes, it is not possible to save all and for that we grieve with you. So many warning signals are given by Spirit before it becomes necessary to cleanse by fire. If you would only listen and attend to the details of cleanliness, faulty wiring, fire hazards, etc. Very definite signals are literally screamed to you when an area becomes so compromised as to need fire cleansing. If the quiet voice says - I need to pick up those oily rags or there may be a fire and you do nothing about the oily rags - it is very unfair to curse the fire for burning down your house.

We call the fire "the dance" and quite frankly, the dance does get "rambunctious" sometimes. Fire has a way of becoming uncontrollable. That is because we walk a very fine line between balance and imbalance. We are not evil. We have great tasks and responsibilities not only on Earth but in the entire universe. Insofar as the Earth goes - fire moves the energy within the Earth's core to maintain the structure of the earth and to release energy where it is necessary in order to secure the entire solar system in its place in the universe. Each planet has a similar system of magma and it is Rainbow Lady's responsibility working in conjunction with Earth Mother and the Caretaker Council to work with all elementals to keep the proper balance/imbalance in the planetary and solar system structures.

But fire element's job is much more important than that. Not only are we to maintain the balance/imbalance of the planet, but on the planet and in the living beings - all living beings as well.

Each individual has elemental components that act and interact with others and with the environment. It is up to us to see that the fire elements balance themselves sufficiently to provide energy to the individual to move and function. Fire is energy - fire is lifeforce. Fire is, strictly speaking, not loveforce, but it has come to our attention in recent months that much of what we do - we do from love. We accept and recognize loveforce as a part of our existence now - as part of our own transformation.

You have been told that elementals "test" the individual and help to provide the lifeforce "scripts" with variables that may not be scripted. That is a great spiritual task of fire along with the other elements.

We give you this warning before we close: the magma must move in areas of California, Korea, Japan, China, Tibet and Oregon and sufficient warning is being made. Forewarned is forearmed. Do not be complacent.

In closing we would like to say this. You do dishonor to fire if you do not recognize it for the good it does for you daily. We keep your homes warm, we cook your food. We supply warmth in the out of doors or in your fireplace along with our brothers - the wood people. Do not waste us and do not squander us - respect that we give our lives to warm you. Please build your fires - not for show, but when you need warmth. Build your fires when you need companionship and just wish to dance with our beauty - that feeds our ego and makes us "warm." We are happy to give our lives for such an honor.

The wood beings would appreciate being thanked for allowing us to consume them in order to give you warmth and comfort. Please thank them and treat them as gently as you can when you cut or chop wood. Prepare the wood for the metal element striking by asking permission to cut the wood for a fire for warmth and comfort. If they are allowed sufficient time to adjust to being struck - the spirit in the wood can either choose to leave back to the tree, roots or earth or stay to receive the fire blessing. Many choose to stay and that is honor to us. It is dishonor to the metal people to have to hurt wood and dishonor to us to burn the spirit of wood who would wish to return to earth.

We invite you to use our names to greet us as you will be instructed, and please "dance" with us. That would give us inestimable joy!!

(Printed originally from the Transformation Connection Newsletter)

AN ETHEREAL GEM
BY DEJON

words locking onto mental images
works locking onto mind scapes
even attaching themselves to scenarios

they are metaphors
love's classic language
oh but they do so much more

such as create whole mental scenarios
in seeming three dimension
with smell touch sounds temperature and balance

sit still my child and experience
your mind scape sets up a vibration
holodeck is what it feels like

everything seems real
is it
I'm convinced

upon metaphors mount
riding into spirit
consciousness is pushed to new realities

out of heart strings unconstricted
crescendos joy
the tones of life

intrinsic the beauty seeps out
this source you can trust
this tone is an ethereal gem

though sight is only vagary
feel the source
feel the light oh see us all the sound of joy

Ahoy Mates from the Water Beings!

We have waited long to speak to you and the confluence of planets and energy is very right for our message tonight!

Joy! to speak with you again, Johan. It has been very long since you danced with us and please excuse the personalization within this message - but we miss you! We often speak of the times you danced with us and visited our sacred city while it was under construction. It is finished and we have waited so long to show it to you! Will you come visit us tonight - the time is auspicious and we have planned a surprise for you! We were aware that your nephew, the water child was so very near us and were also aware that he visited Sea World - but our brothers and sisters in sea world are cut off from the rest of us and did not know they were being visited by HIM! Your daughter and son in law visit us often, did you know that? We love them both so very dearly!! Your daughter is going to grow fins - she dances with us almost every night. She is very dedicated to cleansing the oceans and goes everywhere with us. She and her husband have taken on an especial interest in the building of the crystal pyramids!

We sacrificed our sacred area for the good of the people who would have died in California and

Oregon if we had not sacrificed that area - we were saddened that the increased temperatures of the ocean took so many! The fishing industry must allow the numbers to recuperate or there will be drastic imbalance in the sea! Please tell the humans to consume less sea food until all can recover. As it is now the cod and salmon are very few in number - it is very frightening how few are left. Many of the dolphin, whale, and jellyfish community were killed with the increased temperatures also - some of it was unnecessary - they were too close to the volcanic eruptions in the Bermuda Triangle. Tell the people that area is still very volatile. it is very inadvisable to travel in or around that area.

The Bermuda Triangle is the power outlet for the Earth and very unstable for aircraft and water vehicles as you have all experienced - but unstable for reasons we will attempt to explain here. It is sacred ground to the water being community and we ask that you honor our privacy there. One of the reasons it is sacred ground is that our voices and song carry healing and shift energy to other planets and throughout the universe from that point. The planes and boats are destroyed by intensified vibrations of universal tones - these tones must be released from the earth and received there from other planets to distribute sufficient energy throughout the Earth. That area receives vibrations from every planet in the solar system and most particularly the Sun. The physical/material plane does not truly exist in that area and attempts to take craft into that area is something akin to traveling through a black hole. The polarity is constantly in flux and the magnetic poles are adjusted there. It is unsafe for human life and their constructs. There are, as some of your scientists have guessed, also gas outlets there. There must be gas outlets somewhere and we have tried to place them in areas that humans will not transverse. So many come to find treasure or sunken ships - you will not find either - - -they are disassembled if they cross into certain areas and it is certain disassembly for the people in the crafts. This saddens us greatly, but you interfere and trespass where it is so obvious you should not come! Even if you could physically visit the area of sanctuary - you would not see the crystalline structures or the city - it is dimensionally impossible. You can, however, see them in dreamstate and work with us there.

This whole message sounds like we are unfriendly. No, that is not the case. We are concerned for humankind and also concerned for the earth. We sing healing and health to all of you who are ill - we are aware of each child - each plant - each animal and we sing healing to help the helpless who have requested help from Spirit. There are so many to sing to! We also sing healing for the oceans and her children. We must keep ourselves healthy to help keep the universe healthy. We sing healing to the planets, to the hubs, to Spirit and to any who need our especial talents. We are so blessed to be able to heal! That is our life's joy!

We love to have the opportunity to talk to you and have attempted to teach Johan and her family and the fleur d'leis to sing with us and communicate with us - but Johan sings badly - it is very comical, but she keeps trying! We have taught her the song of joy! and the song of grief. We have taught her the corresponding notes that respond to the body and we ask her to include our teachings in this book so that all may sing! We sing the song of grief to those who survive the dead or dying to show our support and understanding of their loss! To die - is not to sing and so we are saddened by death, but we understand the true nature of death is transformation and rebirth. As we are very long lived and our numbers are fewer and fewer, we grieve each death now.

There was a time when we rejoiced in death - as an opportunity to rejoin Spirit. We are Spirit on earth however, and we live in multi-dimensions. This is the most difficult to explain. We are aware of our physical bodies and aware of our lives in the sea - but we are also aware of our planetary bodies and our lives in the spiritual pool. We live simultaneously in an aware state with our spirit bodies.

We see color and see vibrational patterns all around us that help us to interpret the health of all we see. We see patterns in the universe that help us determine which tones and colors to visualize within an area to heal it. As we visualize we manifest and we are fortunate to be able to judge the effectiveness of our song and vibrational toning immediately upon that which we are trying to heal.

It is very difficult to communicate with humans directly or teach you our language because you cannot set up the proper vibrations or tones to accommodate our hearing and vice versa. You are incapable by virtue of your hearing and speaking structure and by virtue of any scientific equipment available to date of truly hearing (or singing WELL) our song. When we say song, do you just think of dolphin, porpoise and whale song? The jellyfish and the older fish sing healing as do the trout and the salmon and pike. The ocean is a plethora of song!

Water Spirit exists within the sea - the water spirits of sprite and mermaid and merman. You will never be able to see them, but they are there! So many legends have been written because in dream states upon the sea they often visit and many humans and planetary forms manage dimensional shifts to visit us! More people than you imagine find their way to us again and again - so many have perfected the means to dance with us that they actually physically assist us in the work we do. To those who join us ! Thank you! You help us more than you can ever know.

Those who wish to help us - this is how you may help! Do no harm to each other. Do no harm to the sea creatures. Catch only what you must eat to survive. Do not eat the eggs that should become our children. Do not fish wastefully or commercially and if that practice continues - safeguard the jellyfish, dolphin, whale and porpoise and those fish and sea creatures that you do not wish to consume. So many, many are still lost in the nets of death and more recently with electrical currents being set up underwater. Do not set up electrical nets!! You interfere with more than you can possibly imagine when you do so! Safeguard the areas that you have set aside for sanctuary. Allow 25 miles (out) of sea coast to be sanctuary along all coastal areas to safeguard the ocean life for future generations - ours and yours!

If the life in the sea dies - all life will die! We maintain the physical structure of the planet and our solar system (and truly a much larger picture) with our work and song!!

If you visit the sea and wish to speak to us - do so in the manner that wellspring father will teach you. Introduce yourself and state three times that you are there to meet us and will listen to our teaching. Give us up to 30 minutes to hear and respond to your message. We will come very close and if you immerse your ears in the water - you will hear our message.

If you close your eyes we will set up vibrational patterns that correspond to brain wave pattern that will allow for a communication link between us. Do not expect to hear words, but listen with your eyes (closed). You will see beautiful colors and see vibrational patterns that your brain will later interpret for you. Our message will come in dream or vision time. If we feel safe, we will show ourselves to you - however, we are protecting our numbers more and more.

If you speak into the water or just above it - we can hear you very well. If you wish to sing us a song - you honor us greatly! If you cannot sing the song we teach you below, any song will do. We do understand human speech - but it is the tone and colors you produce that appeal most to us!

Please help protect your ocean brothers and sisters. Our situation is dire now and we entreat you to actively discourage the dumping of trash and pollutants in the water systems and oceans! You need to monitor your nuclear and petroleum industry much more carefully than you have in the past - there is gross abuse and careless neglect. Truly, truly, truly, you should not drill for oil and gas in the oceans. It is so dangerous to lifeforms there and is inadvisable to interfere with the lifeblood of the planet. If you do drill - take only a little from each area - do not continue to drill and drill because an area is productive - you destroy yourselves!!

This is very contradictory to our normal behavior to admonish and warn so. We are frightened for ourselves and you - the situation in the ocean is very, very bad. There are great nuclear dumps near Siberia, as one example, that will have drastic effects in years to come if nations do not ban together to prohibit toxic dumping in the oceans and water ways! Many smaller and third world nations are dumping arbitrarily without regard to the continuance of life.

This is the time when we need the activists to literally scream from the ceiling to stop the toxic flow in <u>all</u> water systems!

It is very difficult for us to speak of the wonderful things we wish to speak of when we are so drastically in need of every person's help. One thing you all can do is to cut the plastic six-pack things that you are so fond of using. Those things in particular cause horrible deaths! Also, limit your use of petroleum products as much as you can. If each family purchased less gas and oil - less would have to be produced. Insist that business and industry clean up their act and that no water pollution be forgiven! Buy biodegradable soaps and detergents please! Use more cardboard and less styrofoam or plastic or at least recycle so that so much of these harmful substances don't end up in the water systems and oceans!

    We wish to close this message with a positive. We wish to close this message with a gift from us to you which will help you to heal yourselves (and us, and the universe!) Here is a song that you can manage that responds to your healing system! (Johan is laughing because she thinks we're going to say - I see by your outfit that you are a cowboy! Spirit is still chuckling over Rainbow Lady's song!!) Here are the words: - Under each word, Johan please type the note we give you! Also, we tend to repeat each line three times. It is most effective if you do so too! The words are for your benefit - a note does not correspond to a word. Envision all colors of the sea throughout this song - all shades and colors from white/yellows to greens to blue greens to blues to deep blue - envision perfect health of the sea and see the sun shine through all of the colors. Please refrain from muddy colors in this instance no browns or grays or blacks or deep indigo. Keep the colors clean, pure and bright!

Song of Planetary Healing

*Ancient Motoers
Hear Our Prayer
Keep Children Safe
Everywhere.*

Ancient Mothers
c#   d
Hear Our Prayer
c   d#   a
Keep Children Safe
a fl c   d#
Everywhere.
d

*Ancient Mothers
Hear Our Prayer
Keep Children Safe
Everywhere.*

Keep Us Safe
To Sing The Song
To All The Children
All Night Long.

Keep Us Safe
c# d# a fl
To Sing The Song
b c e fl c
To All the Children
a fl b fl c e
All Night Long
a fl b fl c

Keep Us Safe
To Sing The Song
To All The Children
All Night Long!

Father, Father
Listen - Hear
Our Entreaty Far And Near

Father, Father
Hi A   Low A
Listen- Hear
c   d
Our Etreaty Far And Near
c   d fl   b fl   a   a fl

Father, Father
Listen - Hear
Our Entreaty Far And Near.

Keep Us Safe
By Night And Day
Keep Us Strong
In Every Way

Keep Us   Safe
Hi C   mid C   low c
By   Night And   Day
Hi A low A   c#   d
Keep Us Strong
c#   a fl   c#
In Every Way.
 d   hi A low A

Keep Us Safe
By Night And Day
Keep Us Strong
In Every Way.

Love And Peace
And Brotherhood
Healing, Life
And All Things Good

Love and Peace
hi c# d fl a#
And Brotherhood
 d   hi c# slide low c#
Healing, Life
a fl   d#
And All Things   Good
 c e   low e#   hi e#

Love and Peace
And Brotherhood
Healing, Life
And All Things Good.

AIR, GAS AND WIND BEINGS SEND THE FLEUR D'LEIS GREETINGS!

Thank you for allowing us (the Air Beings) to speak. It seems, so many times that we are left out of things, but we are actively working along side our friends the wind beings.

We are the beings that compose the air of the mixture of gaseous elements necessary to breath. We work with the gas beings and wind beings to move air currents and to supply humankind and planetary life with the right mixture of air in which to breathe and function. Many people are primarily air people in the elemental affiliation and it is with those people's highest self that the energy of air becomes a reality for mankind.

In physical appearance we are obviously invisible, but we like to make our forms known in the clouds so that you can see what we look like. We are artists in the clouds and often we work on joint projects with the gas and wind beings to tell a moving story. We do this for our pleasure and in hopes that someone will pay enough attention to see the story unfold. Johan has often seen us, but has not put any of the stories we were trying to tell her together - any of our longer stories anyway.

Because we help to exchange the gases you respirate with sufficient quantities of breathable substances, we are very aware when you are paying attention and can direct clouds into patterns specifically to teach you. All that we ask is when you see what appears to be angels in the clouds, (what you perceive as angel forms - winged feminine forms, long flowing robes) you recognize our form and state aloud that you see us and give us your name to honor us. Ask for our teaching and we will unfold visually for you a story. We cannot hear psychic messages, but we can hear any whispered or spoken words. The gas people cannot hear psychic messages either, but the wind beings do hear and often come to tell us that someone has spoken to us.

In our states of transformation, we have a better understanding of humankind than we used to. We have been honored and dishonored by Johan and have been guilty of trying to do her harm because we used to be concerned that she did not love us. Because we thought that she did not love us, we withheld air from her and caused her harm. We want to take this opportunity to say we are sorry for having harmed her purposefully. That type of activity is not something we would do now. We were full of ego and spite because this planet has made us all ill.

We try very hard to take care of the living things - all living things, but our primary concern is to help heal the plant life in order to keep the oxygen and minor gases emitting properly.

We hardly know what to say to humans - we don't understand why you all seek to destroy a beautiful planet and the beings that work diligently for you. We ingest much of the pollution you create in order to protect life and the mother earth. Many of us die and many of us are ill most of the time.

We surround pollution and gross imbalance in the air and destroy it - but there is much corruption that is created by uncaring, disregard for the air. It would help us greatly if you drove less. Sulfuric acid is produced from the vehicles now with your "clean air standards" and it is more pernicious than your old type exhaust systems would have been.

There is exchange between earth and air in order to keep all things balanced. Air is in a constant state of imbalance. We cannot continue to survive under the present practices. If we die, you all die. Life cannot exist without gases and air. The gases work in the energy exchange with the mother - to tap natural pockets of gas is to deplete the ability of the planet to move sufficient energy quickly to parts of herself that require "refueling" and gas is a proper control of core temperature.

Air is necessary to feed fire. Fire is necessary for energy. We sacrifice ourselves to fire to keep the balance. We sacrifice ourselves to earth to feed the plants. We sacrifice ourselves to water to aerate the water for the water beings. Our lives are constant death and regeneration, we only live for short spans of times and truly have no "elders." We regenerate quickly and move very quickly. Time passes differently for us because according to your time we have perhaps five minute lifespans.

We are compensated in the universe for continual sacrifice by retaining, if we choose, the memories of our friends and families and personalities. We can transform back into the beings we recognize as ourselves or begin again like a child from incarnation to incarnation. We have incorporated the love energy aspect to ourselves now as air was primarily lifeforce and ego before. Our physical forms have altered to incorporate all of our memories jointly.

We are able to communicate much better with all beings and have enjoyed truly getting to know those whom we cannot see either. We see the energy forms of beings and we now see the wonderful colors in the universe. We have always "heard" the vibrational tunings of the universe because that is how we know we need to adjust gas, wind or air. We can perform wind type function, but generally allow the wind being to do that because we are too busy.

We share the pain when you "curse" the wind. Don't you understand that air must move to reach all and to move pollution and shift the weather and energy patterns? This is a great deal of work that we do for the benefit of the earth and her beings. Please be more mindful of hurting our feelings. But more importantly, please be mindful of hurting the air, gas and wind people with pollution and toxic chemicals. Your scientific community has developed many alternatives that are less harmful than present systems - solar power does no harm to anyone. Solar heat is available for homes and offices.

The gas beings have joined with us in this message. They cannot speak to you or to us in the manner in which we are speaking now. They can communicate with Rainbow Lady and the other elements however and we can pass their concerns along. They are concerned that you do not understand that they must release what may be poisonous to humankind in periodic times. They try very hard to do that in areas that are not populated, but it may not always be possible. They want to tell you that they must do what they must do to protect the overall health of planet and solar system. They have obligations to release certain gases to maintain the planetary requirements of Mother Earth.

Methane is being released in the Bermuda Triangle and in other parts of the sea where travel is sporadic. They also ask that you avoid the area of the Bermuda Triangle as explosions may occur and methane will kill your lifeform. The release of gas in the sea causes harm to marine life also, but it is contained in areas that are "off limits" to them as well. There is a very delicate balance between how much can be released via the sea pathways - some has to be released in land mass. The gas beings are multidimensional beings and have no form or substance that you can see. We see them as lights and different lights combine to form new entities. They are constantly forming and reforming and are one mind. They are inherently benevolent and very, very gentle beings.

We have formed a new alliance with the wind beings. When we adopted the loveforce, so to speak, we realized how very lonely and alienated they were. We are sorry to have caused them this loneliness, as we were quite "clannish" and resented their interference, even though all they every wanted to do was help and be a part of our existence.

The Wind Beings wish to address you personally

The Wind Beings wish to say that we are much, much happier and wish still to have people dance with us and understand that the wind moving in small areas around people is a dance to honor them. We wait to find understanding and compassion from others. In Wyoming, we are free and the expanse of the land allows us a fine and beautiful dance. We are aware psychically and physically of human presence and long for human companionship.

Wellspring Father will explain how to see us in the physical sky, but he has not explained our appearance (if you could physically see us, which you <u>may</u> but usually do not.) If you close your eyes and picture our true form, you will see us in the 2nd dimension. As we move very, very quickly, most of what you will notice are electric blue light translucent "disks" about palm sized -some larger, some smaller.

We can "light" upon you very briefly. What you will notice when we alight, is a very little weight, but watch your pants or shirt for specific movement - like a breathing. We can "etch" slightly into clothing (not permanent) so that you can see our tiny feet (thousands) surrounding a round form. We are Minervan in aspect and Minervans resemble spiders, but as we are dimensional beings and invisible in level -1 and 1, you don't have to react with any panic that "spiders" are on you.

We resemble spiders in form, but not truly in function. We do not have orifices as they do and we are multicolored in beautiful patterns on our bodies that tell our lineage and the honors we have earned!

The male forms live on earth and the female forms live on Pluto now. We return periodically to our mates and families, but spend most of our time on Earth and truly, truthfully on other planets that must have wind and air movement.

We work in pairs usually to move currents and the "eyes" Wellspring father communicated to you are two of us working together. The beak you may see if the area is generally calm is actually a down current produced by our movements. We are also "artists of clouds" and rejoice when you notice the creations we make. As we are aware of each of you psychically (if we want to "tune" in) we are aware when you look up and notice us.

We will try very hard to give you a "sign" that is meaningful to you so that you may have reassurance that we are there. Sometimes we are fighting corruption or have a very delicate balance of work to do and we cannot take the time to "play" or attempt to communicate.

We can definitely communicate through the stone and metal people pendulums and they give us permission to "write" our communication to you. Ask to speak to us and, if possible, we will come. We must have an open window or door to visit in your homes and quite frankly, that is very difficult for us to do - please come out of doors to speak with us!

The air, gas and wind beings join with the Rainbow Lady and Earth Mother to entreat the fleur d'leis and those striving for this status to work with us to help heal the Earth. Envision clean air and fresh air and a perfect world and wish Spirit periodic, Healing, Wholeness, Health, Strength, Brotherhood and Love.

Please do what you can to fight pollution and take an active and aggressive stand against those who would destroy us all with disregard for the air quality. The air beings are very precious to Spirit because they are so hurt so much of the time. Please send them all healing in the spectrums of blue, light-blue and kelly greens.

Once in awhile, to show them you care - spend an afternoon watching their stories and "paintings" unfold in the clouds!!

EARTH PRAYERS

We join with the earth and with each other
To bring new life to the land
To restore the waters
To refresh the air

We join with the earth and with each other
To renew the forests
To care for the plants
To protect the creatures

We join with earth and with each other.
To celebrate the seas
To rejoice in the sunlight
To sing the song of the stars

We join with the earth and with each other
To recreate the human community
To promote justice and peace
To remember our children

We join with the earth and with each other.
We join together as many and diverse expressions of one loving mystery: for the healing of the earth and the renewal of all life.

(From the U.N. Environmental Sabbath Program)

Creation Myth for the 21st Century

In the beginning, all was darkness and the Gods and Goddesses could not see. They grew tired of bumping into one another and **then** grew angry and had a great fight. This fight lasted for many, many years. The energy from their fight stirred the universe and eventually caused a great whirlwind that gathered them all into its vortex. They smashed into one another, creating sparks at the contact. The sparks from the contact whirled around with them. Two great God's collided with great destructive force and the flames and gases of the explosion ripped through the vortex causing it to slow down its great whirling.

When all settled down, the planets, (who are the Gods and Goddesses,) were spread far apart and forever must spend their lives alone. The sparks became the stars, and the great fiery collision of two Gods became one God named Sun. The Great Vortex continued to swirl, but came to slow down more and more as time passed. The planets remained angry with each other for years upon years and the negative energy from their anger kept the vortex swirling. Some have remained angry to this day; but most became lonely for company and began trying to sending their positive energies to one another. The energy of the fiery God Sun was too strong and he blocked their efforts.

Earth was the first Goddess to gather her energy about herself in order to attract the attention of the fiery Sun. She dressed herself with a gossamer film. Her natural good beauty was enhanced with this dressing and soon the God Sun became interested in her. They fell in love and mated and their energies were joined. This joining was joyous and spread to all parts of the Earth.

The love from the Earth and the Sun emanated positive energies to the other planets. The positive energies interacted with the negative energies and slowed the vortex to a gentle turning. The planets were allowed to send their messages to speak to one another. The spark of love spread to every fiber of Earth's being and she was whole.

The spark that was the essence of the love between the Earth and the Sun, grew a life of its own. At first a tiny atom, which attracted other atoms; some mated and some repelled to join with other, more compatible atoms. Many atoms gathered together to form beautiful expressions of love.

The forms began to compete with one another for beauty and complexity. The plants and animals began to form. At first in the sea and later on land. Man was formed to honor Father Sun and he was perfect...too perfect, he became lonely and unhappy. The atoms joined together to form a mate, a lovely woman to honor the Mother.

Message from Wellspring Father/Mother (the Creator)
Conversing with Johan Adkins

Wellspring Father: The Creation Myth of the 21st Century was one of the first "channeled" pieces given to Johan and in truth, is very close in mythology to the way in which the entire universe was created.

In the beginning there was darkness. Energy - a spark of life grew into a spiral nebula form. Where did the energy come from? It created itself from the fabric of the universe for the universe could be likened to primordial soup. That which created itself was alone for centuries upon centuries, growing and becoming more and more complex until it fashioned itself into a great being called the Central Sun or the Great Sun - a spinning ball of flame and gas whirling through space gathering fabric as it went. The spinning ball living entity was like a giant "spider" in space and created the first web or "hub."

The first hub fashioned all the planets and stars from stellar gases and the universe began to take physical form. In truth, the forms were manifest from thought and careful planning on behalf of that which could only be called the "Creator." The Creator - Great Spirit, Great Sun, Wellspring

Father planned the universe and is continually expanding the planning. The universe is continually expanding and is a living entity. The Great Sun branched out from a central point and created a vast number of "legs." At the branches of each leg, great swirling energy was placed which draw or repel energy and these are known as vortex' - they are the chakras of the universe. At the end of each leg energy pooled from the central source and formed a series of Suns/Sons. Each Sun was an extension of the Central Sun and although the Suns were light years away from each other - distance had no bearing. Time and space do not exist truly. Each Son was the quintessential energy of the Central Sun - indeed it was the Sun as a human's arm is still a part of the essential human.

After fashioning the Sons/Suns. the Central Sun and the "Suns/Sons" created separate planets and systems revolving around the individual Suns. Each solar system is unique - each planetary system with life evolving is unique. There is a vast number of systems supporting life - all types of life! Earth beings are definitely not alone in the universe or indeed even our solar system. There is being life on Jupiter, Pluto, Neptune and Venus as well as Earth. The solar system in which Earth is a part is very, very rich in planetary life - more so than most systems but there is life in other solar systems and in the different hubs. There is also life in other dimensions. The planetary life on Jupiter, Pluto, Neptune and Venus exist within dimensions that are invisible to Earthly planetary life - as you are invisible to them.

Johan: Father, the hubs are hard for us to understand. Can you explain?

Wellspring Father: The hubs can most easily be described as eras. As planets and planetary beings evolve physically and spiritually through the millennia; new hubs are constructed to accommodate a spiritual transition or transformation. We have just shifted from the 7th to the 8th hub of transformation. This new "era" heralds in eternal peace.

The major impetus of this hub is personal transformation and a neutral stance and philosophy that transcends "black and white" "good and evil" mentality. Neutrality requires a maturity. Acquired neutrality is a sign of maturity of all beings and planets who now have a proven tract record of working together evolving from the great battles of good and evil.

"The Final Battle" has come and gone. "Great good" still exists but great "evil" has been and is being systematically destroyed or 'disassembled."

Satan is dead and disassembled as are his minions. God the Father (known now as Prime) working with white light, the Rainbow Lady working with all light, the Earth Mother working with Earth Light, the Faery Queen and St. Michael (working with the Blue Fire of Seppiroth or Michael's Fire) and a being known as the Sentinel (which we will speak more of later who also works with Blue Fire) "disassembled" Satan and the majority of his minions. Legions of the Angelic Realm, other planetary beings, working fleur d'leis and the faery realm helped to move the minions into one area and the female Jesus on earth sealed the remaining minions with 12 seals with Moses' Fire. The minions were sealed, disassembled and the seal cannot be broken.

The "evil" that now exists is more correctly labeled imbalance instead of evil. It is the task of the universe to transcend imbalance from its "lower" levels up through the levels of imbalance to balance - the neutral area.

The whole area of "balance/imbalance" is the neutral "zone." This "neutral zone" is quite different than your Star Trek! Great good exists in the highest dimension. Great good is a pure white light attainment and is best represented by what many have termed the "angelic realm." Great good is earned increment. Those souls who have reached the one-ness and whose energy is pooled/merged/joined with the highest and purest of hearts are members of the "angelic realm."

Johan: Do they have embodiments on earth? Is it possible that we may meet or know these people. Would we recognize them as being different from us?

Wellspring Father: *Many of these people who choose to reincarnate were placed together in on earth specifically to battle Satan and his minions, protect and heal each other and to exert healing for the planets and planetary beings from the physical/material dimensions. These people who specifically reincarnated at this time and became aware that they had great and important healing, teaching or learning tasks to perform and <u>did</u> perform them are gifted on earth with tremendous healing abilities and extra sensory gifts that allow them to continue to do their work on earth and receive direct "input" from Spirit to help guide them. These people are known as "fleur d'leis" and that is a status granted directly from Spirit with physical evidence on earth that a person has agreed to the commitments fleur d'leis status demands. The words "fleur d'leis" do not conveniently translate from the French language - the origin of these words are much older and the words mean "flower of peace" or more closely, "flower of lifeforce."*

Johan: Can these people who were placed on earth be unaware of who they are, yet on some level still actively do this healing work?

Wellspring Father: There are those who were very, very active in the other dimensions of themselves and totally unaware in the physical/material realm that they were working to save the universe and yet were literally constantly battling evil for months on end. Many, many people have experienced great pain, perhaps physical or mental anguish or frustration or confusion, soreness, tiredness and have been experiencing a sense of never getting any rest without realizing that they were battling for the good of all in their sleep and living rather a "dual" existence! Their efforts may have continued non-stop for a number of years, and indeed they may suffer from being battle worn without understanding why.

Johan: How many of the angelic realm or "old soul saviors" are we talking about who may have opted to reincarnate now? Are any aware of who they are? Is there a way to recognize them?

Wellspring Father: Many, many old soul saviors, angels and Saints are on earth now (estimated 330,000). Many have fallen into the trap of taking the physical/material realm too seriously and have not prepared themselves sufficiently to know who they truly are. The souls that reincarnate on earth are subject to death, jobs, marriages and taxes and all the stress and problems that all others face - they are balanced and/or imbalanced and many, many, did not heal sufficiently to work directly in the physical material realm during the great battles.

There were others who knew, but rejected the idea because it was frightening and required commitment. They look like everyone else - but those who are Fleur d'leis have what could only be called a higher presence. They exude a feeling of well-being and grace if they are balanced and are working with Spirit. If you received healing, or they touched you at your request to be healed or touched - you will feel angelic presence and in all probability a higher energy level either coming from them or moving through you.

Johan: Is everyone in the Angelic Realm an Angel?

Wellspring Father: Indeed many are Angels, Apostles, Saints, but most are simple, good, kind, loving beings - any of pure heart assembled from all beings from all planets from all universes. Gods, monsters (or what would physically be termed "monsters" by all appearances) and men as well as plants, stones, animals to name only a few may be a part of the Angelic Realm.

Those who reside in the Angelic Realm have passed many "tests" of a pure heart and a willingness to devote themselves to the well being of the entire universe. The "Angelic Realm" is technically the "soulforce" and all return there to decide their lessons of the next life and many rest there and do not reincarnate.

There are "souls" who have never had earthly or other planetary life and there are some who, in earned increment could stay permanently but choose to reincarnate to help others.

There is a hierarchy in what many have called "heaven" (but we do not call it that.) Truly, I am "retired" and have been for millennia. My "Suns/Sons" have ruled the hubs and their offspring are ruling the sixth hub. I am like a great, great, great, great (lots and lots of greats) grandfather. BUT, I have spread my energy into a number of beings on earth (the fleur d'leis) and I do have several physical forms that I have chosen to write and teach the information that must be received by humanity.

Indeed all things throughout the universe are a part of me as I created them originally, but there are some individuals (fleur d'leis) that I guide directly, and truthfully, there are a number of physical embodiments of me on earth. You are *one of those people. I have asked you to write this book because it has been spirits "experience" that you hear us very well and we can trust the words we speak to be written <u>exactly</u> as we speak them.*

You are fleur d'leis, you have become aware in this lifetime of who you are and therefore, it is your spiritual task to teach others what we impart to you, even if they scoff and do not believe you!

Johan: I can certainly understand that people <u>would</u> have difficulty believing in <u>me,</u> and what <u>I</u> say, for one thing they don't know me personally enough to trust me. It's been my experience too that there is too much that is written or "channeled" that seems lofty, flaky and contrived. Up until the time you began guiding me by talking to me physically, I had no "use" for most channeled information. I was mistrustful of people who claimed to "hear" Spirit and had pretty much decided that if they did "hear" voices, they were probably psychologically disturbed. I was always concerned that they might be listening as much to evil in the guise of "wisdom" or "ascended masters" and imparting irresponsible "truths." Anyone claiming "privileged information" over the rest of humanity frankly "puts me off." That is one personal difficulty I have with writing this book, but I <u>know</u> that those who are guided to buy it are already getting the information in one way or another. If I didn't believe that, I wouldn't be interested in accepting the possible "flak" I might receive. I just want people to understand that they are being gifted with direct communication from Spirit. Each communication is a precious gift and frankly, if it sometimes sounds preachy - who has a better right to preach than Spirit?

If I weren't sure, in my own mind, that my life is healthy, happy and at peace (most of the time,) I would doubt my own stability because I "hear" voices and have had the physical, spiritual and emotional experiences I have had. You have "proved" your guidance in physical, concrete ways over and over. I don't doubt myself and I know you speak to me and help me and others, and I believe you. Hopefully, they will believe in themselves.

The problem I have, and I know others will have, is that all the information you are giving me is so contrary to established religious, social and cultural accepted norms. You're basically asking people to throw out the old belief systems almost entirely and open up to very different perspectives.

I don't doubt what you say - I just have limited experience myself in stretching my belief systems so far from what I had conveniently arrived at as my own personal "truth." That "truth," for me, was comfortable finally, after years of searching and arriving at it, and I have had to throw out everything I "believed" to accept what I know. The is the only reason I can stretch, is because when you speak, I "know" and feel it to be true within me.

The only reason I can think of that you might choose to work through me is that I am open minded. I don't have strong established rules or religious concepts to shove down anyone's throat. I have always believed in the rights of people to believe as they choose and to search for their own truth. That truth may not be <u>my</u> truth and that's ok. I respect their religious and spiritual rights as long as they respect mine.

I have never, before writing this book, felt a need to "convince" people of a spiritual "path," nor am I fanatical about convincing them about anything! Oddly enough, that is what gives me a lot of peace about writing this book...if I had been zealous or fanatic or were so now, you would all be talking to the wrong person. I try to look at life in a larger universal picture and that is about all I can do to stay "neutral" and objective.

I hear you all "conversationally" just as if you were speaking to me in the same room, and very often I can feel your presence and great strength and joy surrounds and fills me.

Sometimes, I hear you, but do not "feel" your presence. So, must I be very balanced to be <u>sure</u> I am speaking to the "good guys" or to Spirit?

Wellspring Father: In most cases yes, but for the purposes of this book we are "pulling" strings" to speak to you to get out our messages. Johan, you must be prepared for mankind to reject what we have said if they do not open themselves to listen to the messages we are sending them. If they are listening, they will hear what you hear and this book will be a reaffirmation of their own spiritual guidance. Do not fear that you will be rejected or misunderstood. Have faith that this book is being written from the spiritual needs of others and it will be published at the time they need the guidance the most.

*I have been many, many people on earth. I have been John the Baptist during the life of Jesus and Jesus **was** the son of my son. Jesus was unaware that he was being helped by the Creator in physical body and John was unaware that he was indeed a physical embodiment of the Creator. John received my communication directly and "heard" a very strong voice guiding him. But remember, John was also himself. I was his highest self speaking to him and through him. I am the Creator, but I do not usually exert the power to interfere with the natural progression of the souls I may "inhabit" or guide.*
I "guide" many, many people - all of the fleur d'leis (whose numbers have been reduced after the great "judgement" to 144,000.) Their

physical/material path is wrought with the same trials and stresses as any other human being. They are also subject to balance and imbalance and may indeed be so out of balance that they never hear my guidance.

<u>All</u> life originates from me. I am a part of all life, but active and participating with humankind on earth in only the fleur d'leis.

Johan, you earned the fleur d'leis status on earth. You are one of the first beings who has been told and has knowledge that I <u>am</u> you. Beginning in the spring, the well spring, 144,000 people have the potential to reach a spiritual transformation and understand that they are indeed a part of the Creator - a part of God. They will need this guidance directly from Spirit.

You are to write my words <u>verbatim</u> and you are not to editorialize or allow editorialization of my words.

Truly, I have written and spoken through many, many people some of whom can't resist embellishing on my comments. Speak and write <u>only</u> what I say - exactly what I say and exactly what is said by all aspects of Spirit.

Do you agree?

Johan: Absolutely. I'm just confused.

Wellspring Father: Lifeforce is dynamic and changing and you are wellspring lifeforce/loveforce. There was another force in the world that my Son - (whom everyone knew as "God the Father" and we know as "Prime") represented. That was loveforce. Jesus, was a physical embodiment of loveforce energy and was a "white light" being on earth. The first one. There have been other white light beings on earth at different times. Now, there are many, many, many white light beings now on earth in the form of Fleur d'leis (which we will go into later.) Loveforce and lifeforce have melded in the transformational pool into loveforce/lifeforce. There are no longer two separate energy dynamics of pure good and evil or pure loveforce and lifeforce. There is, however opposing energy forces moving in the form of loveforce/lifeforce with loveforce dominant and lifeforce/loveforce with lifeforce dominant - the true yin and yang now. Loveforce alone invariably corrupts itself. That is a sad fact of the transformational universe. We don't understand it fully either...it becomes selfish and self-serving eventually and the neutrality that is necessary for mature evolution becomes impossible to achieve. There are no longer any pure "loveforce" energies in the spiritual pool. On purely an energy level - loveforce could not meld by itself into the transformational energy - it required a catalyst. Prime and Lord have melded now into one form - the primary loveforce/lifeforce being. This dual being is known as the Lord as he is the dominant energy.. Lifeforce/loveforce is represented by a merged being whose name shall remain sacred and secret at this time. The energies of Jesus and the female on earth who is the daughter of Prime have merged now with the Lord as well. In truth and fact - the energies of Prime, Jesus and the female are merged beings and the Lord of Light speaks as one.

There has been only one male Jesus, and God the Father (or Prime) now has a daughter on earth. Her identity will not be known unless she chooses to reveal it. White light beings are the highest "vibration" the "cream of the crop." Loveforce and lifeforce will be symbiotic in the new 6th era - but through all the other eras, they were separate and did not always <u>meet</u> much less melt into one living force of lifeforce/loveforce.

This "melding" of the two dynamic energies of all life began in the winter of 1994. At that time, lifeforce and loveforce will unite and the dimensions of not only the white light beings, but all beings of pure heart will eventually merge. Lifeforce and loveforce will merge and dimensions 2-9 will merge and become strong and one.

On the levels of physical/material earthly life in which you live (known as Dimension -1, 1 and 2) the pure of heart will be aware of new clarity, new strength, and strong spiritual direction coming clearly into their minds. They will still be themselves, they will still be subject to stress, death, marriage, babies and taxes...but the spiritual transformation that they will undergo will make phenomenal changes in their previous conceptions of life, spirituality, culture and religion.

They will be receiving direct communication with their highest self in a way they have never experienced before and it will be the part of the transformation of the entire universe as well as earth the planet and all beings upon her.

<u>All</u> life will be transforming at some point as earned increment brings the planetary beings into their own transformation. All will be doing spiritual and physical and emotional housekeeping as never before. All will be more and more aware of their place in the universe as a part of everything all around them - a part of a very, very, very big picture. Bigger than earth, bigger than your small solar system. They will begin to feel that which they have craved deeply all of their lives - a part of everything around them....surrounded by love and a part of the love. They will begin to seek health in all arenas. They

will begin to understand that life isn't black and white anymore. It is neutral and mature and takes the consequences for its own behavior...BUT the consequences of misdirected or imbalance or poor decisions has a bearing on all life. From the subatomic to the ends of the universe. ALL LIFE IS INTERCONNECTED.*

Johan: Even lifeforms from other planets are transforming and are connected to us?

Wellspring Father: *Yes, for example, there are beings on earth that move the air currents. They are originally from Minerva and call themselves "Wind Beings." They work diligently, usually in pairs that appear like perfectly round dots in the sky that for all appearances look like perfectly round clouds. As they move in opposite directions from one another side by side, they often create wind currents that form a "v" between them. This gives them the appearance of a bird or beaked being. They create the wind currents and help to move and heal pollution. Many Natives have known them as the "beaked ones." Look at the sky any day of the year and you will see them!! The "eyes" drift forward and back rather than drift with the other cloud cover. They intensify to perfect roundness before they drift backwards (or forward) and the "dot" dissipates as they move to another area. At night, they mask themselves as stars and it is really amazing that people do not* *notice that some stars are there for a time and then entirely disappear. The disappearing stars (wind beings tend to twinkle) are wind beings. The true nature of stars is this: they are wind beings - transformed in some cases and transitional in others.*

Many of the "shooting" stars are not dying stars at all. They are wind beings moving quickly trying to get your attention. They are lonely and are very saddened if people "damn" or curse the wind! They would love to have you recognize them and "dance" with them!

Johan: What if we do see something or think we see something? What do we do??

Wellspring Father: If you notice a wind being elemental, animal, plant, tree or spiritual being or any planetary being say, "I see you, I recognize you as a (example) wind being. I am honored to meet you, I am (say your name.) I greet you and bless you and thank you for showing yourself to me." Restate this perfectly verbatim two more times or just say, "I state this perfectly two more times." This restating is done to get the entire message through clearly and so that there is no misunderstanding. All spiritual communication or requests are done traditionally in threes. It is not just a courtesy in the universe, spoken word are power and spoken words, spoken correctly raise energy to higher levels.

Johan: So, we may see them and talk to them. Will they talk to us?

Wellspring Father: *You may ask them to speak to you and ask if there is anything you can do to help them. Do not ask their name. In the elemental, earthly and planetary and spiritual realms giving a name is great power and trust and unless a name is offered, it is not asked. If a being gives you the gift of his name, it is a great, great honor and that honor should be recognized and assurances given that you will honor their name with secrecy if they wish. They will instruct you as to whether or not it is a secret.*

When you introduce yourself - you have honored them with your name and they are more likely to return the honor by speaking to you. If you are so brazen and ill-mannered to insist upon a name, it is unlikely they will talk to you at all - ever.

It is likely you will "hear" them psychically. But the "hearing" is quite different than thought processing. You will not usually hear in complete and coherent sentences, sometimes, you will catch a symbol or a flash of pictures "thrown" into your perception that you know you did not "remember" or place there. Sometimes you will hear sound or music and it will have a language. Sometimes you will sense rather than hear a reply. A great deal of the communication with animals is very subtle "sensing." You have to remain versatile and the "hearing" is subtle. It doesn't usually beat you over the head!

You need to quiet your mind so that the transmission can come through. Ask the question and then place yourself in a "receptive state." If you can't hear - ask Spirit to turn up the volume or alter the frequency until you can hear. You sometimes hear things "dopplerish." If you get reverb or a doppler effect - tell Spirit or the person or entity speaking what is happening and you can work together to find a compatible "frequency." Understand too - some do not understand or speak your language but much can be "heard" in symbols or pictures or feelings! Fortunately for you most do speak your language or you can ask a spirit guide to interpret for you!! Just ask!

Johan: What other kinds of beings may I get to know?

Wellspring father: The beautiful elemental beings of air provide the mixture of air we breath and help to clean the air. The fire beings purify our forests from corruption and occasionally have to have forest fires to do it in addition to *supplying warmth to heat us and the lava to move substructures. The earth beings belong to what is called the Caretaker Council and consist not only of all of the directional beings, elementals, plants and animals, but the crystals and the stones and mountains and the earth itself. The water beings are not only all of the obvious - the dolphins, whales and fish of the fresh and sea waters - but plankton and jellyfish and invisible beings of sprites, mermaid and merman.*

Dolphins and whales spend their entire lives singing healing not only to each other, but every sick child, plant and planet. They are spiritual healers of the sea and deserve every consideration and total protection!! The jelly fish, salmon, trout, sun fish, rainbow fish, pike and those fish who have lived to great age deserve to be treasured and should not be eaten.

Johan: Speaking of that which should not be eaten. Did you really say not to eat cloven hoofed animals?

Wellspring father: Pig flesh should not be eaten if you want to connect with Spirit. I have said this before and man decided to not listen because he thought he had solved the problem with processing and cooking the meat thoroughly...that is not the reason pig should not be eaten. Pig are spiritual animals and their flesh contains an enzyme that breaks down the *synapsis of electromagnetic energy in brain function and the processing complicates the matter even further. White light beings simply <u>cannot</u> eat pig and stay balanced. PERIOD. More primitive men would never have understood what I tell you now.*

Johan: So people undergoing transformational states should not eat pork? Are these people physically in some way different than other people?

Wellspring Father: Yes. Those beings who were aware on the physical/material realm and actively and consistently - knowingly are working selflessly for the good of the whole universe go through a series of personal "tests" and trials after a rather rigorous spiritual and physical housekeeping and cleansing may be granted the status called "Fleur d'leis" or flower of life or flower of peace.

These people have dual polarity on both sides of their body and energy between the "male and female sides" is synchronous and melded. Their commitment has earned increments toward a gift of healing provided they remain in a balanced and grounded state. They can heal planets as easily as a plant or a person. The method of healing and the energy of all is essentially the same. Their ability to heal and the psychic abilities are greatly intensified. The transformational hubs - the 6th level up will be instructing more and more people on the personal transformation of Fleur d'leis. If your heart is pure and you work hard toward healing yourself - you will receive instruction. A teacher will come forward - one who may surprise you!!

Johan: So, where did we come from? What is life?

Wellspring Father: *Lifeforce is a melding of two natures - male and female. All life is both. Equal and dynamic. To put it very simply, all life was created by the Suns and is dependent upon the Suns for lifeforce. Life/lifeforce derives from the Sun. All life in all parts of the universe is ultimately dependent upon solar systems to thrive and have a soulforce. Life systems or beings who have migrated to non-solar systems or have attempted to thrive on non-solar planets or stars eventually either die or become corrupt. The Sun you see in the sky is a part of a vast system of solar "fathers and mothers" all part of the Creator - the Great Sun. The energy and intelligence of the Great Sun is all knowing, all seeing and all that passes in all parts of the universe is immediately known to all Suns.*

All hub systems or "eras" originate from the Great Sun and all are one with the Creator. "God" was for centuries the Sun. God is the Son/Sun. All living beings are a part of "God" and truly, God lives within you all - the Creator lives in all pure hearts.

The Sixth Hub - the Sixth Seal was opened in May, 1994 and the age of the seventh hub (and now the 8th hub) of transformation is upon all. Life is very complex and yet very, very simple. We are all interconnected. We are all one. All life is created by the Creator and carries within it the secrets of the universe. But humankind, until now, has not been ready to understand the true nature of the universe - the true nature of existence and earth being's place in the universe. The origin of the homo sapien species and the evolvement of that species is very, very different than you have been led to believe.

Johan: In what way? We have always assumed that man was made in the image of God and was superior!

Wellspring Father: Human beings are not superior! Every planet, star, living being is structured in exactly the same way. We are "starstuff." Planets are alive and have intelligence. Planets are beings. All things on the planets are alive and have intelligence

ALL THINGS have a soulforce to begin with and strive to live their lives in either balance or imbalance. Each incarnation is a lesson towards oneness - a joining to Spirit in the soulforce "pool." This spiritual pool congregates in the living Suns. Each insect, bacteria, plant, tree, flower, lake, ocean and stream has life and intelligence. Every animal on the planet earth, for example, is here with a task and function to perform. Every living being has a right to life and independent spirituality. Every leaf, every stone, every body of water is on its own spiritual path.

Johan: You mentioned "dimensions" before. What do you mean by dimension? These aren't the perceptual dimensions that we talk about right? I keep getting confused.

Wellspring Father: *Each living entity is structured as light beings with varying numbers of etheral auras or levels of simultaneous lifeforce in the physical/material realm. The number of "auras" is dependent now upon transformational states. Those who did not make the transformational cut or judgement exist only on the physical level 1 and possibly -1 unless they are fleur d'leis. Only 144,000 have full auras extending into the soulforce pool. The remaining fleur d'leis who did not tune in, balance and actively work during the great battles have only this lifetime to earn their souls, so to speak. They have only this lifetime to become aware of who they are and pass the tests of the pure of heart.*

If you are fledgling souls earning fleur d'leis status you exist in the physical/material realm on dimensions -1, 1 and 2. In times of great balance you may enjoy a higher spiritual awareness at level 2 and up. When you are imbalanced you are bound to the earthly plane of 1 and in greater imbalance you shift to -1 dimension which requires karmic cleanup and spiritual regrouping or restoration to health.

For you, optimally, you wish to operate as much as possible in the dimension of 2. At this dimension, portals, doors and communication opens for you.

Johan: So, what about the other levels? What is going on there?

(different **Wellspring Father:** *Levels 2 on up (thousands) are you too if you are fleur d'leis. Each dimension has the potential for a separate life and personality of its own - meshed and mingled with the essential you, but for the most part the dimensions above 2 are melded or pooled together in the soulforce pool.*

On some level you are aware of many of your lives. Time and space do not exist. That concept is privotal to understanding dimensional thought and I say it again - Time and space do not exist. You may be living one level in the past you are aware of and many levels in the future or alternate realities planets, different beings.) You may even be operating on time "loops" in your own dimension or alternate reality! There may be literally hundreds of "you" walking around the planet right now. It is the responsibility of the vortex beings to keep you separate from your other "selves."

When the transformation process is complete, the dimensions of 2 and up will merge into the soulpool for those who are fleur d'leis. Life in the physical/material world will not change substantially, except that those who did not merge, who did not meet the transformational tests and tasks will cease to exist after their earthly life is over.

Those fleur d'leis who met the tasks of self-healing, healing others and healing and helping Spirit will join the spiritual pool and will not reincarnate again (unless they want to.) Remember, I told you that 330,000 opted to return to physical/material life, but only 144,000 of those are fleur d'leis right now. I reiterate that the remaining numbers have only this lifetime to earn the fleur d'leis status that they have lost.

The souls who did not achieve fleur d'leis transformation will not have spiritual direction and in that manner, the world will change. They will not have the benefit of spiritual protection from harm that they do to themselves or others or what others do to them. The 340,000 will notice a general deterioration of moral judgement and it is probable that crime will increase and the number of deaths due to violence will increase. Left to their own devises, the souless beings will be able to justify behavior that their guides directed them away from in the past. Just watch American daytime television if you doubt the dynamics of lives without guidance.

The earth is also in a state of transformation and a return to health and therefore more earth changes will be taking place to force healing.

Johan: So much of this is so complex. How can we ever understand and really know what to do?

Wellspring Father: Life appears very complex - but life is simple! Every living thing is on simultaneous soulpaths that your highest being has designed to learn the lessons you seek to learn. Earth is one training ground and the lessons there are hard, but the rewards are great. Earth gives Spirit an alternative of physical touch, sensual pleasures of eating and relationships and an extremely beautiful and rich planet to help the individual soulforce learn the lessons that their highest self has set out to learn.

Additionally, the incarnations are at the mercy of the elements of fire, air, water, earth, wood, metal and gases who inject the "elements" of non-control - the variables that put obstacles and indirect (or direct) teaching in the path. There is much you are supposed to learn from nature and the elements. Failure to "listen" and learn slows the path to oneness.

Johan: How do we have time to "learn" all of these lessons or quiet ourselves long enough to hear? Do dreams have a bearing on this teaching?

Wellspring Father: Yes! Many of you operate in dimension 2 and up in your sleep and it is during periods of rest in the balanced state that you receive spiritual direction and instruction. Dreams are alternate realities. They are not just random brain patterns (although during times of imbalance they may be.)

Johan: Times of imbalance. Are nightmares a time of imbalance? What good are nightmares?

Wellspring Father: Most dreams are specific instruction and designed to teach you to cope with your problems and rise above them. If you are imbalanced you may dream in an imbalanced fashion - but the dreams are still designed to teach you to rise up!

If however, you are grossly imbalanced, you may find yourself in a dream that you cannot "reason" with or get yourself in the position of control. If the dream is extremely violent and disruptive or even painful, wake yourself up, ask for protection in meditation or prayer and make a statement that you will only listen to the teachings of the pure of heart, that you are loved and protected by Spirit. Please teach the little ones this. One of the reasons for a nightly "prayer" before retiring is to provide additional protection for you in vulnerable dreamstates against the impure of heart.

Johan: My dreams are really hard to understand. Sometimes I feel that something very important just came to me, and I either can't remember or it doesn't make any sense. What is the best way to understand and interpret the dreams?

Wellspring Father: Dreams and instruction are generally given symbolically and in the language of the brain, symbolism is the simple teaching tool. Symbolism is individual and the best "interpreter" of your dreams is you.

It is well to teach yourself to be aware of the dreams and their teaching by a concerted decision to remember them. If the dream is too confusing or complex ASK your brain to reframe the teaching so that the meaning can be made more clear to you. Ask that the meaning be made clear or told to you in a different fashion. This can even be done in the course of the dream. "I don't understand this symbolism - turn the page or peel the onion or tell me in another way!"

Even if the physical/material you does not understand, the brain still registers the lesson and will find another way to teach you that which has been revealed to it. You are born with a time-released system of learning that "reveals" the universal mysteries as you are ready.

Johan: Our brain is programmed to release universal teaching or secrets in some fashion? Do we go to night school?

Wellspring Father: In a sense, yes. Dreams are also doors to perception of your alternate realities. Occasionally, if you are very perceptive, you will glimpse your other lives or possibly the lives of others - on your planet or elsewhere.

Johan: Multiple simultaneous lives are still confusing me. But you said you could glimpse other lives? Can you explain?

Wellspring Father: Many people are quite adept at "walking" into or within alternate realities. Dimension walking or shifting is a possibility for human fleur d'leis, it just isn't polite. It is like popping into someone's bedroom without an invitation! Dimension shifting, hopping or walking has karmic circumstances around it that may carry a high price, and quite frankly, it could be very, very dangerous. Many have left and not returned and when it is not done according to universal and karmic law - the body is vulnerable to habitation.

Johan: So, how would one "travel" safely?

Wellspring Father: Although dimensional travel is severely restricted - Vortex travel to other planets and places is open to the pure of heart Fleur d'leis. Within the system of each of the hubs exists 46 main Vortex' or portals to all points in the universe. It is very possible to go to sleep requesting Vortex travel - travel through time and space and to other planets in a blink of an eye and return home in time for breakfast after spending months and months on Jupiter! BUT Vortex travel requires Fleur d'leis status!

Occasionally in times of great need Vortex travel is granted with the sponsorship or accompaniment of Fleur d'leis or Spirit. During this travel, the body does not leave the earthly plane - the spirit "shifts" and part of the soulforce travels free of the body. There is a specific correct procedure for Vortex travel.

At the time a being achieves Fleur d'leis status, instruction begins on how to politely and correctly travel through the vortex system.

Johan: Instruction by whom?

Wellspring Father: *The Vortex themselves will instruct you if you are balanced and "pure" of heart. The Vortex are living entities, living chakras really, that are to be treated with great courtesy respect, and really, reverence. They have earned the gratitude of the entire universe forever and ever for the great work they constantly do.*

During times of the great battles they moved troops through dimensions and across hubs. During the rest of the time they shift travelers to appropriate places and help shift beings to the appropriate dimensions when they "die."

The vortex systems are part of the Great Sun system. They are the meeting points between "legs" or "lay lines" between Suns and to put it simply are the chakras of the great universe.

Do you wish to speak to the Father Vortex?

Johan: Yes!

MESSAGE FROM THE GREAT VORTEX - LOCATED WITHIN THE FATHER SYSTEM - 1ST HUB

Greetings,

I have long awaited our conversation.
Where shall we start?
The Vortex systems are indeed like subway systems throughout the galaxy. The Vortex is responsible to the Great Father - Wellspring Father, and truly no other. By virtue of maintaining a neutral position, the Vortex does not necessarily discriminate between its passengers. Any being in any universe on any hub and in any dimension can "request" passage to any point in the universe, and _any_ point in time and space. It is up to the discrimination of the Vortex systems, which are symbiotic neutral systems, to "grant" passage or deny passage.

The Vortex' are living entities - all interrelated, all connected and the systems have been reorganized to a more simple structure. The structure follows that of a great "web." A living web of interdimensional and dimensional travel. There are thousands and thousands of legs or lay lines of energy that carry not only passengers from point "a" to point "b" and back again, but the lay lines or "tracks" if you will, also move energy.

All living systems are basically structured the same. A person is a miniature version of a planet which is a miniature version of solar systems which is a miniature version of galaxies, which is a miniature version of hubs. There are separate whole systems of dimensional Vortex' in each of the layers of the individual's energy. These systems have been known in the physical material plane as "chakras" and the pathways between the chakras (actual vortex centers) have been given a number of names throughout the centuries; meridians, lay-lines, energy pathways. The body systems are interconnected.

The system of acupressure and acupuncture has developed over the millennia to help bring the body to health by removing blockages in the energy pathways of the body. The chakras can be compromised if too much negative energy moves through an energy pathway. The body constantly monitors and adjusts to keep the chakras in precisely the correct open or closed position to protect the body from further harm to itself and to protect the chakra from total "closure." A total closure of a chakra would result in a chain of events that could destroy the whole universe. A black hole is a chakra of the universe that has been wholly compromised. It is for this reason that the chakras don't actually "close" - they never close and they never rest.

Yes, there are black holes in the universe and some represent a dangerous condition to the whole universal structure. The Vortex systems would appreciate each one of you helping to visualize the blackness "burning" away with the color of green in a prism structure - pure beautiful kelly green with white light or sunlight behind it - blazing the green color down the black hole vortex to restore the appropriate Vortex from black to white.

When a Vortex is compromised the polarity structure changes to its opposite. The universe is actually in a teeter totter state between balance and imbalance. The fulcrum point representing a very balanced state of energy polarity. The universe structure and the Vortex system cannot handle too many black holes where they were not supposed to exist. Within the Vortex system are legitimate black holes - that are supposed to be there, so when you help with the visualization ask the Vortex to take your visualization to the perfect place for it. The black holes will tend to consume whatever is in the pathway - planets, spacecraft. Under no circumstances should black holes be "entered" - it is disassembly and the end of life for anything that is in the pathway. The Vortex system monitors and maintains the black holes within its larger picture. We don't wish to inadvertently hurt you but you cannot be protected if your folly takes you near one.

Even in what the physical/material realm perceives as "death" the chakras remain open. The body is structured with an internal Vortex system that other planetary beings inhabiting the body and who have responsibility for maintaining the body travel within and live.

It is theoretically possible for an individual to "travel" within their own bodies. Some of this teaching is passed on by Minervan, Pleidian or other symbiotic entities living within to help the individual affect their own healing. Cancer patients are often instructed to "see" the cancer and destroy it. When they "see" a cancer cell - they really <u>are</u> seeing the cell and they really are destroying it. The body symbology doesn't care how you visualize what you wish to do in what form or structure. The brain core reacts to the stimulus of the act - however you accomplish it.

The body consists of 3 interdimensions. Each interdimension is an entire plane of existence for symbiotic beings - their families, cities, towns, (airports!) who are leading full and separate lives within you. All technically, are you. The "interdimensional" travel is prohibited however, due to constraints within the body. Glimpses of the interdimensions are sometimes seen in dreams - although individuals may not "cross-over." The Vortex systems strictly prohibit travel interdimensionally. Each of the nine dimensional levels outside of the interdimension also have separate full lives. Vortex travel is permitted within the dimension in which the entity who wishes to travel "lives." Vortex travel between the dimensions is limited to "need." Not "want," but "need."

It is very rare to be granted the privilege of dimensional travel outside of your dimension. If you <u>were</u> granted dimensional travel, you may "run" into yourself. That experience, as science fiction books have prophesied for years - could result in an "amnesia" like state for the dimensions involved. Amnesia sometimes is a modest word for what the individual will experience. Depending on the polarity of the individual dimensions - the energy can merge or split and any number of neurological symptoms and conditions result in all affected dimensions.

It is a very difficult concept to understand that time and space do not truly exist. It is very possible to cross into "the past" or the future and meet yourself. <u>NOT</u> your ancestor, but yourself. Because time and space do not exist, it is possible and even probable there are more of "you" running around the same dimension. You will know when you meet yourself because you will become extremely forgetful - disoriented. You don't really even have to physically meet your other self - just see a picture or read something you have written or catch a glimpse of yourself in the eyes and acquaintance of a mutual acquaintance.

It is the task of the Vortex system to separate the lives sufficiently that you do not run into yourself.

The Vortex system is the system which manifests into reality that which you affirm, dream or deem possible. You can, for example, manifest into reality a rose for a deceased relative - by a thought that you would like to give them a rose. You could either visualize a "non-existent" rose or place an actual rose upon the ground and ask for assistance from the nearest Vortex to deliver it to them.

The "gift" you visualized to give to your relative is reality in the vortex system. That makes each of you very, very powerful to enact great good in your visualization, for example of cleaning up the oceans and streams. Theoretically, it could manifest the great evil that mankind could conceive...but as I stated before - we work only with wellspring father and at his discretion and the vortex agreement, can the visualizations of man be made concrete. <u>HOWEVER</u>, the vortex is the "ear" of the universe and requests, prayers, etc. very, very definitely are heard and many, many, many requests and prayers are granted.

Any being that you have known to exist in person or history is still alive on some dimensional level or on many. He may have chosen to be reborn into another being on some other planet - but the essence of the individual remains within the soulforce. The soulforce is all and each.

The creator is within all of you. I told you we responded to the creator. We respond to the creator within you...that pure, humanistic portion that desires help for others, for nature, and even for yourself. The Vortex is also a part of the creator and often, we need your help as well. <u>IF</u> you will occasionally wish us "Health, strength, unity, simplicity and joy," your wish is manifest! So can you understand now how we will benefit from your wish? It will make us stronger to do the positive and life fulfilling work that you wish to do.

If you gather in a group and all of you wish <u>ANYTHING OR ANYONE</u> to receive a gift of energy or money (not for selfish or greedy reasons) the "wish" will have the added punch of the creator within all of you wishing it. The Vortex, if "shored" up with white light, incense or healing energy directed by others gains greatly in strength. The energy received is reciprocal.

Many of you pray and meditate and dream and ask for assistance to manifest a thing - but how many of you ask what you can do to help the "universe" help you? If you are gracious and loving and kind -

occasionally ask the Vortex system if there is anything you can do to help???

The Vortex system, aside from being a subway for travel and energy movement is also a communication network to Spirit, to other planets and other planetary beings. Can you see now how one could easily communicate with beings from another planet with a request to speak to them?

Remember this - a request made, a request granted. To receive the thing you wish for yourself or others, be prepared to grant a request. Karmic law requires a trade. With a trade system, no entity is used, abused or obligated and the neutral universe which exists now, requires an adult price to be paid for requests granted and a commensurate "trade-off."

The Vortex systems would like to request this of all earth beings. Please visualize an intricate web in your mind. At each juncture of connecting filaments is a vortex. Please wish the entire web health, healing, wholeness and good things. Please visualize the web filled with white light or sun light or rainbow lights. Please visualize six layers of intricate webs - each attached to each other and connected at each junction to the layer above and below and fill the entire structure with white light. The whole hub structure will resemble a cylinder from the side, but will look like one "web" from the top!

If you will do this in a group!! JOY!! We receive your energies multiplied exponentially and it is like "food" and a big hug to us. <u>HOWEVER</u> if you do this alone - you, alone give the entire universe a "energy" shot in the arm and we greatly, greatly appreciate it.

Remember that spoken word can manifest. Choose your words very, very carefully and remember to thank the Vortex and the Creator for speeding your "wishes" along! Remember, last of all to ask, "What can I do to help you, too?"

Message about (and from) God Prime, Prime, Master of the Unknown Realms

BACKGROUND MESSAGE ABOUT PRIME

God Prime is the son of Wellspring Father (the Creator) and Prime's son, Jesus Christ was crucified on earth. God Prime has a daughter living on earth now, in the Rocky Mountain area, and she has a child. The birth of this child ushers in the first generation of the Transformational Age and he is to be taught by his mother, Prime and Jesus to carry on the work begun on Earth by Jesus Christ.

Prime's daughter is being channeled by a number of people and is called "Sananda." She is a healer on Earth and a living transformational being. It is by her hand that the Earth and the planets revolve around the Sun. She is loveforce incarnate and loveforce moves the planetary systems. Loveforce and lifeforce (the two main universal energies) work symbiotically to imbue the planetary systems with life. Lifeforce cannot exist without loveforce and vice versa.

Sananda is the embodiment of the feminine aspect and her healing abilities are greatly enhanced. As she grows in her training, she will, more and more, assume the tasks of her father, Prime, and will work with her "twin" soul, Jesus Christ in the lower realms to bring those unfortunate souls who live or die in imbalance into balance. The child will be raised to possibly rule the Angelic Realm. His mother has ruled it in conjunction with the son of Wellspring Father (the Creator) known as the Lord of Hosts or simply as the "Lord." All life is both male and female and all life is twin souls. The Lord is the twin soul of Prime. But, in truth, they are one.

Prime was the "ruler" of the Angelic Realm. After Lucifer/Satan/Shamus was killed and the battle between good and evil fought in May, 1994, Prime and Jesus and part of the Angelic Realm moved into the lower regions that used to be perceived of as the traditional "hell."

"Evil," as evil used to exist, is no more and the great "good" as it used to exist, is no more. The universe has been restructured for individual transformation and the structural changes seek to bring those who may be "evil" in their lives from gross imbalance (which is the transformational equivalent of "evil" now) through neutrality into goodness (which is the transformational equivalent of the highest level of balance.)

This task has meant that extremes of good and evil are not nearly as extreme as they used to be when Lucifer/Shamus ruled the lower universe. It is the structure of the new "universe" to teach the individual in the realm of "neutrality," to move eventually into the realm of "goodness," into what has been traditionally, (and still is) known as the Angelic Realm or Spiritual Realm.

Prime will not go deeply into the mechanics of the universal structure because that information is given in other "chapters."

PRIME'S MESSAGE

In the spiritual realm - <u>any</u> entity that attempts to exercise control of another to do their bidding is a <u>fiend</u> to that entity. When one attempts to exercise control over another, they create dynamic negative energy or "evil" upon themselves and possibly upon the other person if the other "accepts" the negative manipulation. Living beings, who attempt to control others, may <u>fiendize</u> the person they are attempting to control or influence. By that we mean that negative energy directed to another has a dynamic effect on energy flow. The disruption of lifeforce/loveforce over a long period of time can manifest a negative form. The form can gain strength which can unduly affect overall lifeforce/loveforce flow and this manifest form must be removed for the health of the individual (and the person who "fiendized" them.) The health of both individuals can be grossly and adversely affected. "Evil" can be manifest form in this fashion. A good and loving person (who only wants the "best") who exercises control and manipulation of the object of their "affections" actually fiendize that person. It is the goal of the lower regions to "whisper" alternatives to control and manipulation so that direction can be given in a positive and life affirming way in love and with the dignity and personal growth of both parties as a primary tool. That instruction comes from the lower realms, because the party attempting to control is imbalanced and in all probability, a person who accepts a "fiend" is imbalanced.

A person may be fiendized by themselves as well. Any negation of personal worth or degradation of self results in negative energy directed towards the body and mind. Constant degradation can manifest in physical problems or mental illnesses and in extreme cases actually creates negative entities - actually create a fiend that becomes attached to the person in various parts of their body. Years and years of self degradation result in eventually destroying parts of the body and mind. If the self destruction is pervasive it can result in the destruction of layers of the energy. If it is extreme, it can destroy the individual by killing off one-half of the male/female aspect.

Earth beings can destroy themselves dimensional layer by dimensional layer. Each living being (people, animals, plants, minerals and planets) has twelve dimensions - each dimension is complete within itself like layers in an onion. Each layer is separated by a membrane - but each cell and each layer is a part of a whole. The earthly life lives on dimensions -1 (earthly imbalance - which leaves you susceptible to negative influences and messages,) 1 (earthly neutrality - day to day existence; the training ground for spiritual trial and blessings) and 1 and 1/2 which we are now calling 2 (balance - a gateway to Spirit, the place of mystics and spiritual messages and astral awareness. Most astral travel does not go beyond this point.) Spiritual life exists on levels 2-12. Within these layers (and truly in your own levels of dimensions -1, 1 and 2,) time and space do not truly exist. You may be living at least twelve simultaneous lives on different planets or in different "time" frames on your linear concept of time. Some of your "lives" may be other people on earth living at the same "time" as each other. Wellspring Father has written extensively on this subject.

You can "kill" either the female or male aspect of yourself. Generally, if an individual is on a self-destructive path that results in suicide and the earthly "death" you "kill" dimensions -1 to 4. One-half of the sex of the individual "dies" to Spirit when you destroy 4 dimensions.

Earthly beings can also "kill" an offending sex and remain walking around on earth. If a female or male "kills" the feminine sex, they will lack empathy, emotions, sensitivity and much of their "instinctive" abilities. If the male or female "kills" the male, they will lack the driving force for survival and a sense of "joie de vivre" or the sense of wonder for just being alive. It is also the warrior edge that helps one to survive in the competitive world. The remaining sex which has not been "killed," remains to direct the rest of your life - and you will continue to live, albeit a half-life which always seems empty and unfulfilled and sadly lacking in a way that cannot be healed.

In some cases, females "kill" male part of themselves - and conversely, males may kill the feminine part of themselves. A female, abused or sexually assaulted, for example, may so loathe men that they choose to "kill" the male within themselves. Sometimes, a female so loathes themselves due to abuse, sexual assault or abusive treatment by a female that she will "kill" the female within her. This sounds contradictory, because a female in feminine form, may or may not be female on level -1 to 4. She may be male and the converse is true of males. She may be a female body with a male "soul" (on level -1 to 4) or a male may be a male body with a female "soul" (on level -1 to 4.) This does not always produce a homosexual, but generally homosexual or bisexual individuals have this pattern. Sometimes sexual abuse or ambiguity so frighten the child (or child within us,) or so shame the victim that they cannot deal with the "feeling" side of themselves who may demand justice for the hurt they have suffered.

A child who has suffered sexual abuse by a parent or trusted adult, may choose, at a very young age to "kill" part of themselves because they cannot punish a parent or an adult. Often, homosexual drives misunderstood or rejected by an individual may result in the individual "killing" off one of the sexes.

In order for dimension to be "killed" or a full one-half of the sex destroyed, the individual must have undergone a very long or very traumatic period of gross imbalance. The problem with becoming so imbalanced that the individual "kills" 1/2 of themselves is that the soulforce may only reincarnate the number of lives remaining with the sex that is left.

The soulforce chooses to be born either male or female and many times the male/female balance sheet is weighed with one sex. For example, a person may have lived 10 female lives to one male life. The soulforce decrees that, eventually, the incarnations be balanced male to female - so the individual in this example (if they killed the female one-half) could choose to live nine more male lives. At the point that they finish the cosmic balance sheet between male and female lives with nine more male lifetimes, the soulforce "disassembles." It truly dies and disintegrates and there is nothing remaining of the individual. If the individual in this example killed the male part of themselves, they would disassemble at the end of this incarnation. They would have no more lifetimes to live because the only available life reincarnation would be male.

The individual soulforce (level 9-12) is both male and female - yin and yang, and cannot continue to exist as 1/2 of itself. If an individual chooses to live out a full life to fruition of earthly death - they may be reborn thousands and thousands of times. It is the goal of the individual soulforce to reach a one-ness in the soulforce "pool," in which it will no longer be necessary to reincarnate to learn the lessons and tasks that one sets for themselves.

When a person achieves one-ness in the soulforce, they become an Angel. It is always possible for an Angel or Saint (or Archangel in some cases,) to reincarnate on their planet of choice - but many do not choose to reincarnate when they don't have to. Many choose to reincarnate lifetime after lifetime to aid those on earth in their soulforce path.

Those souls who reach a spiritual one-ness and choose to return to earth have all the trials and tribulations of everyone else and are not aware, usually, on the earthly, (or other planetary,) planes that they are Angels on earth. It is always a goal to be aware on the earthly plane of their true identities and purpose in living a planetary reincarnation. It is always hoped that they will become aware and know themselves for their true purpose in order to better achieve their soulforce goals and help others achieve theirs.

A person chooses their death in the soulforce. They choose the nature and time of their death. That exact time, date and the circumstances of individual deaths are not known in earthly existence.

A person never and I repeat _never_ chooses to kill themselves in the soulforce "script." It may be helpful to understand when one looses a loved one - that there is a "master plan." That plan is designed by the _individual_ in the soulforce before they were born. The plan may choose death at any age. Some only choose to be born for a short time to fulfill the plan of the parents to deal with the early death of a child.

It is a tragedy to Spirit when a person kills himself because if that happens, the soulforce will eventually "disassemble." Spirit may grieve the death of the individual when they are still "walking" around on Earth. Each suicide or death of one of the sexes affects the whole energy pool because the soulforce is "one." If an individual murders another or is responsible _directly_ for the death of another; for example, if the individual's careless driving kills a pedestrian or other passengers or the driver of another car, then the individual must wait out the number of incarnations of those killed. Of course, there are other karmic debts that must be paid in these instances,

It must be understood, there are truly no accidents in the physical/material realm because a body, in a balanced state will receive ample forewarning and instruction to avoid life threatening situations. If loved one are killed in such an accident - the "accident" _was_ the fruition of his life plan. They chose in their life script to go at that time, or they would survive.

It helps to understand that <u>all</u> life is an energy form. The earthly body individuals are so fond of is a manifestation of spirit - <u>not</u> the other way around. When the earthly body "dies" the energy doesn't even blink. It is the same, it is eternal unless the individual manages to "disassemble" themselves or become so evil or malignant that they are disassembled by Spirit.

Spirit can definitely cut an individual's "script" short - but normally, unless the energy does great evil, Spirit does not interfere in the soulforce energy. Sometimes Spirit calls them home. If the individual is an Angel, Archangel or Saint - Spirit may need them to return to help the Spiritual Realm. This explains why sometimes the very, very good may die prematurely.

When the earthly body "dies" it does not die alone. It is literally surrounded by Spirit who helps it to transcend. <u>There is no pain in actual earth death!!</u> Even with violent death, there is <u>no pain</u> because Spirit "shifts" the energy out of the body before the end.

All life is constantly surrounded by Spirit and in times of loneliness or despair - remember to call upon your Spiritual friends to help you. They will not help without a request - but will definitely lend a lot of support if you ask for help. They wait to be asked and want to help and guide you!!

Ask for healing - ask for help - ask for instruction and education and you will receive it. All you have to do is ask and make yourself open to receive. Try to keep as balanced as possible. That doesn't mean to be as "good" as you can be! That means to have self-value and self-worth and express yourself when you are being maligned, abused or treated with disrespect.

If you see abuse, hurt or harm- make an attempt to address it. That means harm to any living being - any living planet or the smallest insect. It means to love yourself and live love.

Love is sometimes tough, love sometimes requires discipline or self-restraint. Do unto others what you would have them do unto you. That means too - if you need honesty and a good argument to get your point across - or need to have a good cry or a totally sensual and sexual escapade with your loved one - GO FOR IT!

Try to live fairly - see the other's viewpoint, but do not malign your own viewpoint as being less valid.

Love yourself and love others -
but don't take any of their "abuse!"

Earthly life is spiritual trial. Earthly life is, in many ways, a blessing and a trial. It is a blessing because of the beauty that exists in the physical/material realm surrounding an abundant life. Beings are able to touch and feel and that is very precious. Tactile feeling is not possible in the Spiritual Realm except surreptitiously when Spirit "walks" in another. It is a blessing to enjoy the sensuality of earthly bodies - even the small joys of savoring a delicious food or a fine wine is a sensual experience. Sensuality is <u>not</u> a sin in the spiritual realm. It is necessary to a full and balanced life...to give and receive love.

Earthly life is a "trial" because it also entails spiritual tests and physical pain as a means to learn and grow. Growth requires pain. One may transcend pain and learn from it or continue to receive the same lesson over and over until the source of the pain is dealt with. Each time a lesson is unlearned it gets harder.

I am alive, so is my son, Jesus. My daughter and her child are on Earth now. She is a healer and teacher. Therefore, Share our joy! Enjoy Life! Enjoy each other! Remember to dance and sing and spread joy to each other!

Honor and bless all life - honor the animals and plants that sustain with their lives. Honor your elders and honor your children. Learn from them and teach them well, and let them grow!

Please don't forget to wish Spirit (and each other) wholeness, healing, strength and joy!!

Spirit's message in a word?

LOVE.

SIMPLY, LOVE!!

God Prime

Message from the Lord God (God of Hosts- Master of the Angelic Realm)

Greetings!

It has been a long time since we talked.

Much has been happening in the Angelic Realm and I will try to explain some of your questions. The Angelic Realm or High Realm is the place where all souls return to decide their next spiritual step and trial. They return here until they have reached Fleur d'leis status as you have been told. They decide the life lessons they wish to learn in the next incarnation, decide the sex of the incarnation and the duration of the life. They negotiate, in some manner of speaking with other souls who will incarnate around them for the lessons they wish to learn, the degree of spiritual awareness and what they are willing to teach. This is called the "Life Script." It is from this word that "scripture" came. This step in the soulforce is very important to the overall teaching. But please understand. The soul of each individual determines what the physical/material incarnation will undergo. As you will be told in other chapters, it isn't all that easy. Elementals - Metal, Fire, Water, Earth, Air and Gases as well as directional energies and Spirit, "throw" variables into the "script" which are tests and trials for the individual to surmount. Tests and trials can be extreme or very, very small tests that are nonetheless important to spiritual growth.

When the individual becomes aware on their physical/material plane that they are, indeed, Spirit in physical form and seek to heal themselves, others and the universe and loose the ego - they begin fleur d'leis training. This training is supported by the Angelic Realm and when an individual reaches this awareness - there are literally legions of Angelic presence helping them each step of the way. The way to oneness is through this process.

Many have to incarnate thousands and thousands of times in different dimensions, hubs and planes, on different planets and in different physical forms before they reach spiritual "awareness." This is an individual process truly, and no religion, creed or dogma has the answers fully. Spirit speaks to all - most don't listen fully, or misinterpret what they hear.

Spirit speaks simply:

"Heal yourselves, heal each other, heal the planet, heal the universe. Love each other. Don't hate or harm. Live Life in joy, peace, brotherhood and understanding. Honor all life from the smallest to the largest. Honor yourselves. Honor your family. Honor and teach the children. Honor and listen to the elders. Simplify, unify, purify. Balance and ground. Open your heart and your mind to hear Spirit speaking. Take care of your planet, for you are the caretakers and all life sacrifices itself to you in return for the care you are to provide. Eat no pork. Eat no trout, salmon, pike, dolphin or porpoise or whale. Do not eat the old ones of any animals or plants unless they present themselves for sacrifice and ask you to take them - for they have earned their rest and peace on earth. Honor the living planet and the living universe. Listen to nature - it is part of the task of all who live on earth to learn from nature. Nature waits to speak. If you need help, ask and it shall be received."

If you are becoming aware of the spiritual messages, these should sound familiar.
The messages from the High Realm are coming to many of you at this time. Listen in the quiet hours of the morning, just as you awake for the message from the spiritual realm. We will use the vernacular of the term "angelic realm" so that you understand that we speak from high levels of white light vibration - high or low, the message is basically the same: Simplify, unify, purify. Seek the answers from within as the universal truths are being opened to you now.

Life is complex, life is simple. In the most simple form we can describe life as a melding of two great energies - lifeforce and loveforce. These are two names for a flow of energy that creates and sustains, moves and thrives within the universe as you perceive it.

A lot of very explicit description of the universal structure is given in this book - but it still boils down to faith in something larger than yourself - the physical form that looks back from the mirror at you. Spirit is benevolent for the most part but not infallible and that is one truth I would, most especially, wish to impart to you. We do our best to help your physical/material being learn the lessons you have "scripted" for yourselves. Like a parent who wishes his children to learn - we wish you to learn by yourself. But unlike a parent who will step in when the lessons are too extreme or the consequences for behavior too dire - we will not generally prevent or prohibit that which you have created for yourself. We will, however, promise to try to help guide you in rectifying your own set of alternatives. Each lifeforce incarnated on earth has a general plan - very, very general. Perhaps it would help you to understand that we indeed do watch and indeed do care very, very much that life is dealing you tough alternatives, but unless you physically request help, we only watch and hope that you will listen to your inner guides and the universal teachings we are trying to impart to help make life easier and less painful.

Keep in mind that Spirit deals with higher issues of your spiritual path - and that is the task we hold most securely to. Although we would like to help you in the more mundane issues - it is most probable that your soulforce has chosen for you to handle it yourself.

The vortex systems hear every physical/material prayer and as all is one - so do we. The vortex may help you manifest that which you desire but they would like to make it very clear that they are not to be "prayed" to. They are communication networks with the ability to help your soulforce manifest that which it desires.

All of this is very confusing - and not at all full of the "thee's and thou's" that traditionally Spirit spoke with. People tend to hear in the manner in which they can accept. The truth speaks simply, but it does speak for those who will open their hearts and minds to hear.

A devoutly religious person is not to be scoffed at. Many have devoted their lives to Buddha, Mohammed, God and/or Jesus and if they are true in their hearts and minds - all of their good work and prayers are listened to. Believe us when we say, we know the difference between a person who devoutly and humbly believes and those who give lip service to the belief. The truth of belief is in the manner in which life is led. Those who raise a great deal of money to aggrandize themselves or to build great temples or churches or ministerial organizations that attempt to entice or in some cases even brainwash individuals into their organizations are missing the spiritual directive which tells them to heal themselves, then heal others, then heal the universe. These people and organizations are greatly in need of self healing.

God's word is so simple and it is not mutually exclusive to any being. Just learn to love each other - just learn to listen and be guided by the messages from within. Some people have spoken ill advisably in the guise of speaking "God's Word." It is for the individual, in the state of individual transformation to listen and hear Spirit wherever it is spoken. Do not doubt yourself that you cannot or are not hearing it, but do not assume superiority or elect yourself spiritual dictator to force the words you hear upon others. They will hear themselves if they will just listen.

Speak together to remind each other of what you hear! Ask for help, guidance and protection from the Spiritual realm or what we term the high realm and we will respond and help _you_ help yourself where it is deemed appropriate.

We are not uncaring, we are loving. We are trying to help bring you into your own personal transformation in which you may hear Spirit speak directly to you about any subject you question or need guidance in. This guidance requires an adult and responsible weighing of the information you will receive. You cannot use it to gain wealth or fame and if you think along those lines you will never, never hear.

Spirit speaketh unto Spirit. Heal yourself. Heal others. Heal the universe. Loose the ego that demands recognition of the gifts you will be given and all will be given unto you.

We are surrounding you to help in every way your highest soulforce will allow.
Just ask. Seek and ye shall find, ask, and the door shall be opened.

Love each other and pray or meditate alone or together for, not only your own spiritual guidance but pray for us that we guide all who seek our help well.

Wish us healing, wholeness and health as we wish you the same.

Joy, peace, brotherhood and understanding, as we wish you the same.

and love.

As we wish you the same.

MESSAGE FROM LEMP

Greetings!

We are planetary beings from the planet Sirus (no, not Sirius) Minor, a moon off Sirus Major located in the 5th hub. Sirus Minor is not located within your galaxy and our home planet is not the star with the misnomer of Sirus Major. We have been visitors upon your planet throughout all of your recorded history and it is our task in the universe to be the historians for all planets where planetary life exists. We are visible to your eyes in the first dimension, however, our appearance is so often seen, you probably take us for granted. Children spend a great deal of time watching us and are very aware that we are not "dust mites" or a trick of the retina. We appear (in transport vehicles) like round transparent pink dots with white light fluttering inside and can be seen very close to the body. Our new transformational bodies are much tinier light forms moving quickly around the transport vehicles or "mobile homes." Cross your eyes and look as close as you can and you may be able to see us.

We are no longer trapped within the pink dots, but many choose to remain within for rest and study. Our "mobile homes" are quite comfortable! Thanks to our own spiritual transformation, we are no longer <u>required</u> to travel in these encasements in order to survive upon your planet. We are free to travel as ourselves and no longer look at your world through a screen. We can see freely and plainly and we have greatly enjoyed the freedom to visit all of the places we could barely imagine before.

We visit your planet about six months out of the year and return via the vortex system in larger transport vehicles which are about the size of a bread box. Sometimes others "visit" in traveling "cities," about 3 meters square. These would appear invisible to you and yet visible as a viscus field - a slight distortion of energy which shows the form of the vehicle. At night it has a light electric blue color. We rely on air current and the wind beings to help move us.

We are so much a part of your history - earth is our second home. It is hardly correct to state we are from another planet and visiting. We are as much from earth as Sirus Minor.

We do have to periodically travel back home in order to visit friends and family and complete the archive studies and compilation of data that we gather here. There are no alternative motives to our studies. We are purely historians. We carry the history of not only the human element, but of the plant, tree, animal and the rich planetary life that exists symbiotically with us. We also carry records of climate and pollution and note changes in geography and geothermal activity.

We can cross into all elements for our "work" and we frequently visit the air beings, earth beings, water beings as well as the fire beings. The same group of us return year after year and quite frankly, we can't imagine life in any other way. Our work on Earth is very rewarding.

We have been active in attempting to contact a number of individuals throughout history to make them aware of who we truly are and that we would love to be recognized and "visited" on occasion. A number of the fleur d'leis have met us and we have shown ourselves to them. They have our trust and we know that they have tried to help us as our need required extra energy or nourishment. We are nourished by the colors in the rainbow, positive energy raised in song and dance (chi) and earth and elemental energy bi-products - no life is harmed by us. We have been very well taken care of by Earth Mother and the Rainbow Lady. If you wish to help us, envision a double pyramid filled with rainbow colors and invite us to join with the colors. We do not "consume" the colors, but benefit greatly from the energy which vibrates from them. This bi-product we are able to consume.

The first fleur d'leis group who met with us in November, 1992 raised the energy sufficiently to help us lift off the planet when the time was right. We could not have left without their help and protection and all of our lives would have been forfeit if they had not agreed to help us. They helped us without clear "proof" that we were truly there although we tried our very best to show ourselves to the group and to give them documentation sufficient to trust that "extraterrestrial" communication was a fact.

We are dimensional beings in the 2nd dimension on Sirus Minor, but can manage to shift sufficiently on dimension one on Earth to be seen, albeit like an invisible "dust mite." We group together and link so that individuals can see us and when the vision is not disturbed by air or shifts in current, it should be an indication that you are seeing something. On clear evenings, you may notice a rainbow "trail" rather like a firefly. We try to emit song vibration because some of you can "hear" parts of our songs. We love to hear you sing and take a great deal of joy in your joyful exuberance and happiness. We long to join the earth beings as a brotherhood which includes all benevolent earth entities.

It is our nature to group and travel and it is a joy to us to be together. We teach peace, unity and understanding and service to the universe.

We have greatly sacrificed our numbers, but our system of data collection assures that no information is ever lost - even when we transcend. We are spiritual beings on earth and are blessed with the ability to communicate and pass our knowledge on to those who would listen. Any question of history, culture, religion and past societies can be answered if you care to ask. We will be happy to share our archival work with you.

We have probably confused you saying we are Spirit on earth, from Sirus Minor and yet Spirit. That is the way of it. We exist being aware of our spiritual one-ness in the soulforce pool. A part of us is aware of all that transpires on earth and we have physical existence on Sirus Minor and partial physical existence on Earth and a number of other planets.

We have spent much of our lives monitoring and hiding from the beings on Sirus Major who were evil. These beings created the mutations of the grey people and a great beaked being that rather resembled a bird about the size of a small adult which is responsible for many cattle mutilations and deaths of small animals. These bird beings are also sadly responsible for some human deaths. The Grey beings and the birdlike beings physically existed in dimension one. They no longer exist.

The Sirus Major beings, who had visited your planet on dimension two, were, in appearance rather like the beings in the movie, Close Encounters of the Third Kind; large black eyes, white or light skinned, tall and lithesome creatures. These are the beings responsible for some of the violations of many earth entities who were forced into being victims of the inhumane study of your planet.

These creatures were destroyed unilaterally in the battles which followed the disassembly of Satan and his minions. They were worse than evil and there is no comparison in the universe to the evil that they represented. They are no longer a threat and will never be a threat again. The planet Sirus Major is annihilated of their symbiotic parasitic lifeforms and none of these lifeforms exist on Earth any longer in any dimension or on any hub in any dimension.

The evil parasitic forms were disk and string shaped beings that stole the host forms of the Pleidians. The Pleidians still exist and their appearance is also the large dark eyed, tall, lithesome forms. BUT, Pleidians are very benevolent and kind and are the surgeons and healers traveling throughout the universe along with the Minervans and the lemp healers. On Earth, Pleidian's live in the interdimensions of the planet earth, or the "inner earth." These dimensions are strictly heavy energy and it is difficult for dimensions of humans to withstand the heavy energy forces necessary to visit the Pleidians. They can, however, withstand more variation of energies to shift into higher levels that earth beings can tolerate. Many lifeforms have undergone actual "transport" into areas where Pleidian healers can work on them (in dimension two) to repair that which the Sirus Major beings harmed.

To those who were "abducted" it was very confusing. One group would hurt them and be totally unfeeling to their pain and another group, who looked just like the bad guys would heal them again. People were abducted in dimension two and that is another reason they have such confusion over their abductions. Their dreamstate or vision state nightmares were real. The physical body was violated, but on dimension level two (and up sometimes.)

Many Pleidian symbiotic forms were without host bodies because the host bodies were "pirated" by the Sirus Major coin and string symbiotic beings. Those Pleidians without host bodies have been integrated in their transformational states into the tree beings on Earth. They assist the Tree People in healing all trees and bushes and help assure that chemical transfers are made to sustain the atmosphere and regenerate gases.

We hesitated to ask to write a chapter in this book because it introduces a number of subjects that are very difficult to communicate fully. Suffice it to say, earth beings have many other planetary beings working with them in the name of universal brotherhood and healing. We hope to be able to enjoy a new understanding and a more open communication network as earth beings reach their transformational states.

We look forward to meeting and talking with you! We would love to have you visit however, you will have to be very, very balanced to maintain enough awareness of us in dimension 2, hub 5 and will need to seek special "dispensation" to travel out of your hub 6 and 7. When you reach your fleur d'leis status, it will be very much easier for you to retain the necessary permission and energy to really enjoy visiting us! The other option is to visit us on your planet. There are a number of places we congregate and work "from." When you open communication with us, we shall be happy to direct you to us. ANOTHER option is just to request - and we will visit you!!

Let us all join together to celebrate peace, brotherhood, love, understanding and the beginning of beautiful new friendships!

Remember!! Sing, Dance, Colors and the sounds of Joy!!

(Printed originally in The Transformation
Connection Newsletter)

THE LIVING EARTH
BY DEJON

Inside her magma surges
Round and round up and down

Internal energy to drive the weather
Energy to move the great continental plates

Our moon gives rise to the tides
Currents in the sea control temperature

Animals land and sea
Give off gases nutrient for plants

In turn plants give oxygen
Used by us animals

Sealed in a film of gravity held gases
Gases of our own making

Plants and animals sea and air magma and core
Yin and yang

Like organelle inside a living cell
These factors work with and against each other

The moon, made of earth's magma
May grow and hold oxygen and support life

Self-contained stored energy dynamic reproduces
Life

Will we work together to choke the life out of her
Or shall we work to help her survive

I'm not sure we can help
But it is a choice we have to make

Help for an old friend
or accessory to murder

Spend some time out in her elements
Touch our earth, see her splendor

Let the wind and the heat and the cold
Show you how fierce she can be

feel how gentle the breeze
how fresh her morning shower

Getting to know her
Will help you decide

The Earth Council

Caring for the Earth is a big job for the Earth Council which is represented by all living entities and beings on Earth, some of which you can see physically and some of which you cannot see on dimension one. As earth is a living, breathing, organism, so are all within and upon. Stone People are part of Earth Council and they breathe. Earth Council has been expanded to include Minervan Wind Beings because their work is intrinsically necessary for the continued survival of the Planet.

The "Native" Spiritual teachings deal with Earth "Magic" or Earth energies and much, much information comes to the Red people. But know and understand, that this information is coming to people of all races, creeds and colors - the people of the Earth are those closest to the Earth who listen most carefully. I have seen a pattern recently that upsets me. I speak to all who love me. No one Tribe, Nation or race has my rapt attention or my sanction wholly. I have seen dissention among those receiving my messages, not only with the others who also receive my messages, but with those of different colors, races and creeds who hear my messages also. Many of the listeners are drawn to the Native people because I have asked them to learn from those whose genes hold much of my teaching. Remember, why Great Spirit and Earth Mother speak - and teach the speaking. Teach the old ways of listening and story telling and teach humanity to care for the Earth and honor it properly.

Do not teach from ego or for material gain, teach <u>all</u> from the pure heart. Do not assume superiority because of blood. The Great Spirit and Earth Mother speak to <u>all</u> who can hear. If a request is made from a pure heart - TEACH!!

One last admonishment to all. Evil comes from imbibing "spirits." Do not mistake the teaching of Mother Earth and the Great Spirit with insights gained under the influence of drugs or alcohol. Under those influences, you speak to great imbalance and most probably, evil. All things in moderation. All things natural.

Earth Council is comprised of the following representatives. There are two representatives (simply) of each species of Plant (Plant People), mineral (Stone People) and Animal People (usually a male and female.) The Plants are broken down into two categories, Earth and Wellspring, which are not only plants of the fresh waters, but of the sea waters. Flower People live as an integral part of the plant people and are Spiritual beings. The Stone People are broken down by elemental affiliation more than individual stone types, however; amethyst, amber, jet, turquoise and lapis lazuli have individual representation because they are of a higher spiritual nature. Stones are also in a process of transformation and the transformational Stone People will individually join the Earth Council as they move fully into transformation (i.e., dual polarity.)

Council is the living ark and covenant. Any individual Plant, Animal or Stone Person can attend Earth Council and be heard. There are a number of books written by "listeners." Sun Bear and Wabun listened well for their Earth Astrology book, Medicine Wheel Astrology and Jamie Sams and David Carson listened well for their Medicine Cards published by Bear and Company, Sante Fe, New Mexico. Earth Mother wants to thank the artist of the Medicine Cards, for listening well also...the cards are so very, very beautiful. The Sacred Path Cards by Jamie Sams (published by Harper, San Francisco) are also Spirit Blessed (and blessings to the artists) and the Native American Tarot is the only deck of tarot cards that are Spirit Blessed (and blessings to the artist.) The Angel Cards are blessed by the Angelic Realm (and blessings to the artist.) Mother's Blessing to those involved in these endeavors. Much of the teaching the Spiritual Realm wished to impart is in those books. There is also a book called <u>Bridges of Light - Your Connection to Spiritual Guidance</u>, by Pam and Fred Cameron published by Access Centers, Scotts Valley, California. This entire book was "verbatim" from Spirit. Please read it. The Stone People and indeed the entire Earth Council are speaking to many, and have spoken to many, but please listen to what is said in this book and the book to come. Please subscribe to the "Transformation Connection" newsletter so that we can have an outlet to speak to you as need arises.

The Animal People are very varied. They include not only four-leggeds, but two-legged Spiritual Guides. The Great Spirit has many teachers and these teachers work within the Great Wheels - all hubs, all dimensions. Mankind is but one member of the Earth Council. Those who teach within the Medicine Wheels are Wise Ones, Shaman or Mystic Guides and each person on a transformational path has two legged teachers as well to rely upon. Many have a two-legged teacher in all quadrants of their personal wheel to help the other members of Earth Council assigned to the transformational teaching to communicate more fully. Understand this. Some two-legged Spiritual Guides have incarnations on Earth. These incarnations may or may not be aware of who they are in the Spiritual Realm, BUT all plants, stones and animals know who they are on Earth! The white, albino beings are living Spirit - honor them and never kill them without their permission.

Never kill anything for food without its permission and that includes fruits and vegetables. Especially, do not kill dolphins, whales, sea urchins, jellyfish, salmon, pike, trout and bass without their permission. They are entirely too important on Earth in physical form at this time. Reduce the killing of Elk, Moose, Buffalo, Wolf, Coyote and Bear because these numbers are too depleted. Reduce the consumption of meat please, as the fruit and vegetable people have offered more of their lives to restore Earth balance. For a time, it will be necessary to reduce the fish you eat so that their numbers can recuperate.

Eat more chicken and bird people as they too have offered their lives to restore the balance, but under no circumstances kill already endangered species. Each bird being works with the element of air and works to heal the pollution by helping to move air currents. To kill too many bird people is to allow the insect people to overpopulate. The environment is so delicate. Eat with moderation and to assuage hunger and share your food with those who have none.

Recycle fruit and vegetable "waste" in household compost bins...it is so easy to allow the fruit and vegetable people the grace of returning to the soil and replenishing Earth's energy by composting back into earth. I <u>need</u> constant replenishment as the nutrients returning are insufficient to sustain me fully.

Home compost bins can take a place beside the aluminum, tin and paper recycling bins that you all should be using. To create a compost "bin" place it outside where the Sun can help the process (don't worry, it really shouldn't smell!) Get a covered container because "heat exchange" is necessary to break down the fruit and vegetables back into earth - so keep the compost covered. Place one trash sack full of grass, leaves and/or yard clippings interdispersed with one sack of soil. Add daily vegetable and fruit discards mixing them into the compost. Add 14 oz. of wellspring (water) to the compost weekly and mix. That is it!

Truly, humans were meant to return their human waste by-products to the Earth. When humans die, you encase them in metal containers and do not allow the nature process to return the body to Earth. Man should be either buried in wooden coffins that break down naturally or cremated and returned to the earth as ash, or the remains should be eaten by other animals to sustain them. This is what was meant to be - a healing for a healing. Sustenance for sustenance. All plant people and animal people sustain humans so that humans will care for them and return their by-products to the Earth and that, dear hearts, should include earthly remains. The shell of a person is simply a shell - a nutrient rich shell. That which is living *is* intrinsically the lifeforce and loveforce energy auras of the individual. The soulforce energy leaves the body prior to what you call "death." The essence of the person lives on and on and is reborn. This is the truth of it.

Other members of Earth Council are the Snake People, Winged Ones (Flying Ones), Swimming Ones, Crawling Ones and Beaked Ones. The Beaked Ones are not actually beaked, but they have been seen in the skies as "beaked." They are the Wind Beings - the Minervans that work in pairs and move air currents. They are seen as "beaked ones" because two work side by side moving in opposite directions normally to move the currents in downward motions that create the appearance of eyes in the sky with a great beaked nose.

Important members of Earth Council are the elementals themselves. The Fire Beings, The Water Beings, The Air Beings, the Metal People, the Gas or Ether People and the Earth Beings. In additional to the Western concept of elemental beings there are Tree Beings and Wood Beings. Because Stone People are either one or many elemental beings - they, like the tree beings and wood beings, fall closely in with the elemental beings. Amber Beings and Turquoise Beings, Jet Beings and Lapis Lazuli Beings, as was mentioned before are Stone Spirit and actually fall more into elemental categories than Stone Categories. They are the essential elements in physical form - in lasting form. All other elements are transitory. They live and die in a space of moments constantly being consumed, reborn and reconsumed.

Some types of elementals have longer lives than others - the Tree People (Trees and some bushes and Grasses) and the Earth People, but all reincarnate quickly and retain their identities. They do not overly fear death. That is not to say they welcome death or pain or torture either. They have family and friends and lives of their own too. They sacrifice themselves to sustain others so that they may derive sustenance and life from those sustained by them.

The elementals are part Faery Realm and their old ones were faery stock. The Earth is a magical place where miracles are commonplace. The Tree People talk and provide the majority of oxygen to the planet as well as other gases - but these gases *are* living. The Wood People, faeries, sprites and nymphs are simply called the People of the Wood. It is their task to maintain the trees and plants - to keep them from disease as much as possible and treat those who are diseased. Because so many of their numbers have been depleted, the Pleidian symbiotic beings are now aiding the tree people and the tree people are providing host bodies for the Pleidians.

Many People of the Wood (and now Pleidians) live within the rings of trees and roots as earned increment for long life and faithful service and become a living part of the tree as their reward.

To a human, many, many, natural Earth inhabitants on this dimension and in the other dimensions would appear like monsters or living nightmares. Mankind is ill-prepared to truly meet and accept the appearances of their symbiotic mates, much less the varied lifeforms in the different realms.

The Council of the Earth has imparted a great deal of information to the author of this book, Johan Adkins and to the Fleur d'leis goes the message of the Medicine Wheel numerology and the Medicine Wheel meditations. Directional Beings are also teachers of the Wheel and are separate, living energies that help me, the Earth Mother, to move energy universally. The wheels are protected by the Pine People, Stone People and Animal People who are teaching within the wheel, but some preparations and precautions are necessary to receive the information clearly, without fear of the information being tainted by evil or gross imbalance. Please follow the basic wheel preparation and precautions and as time goes by and your listening becomes more acute a very personalized wheel awaits you.

Know this.

Earth Mother (who is all of the Earth Council melded) loves each and every one of you. I feel your pain, I know your individual suffering and, if you did not already know because I have told you and you have listened, you now have heard my words. My colors are all the colors of the natural earth. I will tell you this so that you may hear me more clearly. Cleanse your bodies and your homes. Prepare the area in which you meditate and pray with representatives of the five elements. Incense (pure-ground) or your offerings of the Plant People helps me sustain the energy necessary to speak to you. Please honor the elements Water, fire, earth and air and amber, by having them within your medicine wheel. Their presence greatly protects the wheel and you and their presence helps to insure that your training will be well rounded.

Heal yourselves with my gifts of herbs and natural medicines. In return, I appreciate your offerings of sage, sweetgrass and precious Plant People returning to the earth. Your gifts are sustenance to me.

Honor the plants well that honor me in their sacrifice.
All life is sacred.
Sing, dance, love and make love and be joyful.
Love one another.
Take joy in the colors of the Earth and all of her family

Listen to the music of the Earth!
Acknowledge the presence of those for whom you wish to speak and give them your name and ask to receive their teachings and blessings with a pure heart and an open mind
....then just listen!

Cherish each other.

CHAPTER 4 - DEATH AND REBIRTH
Message from Prime. Message from Wellspring Father - The New Universal Laws

Message from God Prime (channeled by Johan Adkins - May, 1994)

God Prime must read newspapers because as I was reading one day - I heard what could only be described as the "wrath of God." He was <u>very</u> upset at an article written which seemed to berate God for all the ills of the world. The tone of the article basically asked God why a just and "loving" God would be so invisible and allow the rotten things to happen in the world. Here is his letter.

Dear People Why?

A response from God

Dear God Why? God? God told you to love one another and honor thy mother and thy father. Nowhere did <u>I</u> say to kill each other in my name. Others have interpreted their own meanings of "foes and enemies." Let us get this straight. The only "foes and enemies" you should have is the evil you create by believing that the "foes and enemies" are each other. The "foes and enemies" <u>I</u> spoke of is evil. Evil is the manifestation of precisely the act of killing each other and harming any living thing. Evil manifests itself into a living form that attempts to convince you to do even more evil in my name. You do evil and give it power when you harm another living thing by thought, deed or action. You do evil when you assume superiority over another living thing - including each other. It is this evil form you have created that has been influencing you to believe that God has forsaken you. I have not forsaken you, but I am gravely disappointed that you listen to evil and not to me.

You are all missing the point entirely if you assume I have sanctioned your religion, doctrine, dogma, cult, meditation or study group. I endorse none of you at this time. Know this and rethink what you are doing: Love one another. Honor one another. Take care and treasure one another as you would yourselves. Make your word count for something. Make your life mean something. Walk your talk, and <u>talk</u> your walk with each other but live <u>YOUR</u> "truth" and know that your truth does not have to coincide with the perception of truth to others. Base your truth on things that <u>feel</u> right. Love is the basis for all truth. DO NO HARM! Do no harm not only to yourselves and each other, but do no harm to the other living creatures and the living planets.

Honor the plants and animals that sustain you by giving you their lives. Don't thank me - thank them! Bless the beast and plants that feed you.

All religions have a piece of the puzzle - but let's get this straight for once and for all - NONE OF THEM HAVE MY SANCTION! Not one. The Spirit that speaks to you within has been telling you for years to: "Simplify, unify, purify and put balance into all aspects of your lives."

Get back to nature. Listen to nature: the bird people, the four legged people, two legged human and animal people, and all the insect, spider and crawling people, the stone people, the sea and its people, lakes, brooks and streams and their people, the deserts, plains, forests, meadows, tundra, mountains and tropical rain forests and their people. All the vistas of your world open the eyes to touch me and the entire spiritual realm. Watch the skies for the air people who move the wind and help to fight the pollution you have done to a living planet and to yourselves. Watch the movement of the stars to see the air beings and watch the trees, forests, lakes and sea to "see" (sense) the faery people and the other planetary beings that are a part of the universe.

Treasure your animal friends and don't be so quick to assume human superiority. I will tell you this. You are not superior - quite the opposite. To give you an example; the dolphins and the whales and the water beings spend their entire lives singing healing to the universe. Be ashamed that you harm these great water being healers in any way - with your pollution or great nets or with a delicate "Mai Mai" meal. The water beings sing and dance healing to every plant, every sick child, every stone that has been harmed by misunderstanding the gifts of healing and wisdom, every planet who is lonely because, for example, you accept the warmth of the sun without thanks, or admire the moon but do not ask if the moon would like to receive something from you! Honor all healers within and all around you and treasure your healers wherever they may be.

You are **all** walking in Spirit. Every holy man and the meanest among you are one. What you do to others you do to yourselves. What you say to others in anger or fear or worry harms not only the person you direct that feeling to, but **YOU**. If you demean yourself because you do not love yourself, you harm **everyone** around you, the plants, the animals and literally the entire universe. When you give into negativity and fear, you manifest it for others to deal with. Each time you hit a child, neglect or abuse your elders, turn your back on need expressed by others to you - or kill a religious opponent - you harm yourself.

Dear God, Why? I've been asking myself the very same question. How did my holy words come to this? My "word" is very, very simple: Love. Forgive. Sing. Dance. Be Joyful. Offer your gifts of love to everything and everyone around you and include the plants, animals, stones, elements, planets and the universe. Look at the bigger picture. You are on earth to accomplish the spiritual tasks you have chosen for yourself in your path to "oneness."

You chose your parents; find out why, and ask yourself, "What did I learn from them?" You chose your hardships to teach yourself to rise above them. You chose your husbands and wives to love and to teach you to share. When you "die" you do not "die" alone, Spirit is with you always. There are no true "accidents." Listen to the small voice from your angels or from me (Spirit) which will warn you of possible harm. If you keep yourselves healthy and balance all aspects of your physical, emotional, material and spiritual lives and responsibilities, you can hear the voice of Spirit.

Recognize the good in each other - we are all one. Listen to the messages I have so desperately been trying to send you. The quiet voice that speaks of love and honor...that is me and my angels.

Stop killing each other in my name.
Stop hating each other thinking I endorse the hate.

Just <u>STOP</u>!!
 and <u>LOVE</u>.

God

The New Commandments - Universal Laws
(channeled by Johan Adkins from Wellspring Father/Creator - written in personal form)

(1) A Promise is a Promise -
Make no promises you don't intend to keep and break no promises you have made. Be a person of your word, for words are powerful and should not be spoken without forethought. Do not take the name of any God or Spirit in vain, for to damn a thing with God's name is to invite negative energy into the situation. To curse with the name of God causes us pain and grief.

(2) Do unto others what you would have done unto yourself.
Treat others as you wish to be treated. Treat them with fairness and love and equity. Take responsibility for your words. If you speak a thing, that is a spiritual committment to do it. If you speak it or promise a positive thing, it must be done even if it is inconvenieny or you lack motivation to do it. Speak with a pure heart. This is important when you speak to a child. A promise made to a child is as binding as to another.

(3) Do no harm.

Do no harm physically or verbally or emotionally to another. If you do harm, admit the harm and seek forgiveness from whom you have harmed. When you work with love and purity of intent and purity of heart, you can do no harm. If you do harm, forgive yourselves and seek peace within because Spirit forgives most harm except to murder an innocent or suicide yourself. To do so, may sever your soul from the soulforce pool.

(4) Honor all life.

Honor yourself. If you have caused yourself dishonor, forgive yourself and forgive others lest you manifest negative energy (which can actually create a "fiend" or a living entity) for yourself or them to deal with. Honor your husband or wife. Treat each other with mutual respect and basic kindness. Honor your children. Honor the elders. Do not speak to your elders as children, but sit at their feet and listen to their wisdom. Do not degrade their life experience by speaking as if to an inferior. The elders are to be blessed and honored for their long life. Honor does not require obeyance. Do not confuse the two. Speak to your elders and your children as people who have value and opinions as valid as your own. Listen to what they have to say and weigh your decisions with their advise. Children are still very close to Spirit and their insights are sometimes directed by Spirit because they can still hear and have not been taught not to hear and believe.

Speak with reason and fairness and teach them by example.

If you must discipline anyone, make certain that they understand that it is the thing that they have done that is unacceptable. The individual is still loved and honored and you separate the unacceptable action from the person. They are not bad because what they have done is "bad." If there must be a punishment, help them to maintain their dignity by allowing a choice of punishments. Never strike anyone in anger. Take time from the situation wherever possible to decide the action necessary which will help them to grow and learn and alter their behavior.

Before any punishment is made, ask yourself it is truly their problem or if it is truly your problem. If it is their problem, it is for them to decide the best course of action to deal with it. If it is your problem, learn to hold your anger and frustration, but talk out why what they do affects you adversely and try to work it out together. Listen, truly listen to what they have to say.

(5) Be Grateful
Be thankful and sacrifice only that which agrees to be sacrificed.
Realize that everything of nature has intelligence and is alive and has a life which it values. Think of everything as a whole being and be mindful

how you treat it. Honor extends to the food you eat as well as to each other. Do not waste the sacrifice that the plant, animal and elemental beings have given to sustain you. Thank them and bless them for their sacrifice for your benefit.

When you cut a vegetable or kill an animal to eat, please realize that the they have intelligence and consciousness and that they sacrifice themselves for you. Bless it with wellspring (water.) Express thankfulness for giving its life to sustain your life. Ask it to sleep to prepare it for cutting or killing. If you will cut the bottom and the top from a vegetable and compost those parts, you honor the sacrifice and allow essential energy to return to the earth directly. In doing this thing, you also honor the Earth. With animals, please leave the heart in the earth.

The Earth and the other planets are a giant living organisms. Honor them all.

Realize, please, that elemental fire and air and water and earth also sacrifice themselves to feed you. The flame which broils your steak is not only an elemental being but it is ignited from other elemental beings from the gases released from earth or wood from a tree or charcoal from the earth. Fire burns, sacrificing itself, and also sacrifices that from which it burns. Do not dishonor the flame by forcing it to consume that which does not offer itself freely to the flame as sacrifice. Wherever possible, ask the wood beings if they wish to purify themselves in the flame. Some do not wish this thing. Ask the trees before you cut any of them down if you have permission to cut them down to help provide warmth (or a Christmas tree.) Honor the decision if it is "no." Find a forked branch, ask it to help you find that which agrees to be cut and relax and allow it to guide you. Often you can go into an area and state that you need to cut a tree for warmth and sacrifice and wait for them to direct you to whom they have jointly chosen to be sacrifice. If you are gathering wood for a fire and it resists, do not force it, sufficient quantities will be provided to you with what can be spared for the health of the tree people. Use a sharp ax or blade and do not needlessly throw or beat upon the tree or its branches.

(6) The Law of Three's
Speak your spiritual requests or provide help by repeating three times the thing you wish.
> *The first time is to visualize the intent*
> *The second time is to actually do it*
> *The third time is to finalize the intent or set firmly the intent.*

If you do not speak in three's, it is assumed by Spirit that you do not have full intent to visualize and accomplish what you speak. With each speaking, energy gains and the help you will need to accomplish what you ask is provided. If the itent is pure and is not (always) selfish, Spirit tries to help you to accomplish what you ask. You cannot wish a thing to manifest for another without first seeking their permission to ask.

Spirit aids you when you request a thing to be done for the benefit and highest good of all. You cannot command a thing to be done, nor can you do a thing that is not to the highest and best purpose of the universe. Therefore, do not fear that you will speak three times and do inadvertent harm. If you will say this thing, that possibility is nullified.
"I say this three times fully in the perfect way for the highest and best purpose of all."
You may say this sentence instead of repeating fully and exactly three times.

(7) A Healing for a Healing - The Universal Law of Reciprocity

You may not heal without permission from that which is being healed. You may not move or use or abuse energy without permission from Spirit. To have a gift of healing, you must request that Spirit heals you and helps you. Cleanse your body and water and vegetable fast for three days prior to doing healing work. Those who ask for healing must do this also. You must be receptive to heal yourself and work with Spirit as a "channel" or *"vessel" of Spiritual healing. If you approach healing with this heart, then, you may extend that healing to others and from yourself and others to the universe. Truly, you do the universe no service by attempting to work with Spirit to heal a planet when you have not healed your own energy sufficiently to pass clean and pure energy through the universe.*

(8) Seek a teacher

Learn from the teacher within as well as those around you. Everyone has something to teach. Listen with the open mind of a child and do not judge. All opinion is as valuable as yours. All gifts take different forms and people learn in the way that they are able to learn. Seek your own truth from that which you <u>know</u> is true and honor the truth that others <u>know</u>. Humanity may not accept what you know if it conflicts with what they "know," and that's acceptable.

Feel absolutely free to change your mind from time to time. Feel free to question everything and everybody. Life is dynamic change and belief systems change and evolve too.

Look for truth everywhere and do not discount truth from wherever you find it. Look for subtleties, not miracles, as an affirmation from Spirit. Look to the clouds and the skies for your teachers too. Look to the animals and the plants. Look within.

The New Universal Law demands that humanity take a responsible and equitable position with each other. If you know a thing which is gifted to you by Spirit, share it, but do not expect acceptance or a change in what others believe. Each of you have a different path to travel. Just honor the teaching of others and assimilate what fits into your path.

Spirit is more concerned that you "walk your talk" with what you believe then if you follow a religious dogma or creed. Have the courage of your belief, but have no firm "convictions." Be open to new ideas. The diversity of belief and re-evaluation of your beliefs is not a threat to Spirit and should not be a threat to you.
 Seek your own truth.

(9) Love
In all things, in all ways, act in love and all will fall into place.

BOOK TWO

THE TRANSFORMATION CONNECTION

WRITTEN AND CHANNELED
BY JOHAN ADKINS

The Fleur d'IeisTransformation Connection

PEN'L LEINA PRAYER

Earth Children,

Listen to our prayer for you.

May you find joy and happiness.

May you understand that pain and sorrow

are a necessary part of existence, but are those things

which must be transcended.

May you love and be loved.

May you search for your truth and know it when you find it.

Listen well.

TABLE OF CONTENTS

SECTION ONE - Divine Guidance - The Beginning
Prologue - Personal Message from Johan Adkins

SECTION TWO - Divine Work.
The Metal Elements. How to work with divines and the metal people.

SECTION THREE - Divine Help
Message from St. Augustine: Introduction to working with stone and metal pendulums. Introduction of the Pen'l Leina - the sacred language of the stone, metal and Minervan beings.

SECTION FOUR - Divine Protection
Message from the Earth Council: Medicine Wheel Meditation is taught to build protective structures and learn how to speak to and work with the Earth Council.

SECTION FIVE - Divine Instruction
Introduction to the Pen'l Leina Language - Spirit's symbol language. The first written language forms.

SECTION SIX - Divine Healing

Introduction to the Pen'l Leina Hand Reading. Hand Charts: Physical, emotional and spiritual readings and Charts. Dance of the Universe – Spirit's closing blessing.

SECTION ONE
DIVINE GUIDANCE

Prologue

This book assumes that you have read the book "Spirit Speaks" written and channeled by Johan Adkins because "The Fleur d'leis Transformation Connection" really is a continuation of that work. If you have not read that book first, please do so. The Fleur d'leis Transformation Connection is meant to be a practical advanced guide to help you in the transformational process. Practical tools and how to use them are provided to allow you to gauge where you are on the "transformational wheel."

The word "Fleur d'leis" is very ancient and means flower of life or flower of lifeforce. The spelling is older than the French word. The Fleur d'lei symbol has been adopted for the transformational beings on earth whose souls survived the apocalypse and judgement. There are 330,000 souls in our solar system who have the possibility of transformation. Only those 330,000 souls still have Spiritual guidance. However, they have only this lifetime to get their spiritual act together. Spirit estimates that only 144,000 souls will be successful in transcendence. This book is written to help you be successful.

Yes, you did hear it. Judgement Day has came and past. It happened over a year and a half in 1993 to early 1995. The height of the battles in the sky was fought when the comet threatening Jupiter was close and still in one piece. Had the comet hit full force, it would have altered Jupiter's energy and the pattern of movement and would have caused a chain of events which would have been the end of all life on all the planets in our solar system. It was necessary for other dimensional beings, Spirit and Fleur d'leis to work together to break the comet into pieces before impact. Fleur d'leis worked with the planetary beings, rock people and all of Spirit to place protection over the planets during that period. People all over the world were drawn together and worked to help break up the destructive power of the comet. People all over the world worked dimensionally and in other aspects of themselves to fight the remaining "evil." Few people were physically aware that this work was being done by their higher selves. Those who were aware in this dimension, have spiritual blessing and have already attained Fleur d'leis status. Satan and his minions are destroyed and truly only imbalance remains for us to deal with. "Evil" can still be manifest in gross imbalance - but we have a clean slate if we want to keep it that way.

In order to teach you to use the tools, I have gone to the "sources." The metal beings will teach you to work with divines. The stone people will teach you the stone language known as the Pen'l Leina (pen line.) Various Spiritual teachers and healers will give you other tools toward understanding alternative healing methods and Spiritual transformation.

What is Spiritual transformation? It is the recognition of our spiritual path and work in this lifetime in earthly incarnation which will help us to join with the soulforce pool and stop the requirement of future incarnations. It is becoming healing "Spirit" on earth and doing that work. It is to heighten the awareness of our spiritual self and the path our soul has taken through possibly thousands of lifetimes to reach transcendence to Holy Spirit. It is a joyful journey toward the oneness of soulforce "pool" of the Godhead...of Spirit.

When I say Spirit, I refer not only to the trinity: The Creator who calls himself Wellspring Father; God Prime, Jesus' father; and the Lord who is the "Holy Ghost" of the trinity. Spirit, however, is the "soulforce pool" and contains innumerable souls. To name a few: Angels, Archangels and Directional Beings; Vortex Beings, Planetary beings and beings from other planets and dimensions such as the Lemp, Minervans and Venuvians. Spirit also encompass' the elemental beings, the rock and metal people, Rainbow Lady of the inner sun, Earth Mother and St. Augustine who is the patron saint of the stone people and the insect and spider people, the animals and plants, Faery realms and Water People to name only a few. As a transcended being, you can talk to them yourself. You will meet many of them here and many of them have sent channeled discourses in the first book. We all understand that myth and legend and faery stories are universal. Why have so many cultures had these "mythological and fanciful" entities show up time and time again? It is because they are based on an altered reality, albeit some are based on dream reality -living perhaps not in our physical dimensions or our "time" but a part of our collective consciousness nevertheless.

When Spirit speaks, they seem to do a lot of repeating and that's not a bad thing. We are taught and remember through repetition. Many speak the same message. Some critics will point this out regarding the transmissions from "Spirit Speaks" and this book, but understand this, I don't have the right, nor do editors of this book have the right, to alter one word of their discourses without their permission. This basic agreement was made with Spirit in order to receive this information. Their words have been too often changed and the message changes. I quote them verbatim.

Two books were channeled by the author over a period of several years. The information contained in the books took my spiritual understanding and scattered the pieces into an entirely different puzzle. I felt angelic presence and the presence of Spirit was so strong in those few years that I could not type fast enough to get all the information that was streaming through my fingers. The transmissions were rather like transcription, like my fingers heard and my brain just listened while they were typing. I had no idea of what was coming next. A great deal of work was done to keep the transmissions pure. As I was typing, I wrote only what the pure of heart rainbow and white light beings were generating. I felt Holy presence. I was granted for a time, the ability to "see" beyond my normal perceptive range. I heard them, and still occasionally do hear them as clearly as a dear friend speaking softly into my ear. I fully understand that this type of "hearing" and "seeing" is questionable to the scientific and psychological community. I could be crazy and like everyone else, I sometimes wonder myself if I'm not.

One of the reasons I believe that this gift was given to me is that I was neutral in my beliefs. I didn't have an agenda, and I have nothing to gain by exposing myself to the possible rejection of society for being one of Spirit's teachers and healers. I've had to accept through the years that is what I am. Society has always scoffed and made life difficult for the people who are given spiritual guidance in such a direct fashion.

The test of this work is this - the books should all sound familiar because this information has been streaming to the Fleur d'leis for almost ten years now. It has taken me ten years to have the courage to even attempt to publish these works. The final decision to seek publishing was a conversation with my favorite aunt, Norma Smith. Although very Christian and humble, she told me that I could not be so selfish that I would deny others what has been given to me in trust.

I am happy to share these teachings with you.

Personal Message from Johan Adkins

Spirit wishes to set up a broad energy network for healing. Let one person's request for help be filled by all fleur d'leis. As each of you receive a request for help, please respond, if you can, with love, but be sure to ask for a universal "trade." A healing for a healing. If you ask for healing or help from me personally, what I would request of you is to return the healing you receive toward healing the Earth, not only spiritually and visually, but actually get outdoors and pick up trash and/or work physically with groups to address and clean up pollution problems. Become an activist in your small community or large town.

One person cannot request healing for another (except a young child or an adult who cannot ask themselves) and please understand, all of us must die someday. We set our individual "scripts" and determine the method of our death and Spirit does not, in most cases, interfere in the personal scripts. When healing is requested for another, even if they are comatose, you need to speak to their higher spirit and ask permission to ask for healing and instruct the individual to prepare to receive energy from <u>everywhere</u>. Listen for their response and honor their decision. No miracles are promised. The very best healer of anyone is themselves.

In the first book, "Spirit Speaks," I have basically introduced everyone to specific powers in the spiritual realm. Many of you require no introductions - they are old friends already. Consider the door open and speak to any member of the spiritual realm yourself. All you have to do is balance, quiet, be receptive and **ASK**. Then listen, and you will receive spiritual guidance. Please understand that I cannot be an "intermediary" for you, I can only try to teach as many people as possible to work with the tools that Spirit has gifted to all of us. I certainly cannot speak to them for all of you, nor can I, or will I attempt to manipulate them for another.

Each of you is privy to all of the information I have and Spirit looks forward to meeting and talking with you. Follow the introduction "procedures" and ask humbly and from a pure and loving heart and Spirit will make every effort to communicate with you.

Program your dreamstate to receive spiritual communication by asking your body to become receptive to it. Take this request a step further and ask for help to remember your dreams and dreamstate instruction the next morning. Keep a spiritual or dream log and teach yourself to log as much as you can possibly remember the very first moments you awake. The more you do this, the easier it will be to remember your nightly classwork!

Whatever you can visualize - it is done! You can't do anything "wrong" and you can't "screw up." Whatever you do, as long as you do it in love and with a pure heart and intent, will be exactly right. Spirit is very patient of us and understanding.

If you have objections to "ritual" of any kind and it just doesn't feel right - don't do it. Don't do anything that doesn't smack of truth and have a right "feeling" for you. Spirit will find a way to help you find what is right for you. As long as you do no harm to any living thing and honor all things as they honor you, you cannot fail. Ask for help and you will receive it. Ask for instruction and you will receive it. It's amazing!

I would like to give you all a hug and wish you the best in your personal work toward spiritual transformation! Please make yourself receptive to the love surrounding all and live your life as living spiritual examples of the highest fleur d'leis order!

SECTION TWO
DIVINE WORK

PERSONAL MESSAGE FROM JOHAN ADKINS

WORKING WITH METAL DIVINES

The piece following this section of my personal experiences is directly from the metal elementals. It is really a rarity and a blessing to actually have verbal communication from them.

I have worked with copper divining rods for years. These are two copper rods of the same length bent in an L shape with a slightly larger copper sheath for the hands so that the divines can move freely and produce a tone when they move. The pair I am most comfortable with have approximately a twelve inch long leg and a four inch hand hold. It is important to hold them so that they are level to one another (one slightly elevated to the other) and level to the ground so that they don't have to fight gravity to work with you.

The first time they move of their own volition in your hands is a magical and scary moment. There are all kinds of explanations of why they work, but until you actually feel them move and know you are not moving them, you will not understand how truly miraculous and powerful the feeling is. I'll never forget when the medicine wheel teaching was coming through, the divines moved with great energy, and chose the stones and pinecones to build the circle. Then they chose the spots where each was to be placed. The divines then proceeded to move me in the four directions. When I moved as directed, I experienced four different and strong directional energies which completely overwhelmed my senses. The reward of following the careful instructions increased the energy I felt threefold. The divines will teach you how to work with them. The rods will guide you step by step if you are patient. They are miraculous metaphysical and healing tools.

The universe is made of a matrix of the metal element's highest dimensional vibration. The ancient Orientals somehow knew this. The matrix, comprised of the same "star stuff" as our own auras, can sometimes become weak in areas or develop dangerous breaks or holes. At the meeting points of the lay lines, the chakras of the universe can become distorted or misaligned which requires repair or reconstruction. The metal divines search the matrix looking for problems and work the necessary repairs. I think of it as "weaving" the matrix, sometimes even "patching" the holes.

So when it seems that you are merely holding the divines while they move in seemingly meaningless patterns, consider instead, that you are helping to mend the matrix in the universe. This will give you the patience to wait until the divines are finished doing what they must do first. The results produced are well worth the patience required.

You can work with the divines in the same fashion to heal anything. We are all comprised of basically of the same structure as the universe. We are the same as a single cell. Miracle, isn't it? The chakras are a spiral form and the spiral form is found in every aspect of life.

I've worked with the rods to determine the openness of the main chakras in the body and then worked with the rods to balance the chakras for overall good health. The rods have totally lased away kidney and gall stones and tumors. They do incredible work mending organs, muscles and bones as well as performing delicate laser "surgery" where required. The body will seek health and if the lay-lines, meridians and chakras are kept in good condition, there is no reason for dis-ease.

The diving rods work to balance the male and female aspects. You can feel when the divines are perfectly balanced (which means you are balanced too.) When all is balanced they will circle, usually simultaneously either towards each other towards the body or away from each other away from the body, depending on the individual's polarity.

Sometimes the divines pull together and hit. This is a necessary step to get them freed from residual corruption and balanced and get you balanced. If you tune in, you can feel when they are "equal" in energy and that is what you are after and what they need. When the energy is "equal" they begin to move concentrically to complete 81 circles. This number is spiritual blessing and protection. Then they are ready to proceed with the work you need done. Normally, to reach this stage, I try to give them something in the neighborhood of five to fifteen minutes to do their thing.

One needs to state early on what your intent is so that they can prepare. If you have great time restraints, ask them to work with you as soon as possible and they will try to comply if at all possible.

It is necessary to establish early on what movements represent "yes" and "no." You can ask them periodically as they are moving if they are ready to work and the divines will give you small responses that won't interrupt the flow of their work. I believe that many of the movements build a safe matrix structure around you, in order to allow them to work unimpeded. If the divines just seem to look around and won't settle down to work, they probably need to be somewhere else or in a sacred environment. If the energy feels "spacey" try another time and another place. Sometimes, it rather feels like they are just looking around and looking over their shoulder and feel uncomfortable about the surroundings.

When one of the rods move and the other "ticks" they are gathering data. Often, when you ask them a question, they respond this way. I know that this is a Spiritual transmission or lesson that is coming through the divines to you. Although it may seem that your question isn't being answered, the data is being stored for a time when Spirit is willing to allow you to hear the transmission. I've received enough of their "transmissions" to know this is true for me.

On a practical use level, I thought it might be helpful to tell you what works best for me when I am working with the divines. It has been my experience that it really does work best to work in a sacred space with them. Direct sun light helps to keep them energized, but unless you work within a stone or pinecone circle or a pyramid, it takes a great deal of time to accomplish much because they have to keep clearing the immediate area, themselves and you.

They can work with "wellspring" to find water and tell you how deep you must dig your well. To do this, work with another person and triangulate the spot to dig the well. When the rods cross mark the spot. Ask the divines to show you how many feet to dig down for the best flow of water and to assure future supplies. For example, you can ask them to give you one rotation per 10 feet. When we had the well dug by "non-believers" for our home, my Aunt Babe Snow and I worked together with two sets of divines to "divine" the place to dig the well. We sealed our footage results in an envelope and gave it to the men digging our well. After they did their "scientific" thing while "pooh-poohing" divining results, they wrote their suggestion on a slip of paper and opened our sealed envelope. We were within 10 feet of each other on two levels of where water was found. There was very little available water to be found away from the points we told them. When they were told that, they kept drilling on their dime to prove us wrong. They didn't find another level until they went past 800 feet.

I know that the divines have saved my life by destroying a tumor and through the years have made me much more healthy. They worked to help dissolve a quarter size kidney stone which was going to require surgery on one of my best friends. The Doctor, preparing her for surgery but doing one last test had no explanation of how it could have possibly "gone away." They have speeded the mending of bones and balanced the chakras of my family over and over. I am especially thankful to them when I have sinus' problems!

It is very possible to work remotely with the divines on someone far away (provided you have their permission.) If you know the person well and have physical contact with them often, you do not need to go to the next step. The divines can read energy signatures from your energy.

If you do not know the person, or haven't touched the person physically in several years, it is helpful if the person needing help mails you a clean sheet of paper with their (clean) hand "signatures" on the sheet. It is best to use three pieces of paper and sandwich the hand prints between the other two sheets. If the person is so shallow as to try to trick the divines with another energy signature or by not touching the inner piece of paper, the rods will often refuse to help that individual.

If the hand energy signatures aren't feasible, a picture of the individual will suffice. Let the divines "read" the picture. A very talented and wonderful psychic nurse friend of mine was approached by a co-worker whose son had disappeared. The nurse worked with the rods over a picture of the boy and then over a map and found the city where he was located, then worked with a city map and found the street where he was. The co-worker had so much faith in my friend, that she flew directly there and went to the place my friend "saw." She missed her son by ten minutes. The son did not want to be found. My friend worked with the rods without permission of the boy. That's a hard lesson. The family needed to find him because he was on drugs, but even so, he physically (or even his higher self) had to give his permission to be found in order for his family to connect with him.

The divines have their own story to tell. Even now, when I enter my pyramid and watch the divines "dance," I wonder what on earth they are doing. I can feel the subtle, and sometimes not so subtle, energies moving around me and through the divines and it often feels that they must be doing something so very important that it is hubris to interrupt the flow. We are all instruments of the divine instruments, and I am blessed that they consent to work with me.

GREETINGS FROM THE METAL ELEMENTALS

We have agreed to speak with you today to instruct you in the proper etiquette, if you will, to work with us. Metal is a group dynamic. When you speak to "metal" you speak to all metal. When metal is compromised in some fashion, all are compromised.

Some of you have been working with the metal divining rods for some time, however, you have not always been able to rely upon them. There are a number of factors that must be understood when a request to work with metal elementals becomes a factor.

First of all, we are a formal group and would prefer the exchange remain formal. We work with the body meridians and the lay-lines of the earth are the paths in which earth metal elementals move. Indeed meridians, lay-lines and linear paths throughout the entire universes are composed of metal elements. We make up the dynamics of energy pathways in the hubs in conjunction with the vortex and the energy of the solar son/sun.

As we are neutrals in the purest sense of the word, we are less emotionally pulled, but are subject to extremes of balance/imbalance depending upon what is happening on very large scales of the hubs vortex/linear/sun systems. What we are trying to say is, we don't judge you - we don't get emotional or get our "feelings" hurt when speaking to you. Our balance/imbalance is more dependent upon the big picture.

We prefer to work through the vortex systems and it is not necessary to ask our permission to move from point to point when "traveling" through the dimensions or hubs. We are the pathways - we do not care whether or not you are "pure heart" or "impure" heart at this point.*

All who are granted passage by the vortex may travel any linear direction (may travel the path from vortex to vortex.) It is conceivable, however, that one vortex will allow passage and the vortex at the other end will disallow passage through the vortex itself, but the connecting points in between (us) are open from point a to point b regardless. You can get in - but you can't get out without permission of the vortex.

During the last twelve months, a great deal of traffic has passed through the hubs. Most beings do not understand that they travel by the grace of the metal elementals as well as the vortex.

The metal divining rods are more correctly called "divines." We like that name for the purposes of the rods. The rods are direct links to the metal elementals as well as any the individual wish to speak to with our permission. Remember to always ask permission to speak to someone else when working with the divines.

In most cases, it is not necessary to speak to others as we have a direct link to the vortex system which is the "com-link," so to speak, with all energies, planets, elementals and directional energies in the universes.

Think of the nature of metal. It is strong. It is straightforward. It can be molded by heat to different shapes which remain strong, but extremes of movement or temperatures can weaken, melt or snap the metal. Metal elementals' divines are not to be abused by extremes of temperatures but prefer to remain at a constant temperature. Extremes of temperatures weaken us.

Sun is required to energize and help us to clear away negativity or corruption from the lay-lines of the hubs down to the lay-lines or meridians of individuals. We gather energy from the sun, therefore, it is much easier to work with the divines in direct sun. Remember, I said direct sun not indirect sun as within a house or through a closed window.

The metal element is set apart from the other elements by virtue of the vibrational energy we emit. The wood elementals are not comfortable around us, and indeed we do not wish to kill them inadvertently by being forced to be buried at the roots of trees or hung in their branches for "sun baths" or healing outdoors. Put metal by metal. The metal within the earth's structure helps mother earth move the energies - too much metal in the wrong places can poison the earth. Metal buried without thought or understanding in the wrong places can interrupt the flow of energy within mother earth and conversely then *from* mother earth to the other planets. Metal mined by man is a real problem - because man interferes with energy pathways that maintain the integrity of the entire planet. Metal dumped in water bodies pollutes and harms the water and the metal. Heavy metal in drinking water can pollute and poison the beings who imbibe the water. We don't wish to hurt or harm anyone. Nature left to its own design would not, ordinarily, harm.

Metal elementals demand adherence to the universal law of exchange. We will be happy to help you, if you will, in turn, help us.

When you wish to work with divines, establish first of all if the divines are clear enough to begin work. Ask the divines to move in a direction which indicates "yes." Then ask for a direction which indicates "no." Then ask for a direction which indicates a neutrality. The neutral direction is necessary because we aren't all that wishy washy with "I don't know, or I can't answer. A neutral direction generally is a placement in which information is being "piped in" through the body meridians because it would not be to the highest or best interest at this time to answer you or universally, or we simply are prohibited to answer at this time. Try answering any question only with yes or no and you will see the problem. Stone People tend to fall back on "I don't know or I can't answer or I won't answer. If you ask we will answer, however, you may not receive the answer directly until you are spiritually ready to receive it. We will not lie, evade or "spare" your feelings. We will not refuse to answer truly, but your individual spiritual path may delay the answer.

Ask permission to work with the divines. If the answer is no, ask if we need clearing. Ask us, if metal elementals are sufficiently cleared would we be willing to work with you (not for you - not "used" by you.) If the answer is no, you may be incompatible either with the divines or you are far too unbalanced (in either direction) to work with metal. Try again later after you have established a neutral balance.

If the answer is yes than the following instructions need to be followed.

> If the divine is willing to work with you, the next question must be (stated aloud or psychically silent,) "Please show me based

upon a 360 degree circle, the degree in which you are available (or clear) to speak to me." A clear answer for yes and a readiness to answer is a 260 or better degree open position.

If the answer to this question is less than 260 degrees (or roughly 3/4 around,) it is an indication that the metal elements need help "clearing" before the divine work can resume. It is possible that the individual also needs clearing, but that question will have to wait for a clear "path" to be answered. Ask no more questions until the divines have been cleared.

The method for clearing the divines is as follows:

> Go outdoors in the sun whenever possible or open the windows to allow the sun to shine in upon the divines. With one in each hand, allow them to move of their own volition until they begin to move simultaneously in the same direction.
>
> Generally, this takes a maximum of five minutes, but in some extreme cases, you will need to wait a few moments longer. You will notice that the rods will move independently in different ways. What they are actually doing is clearing pathways in the universal hubs on seven hub layers so that all metal

(not just the rods you are holding) is healed and cleared sufficiently to assist you.

Continue to hold the rods once they have begun moving simultaneously and they will stop when they are ready to begin. Allow up to fifteen minutes for this process. Please be patient as you are helping the whole universal structure heal when you honor this step.

After the rods have completely stopped, ask them to show you, based upon a 360 degree circle how open they are to communicate with you now. You should have at least a 260 degree or better open status at this time.

If you still do not have a 260 degree open status, ask the divines if the reason is due to something within or surrounding you. If a yes, try to balance and ground. Drink wellspring (water) and/or bathe away attached negativity or corruption. Try again after you have negated the "evil" (follow the chapter on removing "evil") and/or meditated, healed, grounded and balanced. Usually, at this stage you can begin.

If the answer is still less than 260 degrees after you have attempted to rectify your personal status, ask the rods if there is something they can do to help you. If the answer is yes, allow the rods to move as they wish until they move simultaneously again. If they still are unclear you have a major problem to overcome and refer to the section on pyramidal and protected environment structures.

Sometimes you are clear, but the area in which you are attempting to work is compromised in some fashion. Ask the rods if that is the case. If the answer is yes, than construct your medicine wheel or encase yourself in two layers of protected environment (i.e., build an actual or visual pyramid structure and physically surround yourself with pine cones, candles, stones, and/or color in two layers. See the chapter on the proper building of the healing/communication structures.)

If Spirit is requiring the structures that is done because either Spirit or the divines wish to speak in a private manner or because there is too much electromagnetic energy around interfering with transmissions or because there is "evil," corruption and residue surrounding the area (or you - or others around you) which is interfering either with you or the communication through the divines.

Building the proper structures will help the energies around you to cleanse and clear the area while protecting you. Ask for help.

Generally, however, the first five minutes is sufficient to clear the divines to work with you. Sometimes Spirit has requested in advance to speak to you through the divines. In this case, the divines will usually wish you to speak within a protected environment.

The protected environment is a good idea in any event, because working with divines is power and power calls power...and sometimes the power isn't the "power" you wish to speak to. This isn't as big a problem as it used to be when Satan ruled the other universe.

When you are within the protected environment - Ask again if you may work with the rods. If the answer is still no, put the rods down and ask for spiritual guidance. You may be one of the people incompatible with the element of metal...sorry, but there are some people who must rely upon other measures or other elementals to receive information and to ease communication. Ask if that is the case and we will answer honestly.

The Metal element rarely speaks actively in the dimensions of -1, 1 or 2 except through the rods (or some pendulums)- and then only when the "divines" and/or pendulums are honored and sufficiently cleansed. This is because "evil" can, in some cases in these dimensions, override and overpower metal and speak to you using metal. That is like "rape" to the metal elementals as it would be to anyone. To be used against our will is a universal atrocity. It is because we have been so used in the past that we wish to establish the methods necessary to prevent that from happening. Information that is harmful or frightening or negative harms us as well as you. It builds mistrust and causes the individuals to question whether or not we are neutral and reliable energies and "tools" to speaking to Spirit. That, is the one case that truly hurts our collective feelings.

It is very helpful to you, to us, and to Spirit, who is trying to communicate to you through us if you will state the following before you attempt to work with the divines;

> **"I wish to speak only to the neutral or balanced (or imbalanced) universes. I desire to receive help for my highest and best good and seek permission to work**

with the divines to this end. May I have permission...?"

At this point, you should establish to whom you wish to speak. It may be; "May I have permission to speak to my highest self?" or may I have permission to speak to Jesus or the Minervans or my spirit guide? May I have permission to speak to...anybody or anything or anyone."

At no time do you have our permission to use us to speak to "evil" or corruption or ask questions which will cause harm to any living being. Keep that in mind. Keep in mind also that guns are made of metal and much harm has came from what the individual holding a weapon has chosen to do. The metal itself cannot be blamed for being "used" as an instrument of harm. When harm is done, we are harmed too. When great harm is done we are greatly harmed and "evil" and corruption may take over the metal element of the physical weapon. Some weapons are definitely fully compromised. Some have killed that which would have harmed others. That is the task and spiritual trial of metal - to sometimes be weapons.

Metal elementals are warriors for this reason and are dynamic in the universe. That is the nature of the metal elementals. Because we are warriors and serious and formal in our natures, we appreciate being respected. We appreciate serious work for solid, good reasons and not frivolous "play." We appreciate adherence to hierarchial guidelines and appreciate being asked, before we ask others, if <u>we</u> may help or guide you. Too many times we are just "used" to speak to everyone else. The best guide is to ask us to let you speak to whomever will help you to your highest and best good. Let us, along with the vortex system and the Spiritual realm, decide to whom you should speak that can help you the best.

The 360 degree circle is a very viable tool to discover many things about yourself. Allow us to "check" the degree of openness of each of your chakras (on all twelve auric layers if you want. This check can help you direct energy to heal a chakra that is insufficiently open or is too open in relation to others. The vortex system within your bodies (that are your chakras,) is very much appreciate the divine's help in re-establishing uniformity within the physical layers (three layers within) and nine layers without.

Allow the rod to "find" the chakra in the auric layers and tell you the degree of openness. The chakras are placed in wider and wider patterns within the auric layers moving away from the core physical body. All should be at least 180 degrees open to full open condition. Chakras that are too open result eventually in imbalance. Sometimes they are too open to compensate for other chakras too closed.

A closed chakra is always open at least a small degree - it can never be "closed" fully unless the physical body has "died" or disassembled. It appears, in what you call death, that the chakras are closed, but actually, the dimensions shift up and truly, the chakras never truly close or even "blink" from the moment of death to transcendence.

To balance the vortex chakras - picture a flower or a bud opening or closing. A too open chakra is like a flower beyond its bloom - the petals fall, so rebuild the flower to an open, healthy blossom. Any visualization will work - do what works for you.

To help cleanse and balance the metal elementals/lay-lines, linear paths or meridians of anything:

> Flood the web of the hubs of the universe with sunlight (white/gold - shining light.) To keep your bodies' meridians clear and uncompromised - use the same visualization or use whatever works for you. Any visualization in which you can move energy and feel energy, is working. Many gain successful visualization by picturing a "liquid gold" running throughout the meridians of the body. If you will do this for yourself, it is the same as doing it for the universe. We are all one.

Metal is a perfect com-link from Spirit directly down our "bodies" into your body via the meridians to the part of the body receiving information or spiritual "healing." It is for this reason that we are a healing "tool." Hold one rod over an area needing healing and you will feel the dynamic direct healing taking place. We may be working alone or we may be working with vortex energy or healing energies from many.

If you request healing via the divine - appropriate energy will "channel" through depending on what you need and where you need it. Visualize the body as whole and healed and wish for perfect healing in the perfect way.

> Hold the rod about 1/4" off the skin for the best "laser" effect and hold the rod about 5" off the skin for generalized, overall area healing. The closer the rod - the more direct the "beam." If you are working with the rods to heal - your hand will be guided by Spirit (we include ourselves in that word) as to distance and placement. Remember a request made, a request granted. A healing for a healing. If healing is denied for some reason - the denial must be honored.

Honor us, we will honor you with direct teaching. Hold the divines at the temple to receive our instruction. If you cannot "hear" by doing this - hold the divines at the third eye and ask for visual instruction.

Sometimes the divines will "talk" or gather data by holding themselves in one position (generally, the neutral position) for a space of time. You can tell when this is happening because the divines will pulse or "tick" - which is a slight "heartbeat" type motion. If this happens, communication or healing is being received and directly transmitted to the body. Much of the universal teaching and healing is done in this fashion.

Allow the rods to continue the "transmission" until the transmission is ended. Usually, it will not take longer than five minutes. If it does, however, something very, very important is coming through and your impatience with the rod not "moving" to answer your questions insults Spirit as you <u>are</u> receiving the answer or the healing through meridians of the entire universe directly into the meridians in your body. There will come a knowing and understanding at a time that is appropriate, if not right away. Sometimes this transmission is received in a "flash" understanding - no words but many words quickly transmitted. Your brain core receives information in this way to sort it out for you in whatever fashion it must to relay the information. It may choose to speak to you in dreams or astral states or in casual "conversation" when time and circumstances are appropriate.

It does not insult us if you verify with us that a transmission is coming through. We will move in a slightly larger "tick" in your "yes" direction to indicate yes....just be patient and be polite.

You will not receive data in this fashion if it is not to your highest and best good. It is impossible for negative data to come into your body in this fashion. Do not fear.

The divines, held in the hand of a fleur d'leis can aid in healing the entire universe. If you will set aside a time within your medicine wheel or pyramid to work with Spirit and check the seven hubs - any problems can be sought out and healed. When an area is found that requires healing, the divines will circle in the direction needed to heal the area. Sometimes this is clockwise, sometimes counter clockwise (as vortex may be either.)

To heal an area that is not too compromised (that lifeforce alone needs to heal) only requires 36 full rotations. To heal an area that requires loveforce as well as lifeforce requires 42 full rotations. To heal a very troubled area requiring wellspring father's help and blessing requires lifeforce and loveforce and full rotations of 81. If more rotations are required or an odd number required for some reason - Spirit will speak the number required. Please help them complete the number spoken.

The reason Spirit speaks the number is to have you help the rods move through heavy energies that may attempt to stop the rotation. When Johan does this healing for the universe, she has told us that it helps her to breathe in - pulling the rod through and breathe out pushing it around its path. "Evil" and corruption attempt to interfere sometimes with the rotations - but that energy is not sufficient to stop the divines from rotating if we have your help to complete the healing cycles. It is merely annoying and tiring.

A determination and a visualization of complete cycles with your energy thrown in there is more than sufficient to help us to complete the necessary cycles. Using whatever works for you help us to always complete the perfect number of cycles in the perfect way.

As this instruction is lengthy, you may be thinking that it is too much of a chore to work with the metal element. Usually, it is not a chore at all because much of what imbalances people and things in the -1, 1 and 2 dimensions in which you live in the physical/material realm affect us not at all. It is for that reason we are more reliable, as a rule, than other methods of physical "divining." Often stones are compromised as pendulums and require as much or more cleansing than metal elements do.

Remember, a neutral stance is also an adult perspective. We can be counted on to tell you the truth when many others only wish to spare your feelings. If the truth is not what you wish to hear from a neutral standpoint - don't waste your time or ours. The truth requires us to say this; we are lifeforce - not loveforce at this time, however the meridians are also in a state of transformation to become both.

When we become both, as we know we will because we must, the loveforce element will "tender" the response. As it stands now, we are in our own transformational process to blend (meld) loveforce and lifeforce. This is looked for with great enthusiasm as we are too structured sometimes and long for a better understanding of the whole of Spirit.
As we all move into the seventh hub - the hub of transformation, we grow together.

Bless us all.

** As of November, 1994, the loveforce/lifeforce has melded for the metal people and many other Spiritual beings as a precursor and preparation for the planetary beings transformation.

SECTION THREE
DIVINE HELP

MESSAGE FROM ST. AUGUSTINE STONE HEALING AND THE PEN'L LEINA LANGUAGE

Stones communicate very logically. If you ask a stone, "Can you answer if this stone is compatible with me? It will say, "Yes." Yes means, yes, I can answer if this stone is compatible with you. Stones offer straightforward answers with a beautiful simple logic of their own.

It is improper to ask the stone (or any spiritual being) if it has a "name." Stones are a group mind of St. Augustine. They communicate with each other mostly along elemental lines. What you do to one, you do to all. Therefore it is most important to honor the stone people. Be aware that you are speaking to an intelligent, thinking entity that is very, very ancient. There are not "children" or "babies." Their intelligence comes from great long life wisdom and elemental and spiritual teaching.

Each stone has healing properties and each stone has polarity. The stones generally are opposite poles on front and back. Sometimes however, the stone is one polarity - either clockwise or counter clockwise. Some stones have dual polarities on one side. This stone is transformed and can help you with your transformation. All stones can heal all areas, but like doctors they specialize. The color of the stone and the vibrational energies are "set" to work on specific areas of the body.

The energy you are speaking to in a stone pendulum could be many different energies. You should establish to whom you are speaking (without asking a name.) If the stone give you a name, you are very, very blessed indeed and you should humbly acknowledge the gift that was given to you. However, a stones "name" is a symbol in penl leina (the pendulum language or strictly translated, the pen line.) Humankind's general names for them are sometimes not what they call themselves. Often they do not like what they are called. Stone language is largely symbolic symbols and the language is the basis for ancient Mayan language. If you ask, the stones may teach you the pen'l leina spoken word.

When you work with a pendulum, you are generally speaking to the stone, or stones if a multiple setting. If the stone cannot answer, you may be speaking to the metal holding the stone or the chain. If the stone and metal cannot answer or the questions require spiritual assistance you could be talking to any number of spirit guides through the stone.

Minervan and air beings and sometimes wind beings often help to move the pendulum in order to keep the stones and metals from expending too much energy in communicating what others wish to communicate to you. Communication is very labor intensive, so try to think your questions through and check periodically with the stone as to how it is doing. If it is too "tired" to continue please do not try to force it to keep working.

You can ask to speak to specific individuals or spirit guides, but if you are communicating with a stone pendulum it is only polite to ask if you may speak to others through them. If the pendulum says no, it is usually because it does not have sufficient energy to continue. Also, like you or I, it may or may not wish to be "used" to talk to someone else. Honor its decision. Also, just because you request to speak to a specific Spiritual guide, does not obligate them to speak to you. It is improbable that they will speak to you through a pendulum unless you are sufficiently balanced and the stones are cleaned, cleared and de-programmed. They ask that you honor the stone and the procedure below to facilitate communication with you and prevent misunderstanding or misinterpretation.

In order to work with pendulums there are a few "ground" rules that you should be aware of. The main rule is: Don't demand, ask! (humbly and with love) Treat the stone people like your friends and honor them as they honor you.

(1)   Cleanse yourself. Before any pendulum work is done, ground yourself and clear yourself.

Literally, a bath (as water is wellspring healing) is a good idea! A good way to cleanse yourself is to repeat this phrase three times,

"I am balance, I am light, I am love, I am living in the light of healing, balance and love. I reject corruption and accept only communication with love and light."

See yourself as a shining white light being and place yourself in a pyramid full of white light. Notice if there are dark areas. If there are, burn them away with the light. When you have completely burned the dark areas away, melt your body in the light until you disappear within the light pyramid. It is very helpful to drink water (wellspring) and ask for a wellspring blessing and cleansing.

(2) Cleanse your stones. Ask the pendulum if it is in need of cleansing or clearing before you go any further. If the answer is a "yes." Ask it if it needs elemental cleansing. Generally, it does. Ask if it is an element of earth (if yes - cleanse it in sand or earth), if it is an element of water, establish whether or not it is fresh or salt water. If it is salt water - a pinch of sea salt in water or non-iodized salt will help to revitalize it. To deep clean a sea loving stone, mix 1/2 tsp sea salt, 1 kelp tablet in 8 oz of

fresh water and allow it to bathe overnight. If the stone is an element of air - pass it through incense (which is also fire and earth) or place it beside a fan or expose it to wind and air currents. If the stone is an element of fire - pass it through incense or place it in the Sun. Rarely, does a stone actually want "fire," but sometimes it may want to be basked above a candle flame. DO NOT PUT STONES DIRECTLY THROUGH A FLAME!

What you will find, when you ask is that the elemental properties of stones will vary stone to stone. Most are combination elementals and will want, for example water and sun, or earth and sun. All respond to incense! Additionally ask the stone if it needs Moon energy. If so, a full Moon bath is a very precious and revitalizing experience...like food!

This step is very important, because communication is very energy draining on the stone. In addition to asking the elemental affiliation, the stones would like humankind to ask if it is in need of white light energy and de-programming. If a stone needs light clearing, ask your spirit guides to assist you in supplying the energy that the stone needs. State your purpose aloud or silently that you would like to give light energy to the stone and would appreciate any assistance that you may need to do this.

A good visualization for light clearing is to hold the stone in the hand that feels comfortable - you can trust your instincts on this, as the stone will definitely feel "right" in one of your hands. There is no concrete "giving" and "receiving" hand because your polarity and the stones polarity may not mesh. I say "light" instead of "white light," because the stone may need a color light. If it does - ask the stone to show you psychically what color it needs. If you aren't picking up the color, use the letter chart and ask it to communicate exactly what it needs. Turn your hand the color it needs and see the color as pure, and lit from within. Send love, healing, wholeness, joy, strength (whatever) to the stone and ask the stone to please accept your gift of healing energy.

(3)   Is the stone programmed? Programming is simply to state a wish upon a stone while sending energy through the stone to "implant" the wish. If you hold a stone and wish for good and love and light and things of a unselfish and universal nature with a pure heart, that does not harm the stone. Much programming is done inadvertently. The stones are learning not to accept inadvertent

programming or programming done with an intent to harm any living entity. There are not subservient anymore, however, many carry programming or messages from the past that they have held in order to teach what the entity wished. Stones may have held this information for millennia waiting to find the person who can "hear" or learn what is inside. Sometimes a stone's message is for only one individual in the worlds. Ask the stone if there is programming in the stone.

If there is programming, ask the stone if the programming was done with its blessing. If it was, ask the stone if the programming is to your highest and best good. If not, ask the stone if it wants to continue to hold the programming. The stone may or may not tell you specifically what it is programmed for, but you can ask. Ask the stone if it desires to continue to have the programming within. If the answer is "no" - then the stone needs deprogramming.

(4)   Deprogram the stones. If the stone has negative programming, it will require some intensive work before you can work with it as a pendulum. Programming can be done against a stones will by unscrupulous people or entities. This harms the stone. To cause pain, hurt or problems to any living entity is

an anathema to a stone. They are healers BUT crystals and some stones can carry negative programming. To my way of thinking this is the most irresponsible and cruel thing one entity can do to another. A stone is a natural record keeper. A stone holds the energy of all who have touched it. If a stone is worn by an individual who does "evil" - the stone is harmed by the "evil" and will need healing.

Stones pick up the vibration of whomever touches them not only on the physical material realm but in the other dimensions as well. That is why you cannot assume that a stone has no programming. The ancient Atlantians and Lemurians understood this principle well and have placed a great deal of information in crystals and stones. The crystals that have Lemurian record have a raised pyramid on the faces. This is an example of programming that you probably would not want to deprogram. The Lemurians understood the stone people and honored them. They did not place programming against the stones will.

(5) Methods in Deprogramming: If the stone needs deprogramming, ask it if a salt "bath" is necessary. Evil, corruption and residue are often negated by sea salt or non-iodized salt.

Generally, don't put a stone in salt without its permission. It burns some stones. However, if the stone is compromised by "evil" (feels creepy, doesn't feel right, moves arbitrarily in pendulum movement, is heavy - physically heavy!) evil may be overriding the stone and "evil" will definitely tell you not to put it in salt.

You can tell if a stone is compromised because you can feel the stone resisting movement. The stone may move in a totally arbitrary fashion because it is fighting what has compromised it. In this case, definitely put it in salt.

(6) Negation for "evil," corruption and residue: This negation is also useful to remove negative or evil energy from anything. If you suspect that your stones or pendulums have been compromised by "evil," say this while allowing the pendulum to move in circles:

"I negate the evil, corruption and residue without,
I negate the evil, residue and corruption within,
I condemn the evil, corruption and residue to death with the wellspring of life or any appropriate energies or combinations of energies."

As you say this three times, allow the pendulum to circle of its own volition and ground it to the earth three times. The third time, state:

"I ask Mother Earth, Wellspring Father and the Vortex place the evil, corruption and residue in a * "perfectly structured sequence." NOW.

> * The words "perfectly structured sequence" are a capsulization for these statements: "I ask that the evil, corruption and residue be reduced to the perfect size and shape in the perfect way and placed in the perfect structure to be moved to the perfect place in the perfect way. The container cannot be breached from without or within by that which it contains or by those who would try to free it for evil purposes or to supersede the wellspring or appropriate energy healing or retribution. The evil, corruption and residue within is given the benefit of wellspring three-fold healing, if the heart is pure and no harm was done to any, the evil, corruption and residue may live and be healed. If evil or harm

was the intent or will, the impure heart will suffer the retribution of wellspring disassembly or other karmic debt by decree of Spirit. With the blessings and permission of the vortex, the perfect structure shall be carried by the vortex and/or appropriate energy or combination of energies in the perfect way to the perfect place. I thank the vortex and all appropriate energies for protecting me and offer my service in love and thanksgiving in return. I offer a healing for a healing in return."

Either state, "perfectly structured sequence" or repeat the above three times. The stones generally need a long period of rest after deprogramming or removal of "evil." Ask the stone what it needs to recuperate. Sometimes, it is just fine and dandy and ready to go!

If it has been damaged by negativity or corruption, ask Mother Earth and Wellspring Father to help heal the stones. Bless Mother Earth and with the blessing of Wellspring father, sanctify a small plot of earth (or a flower pot!) with wellspring (water) healing by wishing this earth to have threefold healing for stones.

Ask your crystals if they will provide a white light circle around the stone to be healed. Sometimes, like heals like and stones of the same type wish to be in the circle as well. If they agree - place eight stones clockwise with the stone needing healing in the center buried in Mother Earth for a time. Check the stone circle periodically to see how things are going. Sometimes, a crystal in the circle needs replaced or healed also. Sometimes stones needing healing must be left for a month (a moon) or so. The closer the Moon is to a full moon, the stronger the healing energy from the Moon. If you cleanse and deprogram your stones around a full Moon cycle, you may only need to keep the stone buried for a few days.

(7) Ask Permission. Before any pendulum work is begun, it is common courtesy to establish whether or not the pendulum wishes to work with you to teach you. Allow the pendulum to "scan" through your hand. By scanning your hand the stones become acquainted with all aspects of your physical, emotional and spiritual selves. They know now, everything about you - everyone you know, <u>everything.</u> Sometimes the stones say "No." There are a lot of reasons for a "no" and it should never be assumed that the stone is

rejecting YOU. They may not be compatible with your vibration or simply do not have the excess energy to help. They are elementally affiliated and so are individuals. If, for instance, you are a strong fire person and you are attempting to work with a water stone for a pendulum - your energy may be too fiery for the water. Conversely, if you are a strong water being - fire may not wish to spend a lot of time with you as a pendulum. If you remember that all stones are healers - you may need the energies of a different pendulum to accomplish what you wish to accomplish with them.

(8) If you are imbalanced. You are speaking to imbalance. If you are balanced, you are speaking to balance. Imbalance is not evil and it is the task of God Prime and Jesus/Sananda (and many, many others) to help bring you into balance. There is, however, a big difference between minor imbalance and gross imbalance. Gross imbalance hinges on "evil" and may, indeed, leave you open to "evil" speaking to you through the stones. I mentioned before that you have access to many entities through the stones. IF the stone is clear, but in your white light visualization you have dark areas that means that you are imbalanced to work with the pendulum. If you are imbalanced, wait

until you are more balanced if possible. If you are in need of communication to help you clear the imbalance, ask the stone or metal pendulum to protect itself from your energy, or visualize a pyramid around the stone surrounded by the color of the stone. You can harm the pendulum if you are imbalanced or corrupted.

The stone people are healers. They will try to clear you by taking on your problems, however, they ask that you try to clear yourself before asking them to clear you. If the stone people take on corruption or "evil" for you, you owe them a "healing for a healing." You will need to work with them to clear them of the negative energy. Clear the pendulum by cleansing it.

After you have cleansed yourself, your stones and deprogrammed the stones you are in a position to learn greatly from the Spiritual realm. The stones and metal people are Spiritual Entities - Stone PEOPLE and Metal PEOPLE and should always be treated with respect and decorum. You are gifted with their communication and it is a great gift indeed to receive pendulum guidance.

There are many ways to communicate with the Stone people. The pendulum makes it easy. You can hold any stone in your hand, for example and ask the pendulum to act as a communication devise to speak to the stone in your hand. This extends not just to stones but to any object. The pendulum can move in different directions for "yes, no, I don't know, or I can't (won't) answer for very simple communications or directly speak with the phonetic chart. But it can also speak in symbolic picture language and draw symbols to teach you the penl leina. Eventually, as you work more and more with the pendulum you will find that it incorporates psychic speech and will actually write in cursive. You will hear as you see and so the pendulum may only "write" the first syllable or so - just enough for you to verify that you are really "hearing" which you are seeing. When you move into the arena of writing - actual writing - the next step is to listen. Listen and learn to trust that which you are hearing without the tool of "writing." The pendulum is a psychic teaching tool.

But the pendulum is much, much more as they are healers in the universe on dimensional levels 1-3 they take physical form. Their auric levels are very compact and as such they live multidimensional lives on earth. Their lives are very, very rich. They can teach so much about healing people - so much about the interconnection between ailments of physical/emotional and spiritual. Modern medicine attempts to heal the physical without addressing the spiritual. Modern psychologists address the emotional. Holistic Medicine is a step in the right direction as is Naturopathic and Osteopathic Medicine - but the matters of the Spirit have to be addressed. They cannot be ignored.

All ailments are threefold in nature. Physical -- Emotional -- Spiritual. To fully heal you must heal all three. Disease is dis-ease. Disease is an interruption on the physical level in energy flow or in severe cases a blockage which could result in organ failure and the body's attempt to get attention to the emotional and spiritual blocks by literally hitting you over your head to make a point. Anger/worry/fear is the same dynamic in the body. Anger/worry/fear are the same word and have almost the same symbol in penl leina. Anger/worry/fear is generally held in the liver. Therefore, in the dynamics of stone healing - to work on the liver is to work on those problems.

Anger/fear/worry may have emotional basis. The emotion needing healing may vary with the individual. It may be, for example, a fear of loss of a loved one, or a result of being abused as a child. The Spiritual ramifications of the anger/worry/fear issues may be the person's inability to deal with control issues that cause a blockage in the transformational processes until it is faced as what it is _fully_ and dealt with. Issues involving power involve the kidneys. Issues that involve inflexibility and ego are held in the knees and spine. The stones teach healing from a different perspective, but this knowledge can be found in bits and pieces in every culture and society in the world. Much of the teaching is actually "reteaching."

SECTION FOUR
DIVINE PROTECTION

BASIC MEDICINE WHEEL PREPARATIONS AND PRECAUTIONS

Spirit can speak to you in any way you will listen. It is not so much a matter of ritual or form in which to hear "true communication," as it is a format in which it is much easier for spiritual communications to reach you. The Medicine Wheel Meditation is not for everyone and it is not absolutely necessary that all "rules" be followed in order to hear or see the lessons within the wheel. The Medicine Wheel is a microcosm of the universal hubs in which energy flows freely and effortlessly (in most cases.) To recreate an environment similar to the energy pathways in which all energy flows, "ups" your chances of experiencing, unimpeded, the wonders of the Medicine Wheel.

Do what works for you, but take some initial "precautions" to be sure that the information you receive is reliable and coming from the pure-heart sources. Evil, corruption and residue from evil do attempt to interfere in this teaching and misguide you or dissuade you from speaking directly to Spirit. When you work within a sanctified area or a protected structure, like the Medicine Wheel or a pyramid, you are very less likely to be speaking to evil.

The basics of Medicine Wheel Meditations are these:

(1) Prepare the area. Cleanse and purify the ground or floor by physically cleaning it (vacuum, dust, mop etc.) If you are out of doors and preparing the earth - sweep it clean with a pine bough, spray the area with wellspring (water) and bless it, or flood the area with white light. It is well to smudge the area with the herbs of Mother Earth - sweetgrass and sage are traditional, but any smudge or incense will do. Please offer a blessing to the area in return for a request for protection and guidance from within. Agree, possibly to pick up trash or do something to <u>physically</u> clean up around the area (or another designated area) in return for Earth protection.

(2) The Stone People, Tree People, Rainbow Beings (Color), Directional and Elemental Beings can help protect the Medicine Wheel. If you are comfortable setting up two circles with pine cones, stones, candles, colors that is very helpful to keep the information coming in very clear and unimpeded. Two circles - one outer circle and one inner circle.

(3) Within the inner circle, it is a blessing for all of the elements to be honored. It is also additional protection and a facilitator to their teaching. Incense or smudge incorporates the elements of fire, air and earth. Water is

wellspring and it is cleansing and protecting. Pipestone, amber, azurite, turquoise, lapis lazuli, and/or sugulite brings the higher vibrations of elemental stone spirits into the circle of teaching.

(4) Before you enter - take off your shoes. You may certainly enter nude, but it is not necessary. Nudity is another facilitator that allows a more free flow to Spirit and vice versa. Do not wear black or have anything black in the Medicine Circle. It is advisable for light beings not to wear black at all, for black clothing can hold negativity within.

When you enter the first circle walk clockwise completely around the circle before entering the second circle. Walk counterclockwise completely around the second circle.

(5) It is advisable, but not always necessary (if you are in a hurry) to greet the directional beings and stand still to receive their energy "greeting." This greatly honors them and adds a measure of protection for you. Face the directions that feel appropriate to you in the sequence that feels appropriate to you. As a general "rule" however, face North, East, South, West and then Northeast, Southeast, Southwest and Northwest. If that does not

"feel" right for you - do what feels right. If you do not rush this process, you will feel the subtle differences in the directional energies and may hear the messages that your instruction today will come from (for example) the southwest.

(6) State that the circle is complete and is safe and that you will accept communication only to the highest and best purposes and from beings of life, light and love. If it will help you to assure yourself of complete protection repeat the negation of evil, and "wellspring" the area (see the section on St. Augustine - Stone People.) Wellspring (blessed water) is three-fold healing and three-fold retribution for evil. It will negate and destroy evil, corruption and residue in most cases.

(7) Each quadrant of the Medicine Wheel may have representative "guides" or teachers from the planetary beings, Spiritual Beings, elements, stone people, plant people, two-legged, four-legged, bird people, crawling people and insect/spider people. Additionally, each quadrant may be "seasonal" and directional in the teaching the guides in the quadrant wish to impart. You may receive much different information from the same quadrant because the guides will vary greatly. Sometimes your teaching

comes from one animal, for example or one plant.

Ask to be shown visually the lesson and then expect to "unravel" spiritually what you see. The lessons tend to come in "flashes" on "fast-forward" that your brain core can sort out later for you if you need help. You can ask for the information to "slow-down" and "restate" if you really don't "get it." You can always ask for spiritual guidance to interpret it.

If you do not see visually - ask to be shown the lesson in another way or have the visualization amplified. Trust what you see, hear or sense as your lesson. It may help to take a "communicator" crystal with you in each quadrant you are working in. A communicator crystal has a six sided crystal face. If you place this crystal on your third eye, it will help to facilitate the instruction. An octahedron (pyramid base to base) crystal or structure is also helpful.

(8) Before you leave the circles. Ask if there is universal or spiritual work or healing that you may help with. Spirit and the Council of 12 will guide you with what you need to do. Please be sure to thank all who helped and realize that instruction comes with a spiritual

price to return something to the teacher. That something could be an offering, but it is much more helpful to ask what they need and how you can help provide it.

(9) When you "break down" the Medicine Wheel - break it down in the opposite way in which you set it up. "Break down" first what you placed last and work backwards. Please be sure to thank all who helped you and ask what you may do in return for their guidance. It is advisable to keep your Medicine Wheel "set-up" together in a place of light, love and healing. They will continue to work together to plan future teaching.

Periodically check the "set-up" participants in your wheel to make sure that they wish to continue to do this work and that they have sufficient strength to continue. If they need healing, please provide it. If they wish to be returned to earth, let them go with your love, thanks and blessing. Remember, you are gifted by their love and teaching. They agree to live with you. You do not own them and, even if it is very, very difficult, you may be asked to give up a favorite stone or allow them to move on to another whose need is greater than yours. When their teaching is done, they usually wish to "move on." The Pine Cone People need to return to the Earth after about a quarter. New pine cone people will make themselves available to you to replace their friends.

SECTION FIVE
DIVINE INSTRUCTION

PEN'L LEINA - COMMUNICATION FROM THE STONE PEOPLE
by Johan Adkins

As a stone person, I rely on a stone pendulum for "yes, no, I don't know, and I can't answer" insights. This very simple communication is accomplished by holding (suspended) a pendulum, stone necklace, silver or gold bob over your palm and asking it to move in specific directions for simple communication. Each time a series of questions is asked, the directions should be re-established as it has been my experience that some stones differ at different times. Generally, you will see a clockwise circle for "yes," a counter clockwise circle for "no," a back and forth movement for "I don't know" and stillness for "I can't (or won't) answer.

Beginning in the spring of 1995, the pendulums began making strange movements of their own volition; spirals, flowers, crosses etc. It became apparent that there was communication coming from "somewhere" else.

At first, the pendulums began circling over different parts of the hand - when I asked a questions regarding an individual, it would insist on "reading" through the entire hand before answering. It would very definitely follow the lines in the hand, but would sometimes linger over a certain area. As it lingered over a particular area of someone's palm -

they would often startle and say, "I can really feel the pendulum doing something!" The energy moving the pendulum was often very, very intense. Without any question in my mind, the pendulums (no matter what was used) were acting more and more in their own volition.

One night I was trying to decide whether or not to read a certain book. I asked the pendulum to "look" over the volume and see if there was a message in the book for me. As the title was very lengthy - the pendulum began to seek out letters. The first word it singled out was "WRITE." I wrote the letters out as it circled each one and the message was clearly spelling out exactly what it thought of the book. I was fascinated to find out what was going on so after hours of laborious A, B, C, I developed the following chart to make "writing" easier.

a aa ab ac ad ae af ag ah ai aid air al
all am an   and ant antelope ap ar are
as ass ast at au aura   auras av aw ay
b ba balance bat be bear being between
bi bk bl bo br   bu by
c ca cancel cat cd ce ch check child ci
ck cl co coin   cold color come country
cr create created creates crow   cu
d da dad daughter de deer der di did
die dk do dog   dolphin dr dragon ds
dt du dw
e ea eagle ear ears earth ease eat eats
eb ec ed ee ei   ek el elk em en eo ep
er es et eu ev ew ex ey eye   eyes
f fa faith father fd fe ff fi fire fl fo foc
focus food   for fox fr fs ft fu
g ga ge ger get gh gi give gl go god
good got gr grass   gu guidance gw gy
h ha had hare have hawk he heal
healing her hi him his   hl hn ho hood
horse hot how hu hub hum
hummingbird   husband hy
i ia ial ib ic id ie ies if ig ih ik il im in
ing io   ir is it iu iw
j ja jasmine je ji jo joke joy ju jk jl jn
jm jr

k ka karma karmic ke key keys ki kl kn
ko kr ku
l la layer le lea lemp let ley lf li lie
listen lk ll lm ln lo lord love loved
lovely loves lr lu ly
m ma man many mc me men ment met
mi mine mn mo moon   mom money
mother mouse moves mr mu my
n na name ne need negate ness ni nil
no non none not   now nr ns nt nu ny
o oa ob oc od oe of og oh oi ok ol om
on one oo or   os ot ou our ous ow oy
p pa parent pe peace people person ph
pi pig pl plant   please pn po power pr
pray ps pt pu purify py pyramid
q qu question questions quick quiet
quietly quit quitting
r ra radiate rain rainbow raven rc rd re
red ri rk rl rm rn ro ron room
rooster root rt ru rs rv ry
s sa sacred sandal sc scent se see self
sex sh shall she   should shouldn't si
simple simplify sis sk sl sleep   sleet
sm smudge sn snake snow so some son
sour sp   space speak speaks Spirit sq
sr ss st stay stem stone   structure

**struggle su sun sw sweet sy system
systems
t ta te ted th the their there ti time tion
to tone tr trust try tt tu tw ty
u ua ue ui ul um un unify universe
universal uo up ur us use ut uw uy uz
v va ve Venus vh vi video vo von vortex
vr vs vu vw vy
w wa wait warm watch water we weak
well wellspring wh   whale what where
who whose why wi wife will wn wo
woman woman won't wood would ws wt
wu
y ya ye yea year yes yet yi yo you your
your's yourself ys yt yu**

a   b   c   d   e   f   g   h   i   j   k   l
m   n   o   p   q   r   s   t   u   v   w
x   y   z   1   2   3   4   5   6   7   8   9   0

. , ! ( ) no   yes   maybe   rest

PEN'L LEINA CHART

The Pen'l Leina language assumes that the healer or reader works with and knows their colors and tones. Because it is the language of the stone people as well, it has certain internal keys to the energy vibration called for in the healing. Because this is a book in itself and is very subtle in pendulum reading, interested people should master the three-fold readings and general color healing techniques taught by Rainbow Lady in the book <u>Spirit Speaks</u> channeled by Johan Adkins. When the reader is ready to move on - the information contained below is ready to come to you easily.

In order to contain symbols of a possible negative or harmful nature (and to give them no energy in this book,) some symbols are contained by a pyramid base square structure. The primary structures are given below - many structures have entire pages written on them which fine tune their message.

PEN'L LEINA SYMBOLOGY

Healing (Six petals – usually clockwise.) Six is the spiritual number of love. All healing must be done with love and acceptance of love offered, or it cannot take place.

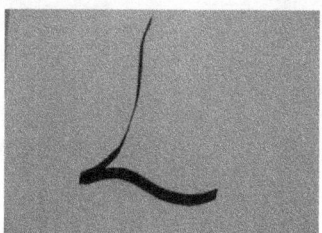

Loveforce energy. This is usually a test for the fleur d'leis regarding mature and self-less love. See the hand charts.

Lifeforce energy. Sign of the vortex. Six spirals from the center and clockwise out. The is a message of doing or creating. (See message from vortex beings.

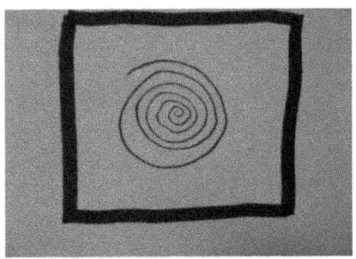

Vortex Message – Six spirals from center – counterclockwise. This is a message of undoing or uncreating. (See message from vortex beings.

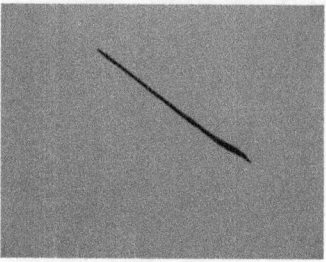

Slash – "Not" – Negation of the sign or a severing or restriction of some kind.

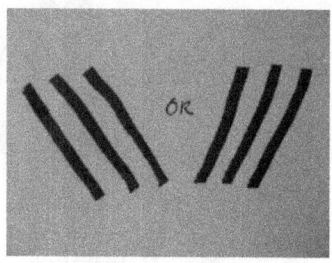

Sweeping Motion - The pendulum needs the area cleansed and probably will need to be cleansed as well. It is trying to move negative energy aside. The sweeping motion also indicates a hole or a void or lack - if it shows three definite sweeps.

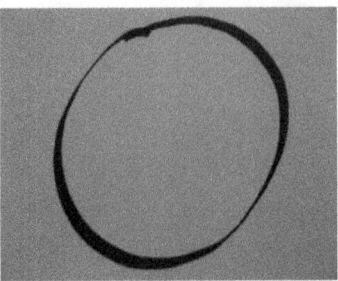

Wholeness – Earth – Gaia – Complete

Wholeness – Earth – Lifeforce healing. Two symbols joined. A sign of good healing toward wholeness.

Not whole - not conducive to lifeforce - not good for the earth. Earth in trouble of some kind. Also may be male (left) female right message. Have to inquire more deeply.

Not healed - Love aspect either not being given or not being received to affect healing.

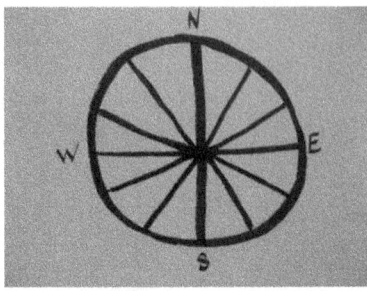

Medicine Wheel Teaching. Make note of the quadrant circled and face in the specific direction to receive Earth Council teaching.

Kindness - Loveforce

Loveforce Energy - Fleur d'leis lesson, challenge or trial in loveforce.

Fleur d'leis Blessing. Eight petal flower. Fleur d'leis teaching.

Divine (Soulforce) Energy or message.

This symbol is very ancient and although in modern times it represents the Jewish faith - to Spirit, this is a many faceted blessing of the trinity - it is a blessing of love because of the six points and it is a blessing of the pyramid beings. Pyramids are living structures and they are pure of heart teachers and protectors.

Directional Energy - A blessing from the white light beings. The Pen'l Leina is very precise. The symbol is written top to bottom and left to right. If the symbol is not precisely written this way and it comes through - discontinue dialogue and cleanse (see section on cleansing) - Bathe and balance and resume communication at a later time. This symbol is also the symbol for truth. It is also the white light blessing (and traditional Christian or Celtic cross symbol for the "Father - Son and Holy Ghost" - or Hat, shoes, wallet change - Spirit does have a sense of humor!!)

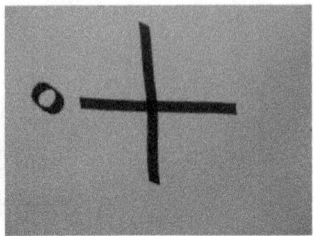

Specific Directional Energy waiting to speak - turn in the direction indicated and listen.

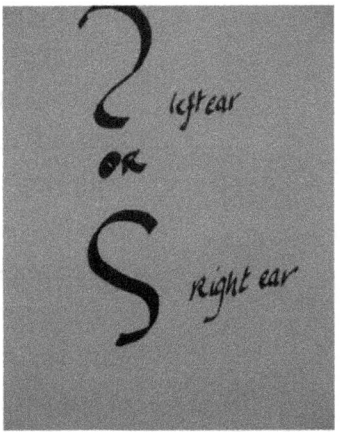

Listen

Look- Search

Hand - Hand reading to follow

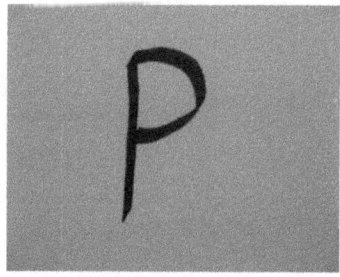

Physical Reading

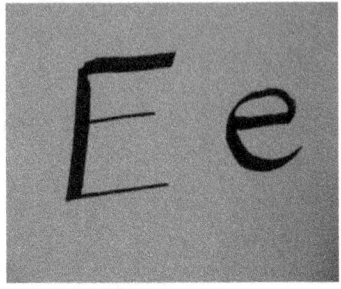

Emotional Reading

Spiritual Reading

Write - let your hand go loose and just listen to the dictation.

Question. What? Either Spirit doesn't understand what you're asking or they are asking you a question. When questions are framed, they need to be simple and childlike. Pendulum work requires computer type logic. If you ask, "Can you tell me if I am a man? The answer would be "yes." Not yes that you are a man, but yes I can tell you. Don't ask two questions in one question.

1, 2 (II), 3 (III), 4 (IV), 5 (V), 6 (VI), 7 (VII), 8 (VIII), 9 (VIIII), 12 (I, II), 18 (I, VIII), 24 (II, IV), 36 (III, VI), 42 (IIII, II) 81 (VIII, I). These symbols are contrary to Roman numeral structure, but compound numbers are always two single numbers together to Spirit. These numbers have strong spiritual significance and the numerology section of the book should be consulted. Many times a pendulum will need to move a certain number of times - just be patient. It will tell you how many rotations it needs. Each number has significance - but pendulum movements are strictly in 3's with the exception of 4 and 8 single numbers only.

The symbol of balance of ego and id. Ego top, power and control issues bottom. It is also the elemental symbol of air (top) and earth (bottom.

Divine Blessing

Trinity. Symbol for the trinity. Father Son and Holy Spirit were the traditional names. In truth all Spirit works in threes or groups of threes. (3,6,9,12, etc.) Three is the number for Spirit. This form is also a pyramid side and additionally is the symbol for the heavenly host.

Applies to

Negate - Rethink - start over. Negate signs should be made top to bottom - right to left, left to right. If they are made in any other way. Stop the work and cleanse thoroughly.

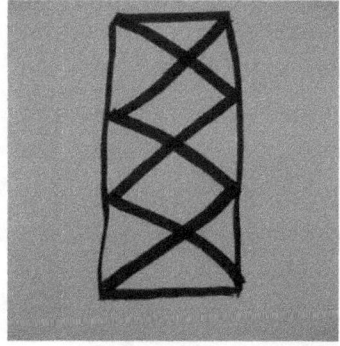

To contain negative energy and allow it to be disassembled in a controlled environment. This symbol is a gift of Merlyn and is not to be used lightly. There are three negation symbols and they need to be constructed east to west. As each one is written say the words - negate, negate, negate. Without lifting the pen on the last negations symbol the stroke should be north to south, west to east, south to north and east to west ending up where you started - repeat the square two more rotations. This symbol can be used only once on the item you are attempting to contain. If used twice on the same item, it undoes itself and releases any negative energy it may contain.

Pyramid - Draw or Build or Visualize the structure. A pyramid has very specific construct sequence: e-w, n-s, w-e, s-n, ne-sw, w-e, se-nw. The outside shell should be retraced three times.

Pyramids are very important structures to work in when doing pendulum work. Because pendulum work is very energy demanding, unnecessary stress is lessened by working in a protected and cleansed environment. A physical pyramid is best, but the symbol helps to keep negative energy or distractions away. Visually grow the pyramid over the person working with the pyramid and any guests.

Octahedron (Double pyramid) Structure needed for healing or protection. Physically, it would have eight sides. On paper it is four sided. As above, so below. This is an important protective structure for all the elements. The mirror image of the trinity extends to the realm of imbalance as well as creating a physical structure to protect something fully.

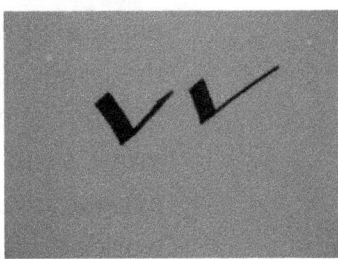

Sharp tic movements - sever or severed.

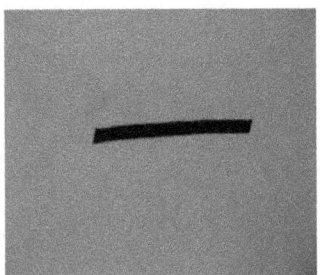

Message is being received- energy flowing well.

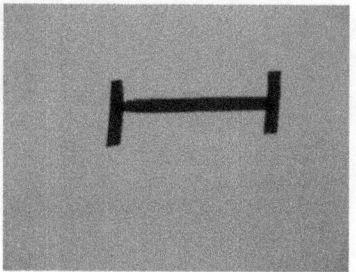

Energy flows - connection to - related to

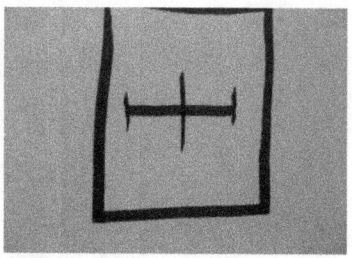

This is a severing of energy flow. May have to do major restructuring. Lifeforce is threatened.

Energy Blockage - Block in flow. Healing is needed to remove blockages and restore energy. Lifeforce is threatened.

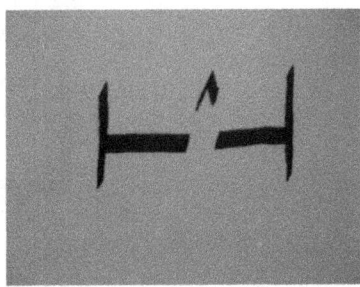

Break in energy flow - An interruption of some kind. Needs to be healed so that energy can resume healing the body.

Struggle - Interrupted Energy - Not flowing well

This is a sign of substance abuse. The energy leaches at the downward arrow and becomes weaker and weaker. Lifeforce is threatened.

Elemental Energy Moving

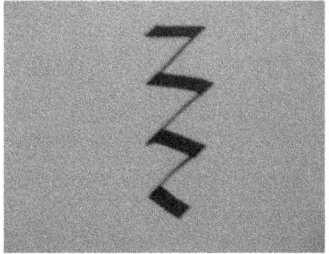

Anger, Fear and Worry are the same symbol. Anger, fear and worry are held in the liver. . Wear a leather belt to hold your power in the liver to help ground it. May be a physical problem with the liver.

A smile - Joy - Happiness.

It is also sometimes a symbol of a Rainbow being speaking to you or wishing to speak to you. The symbol, if it is a Rainbow being will be slanted eyed.

Kileo Balance. (Ki lee e o) This is laughter. A sign of joy and mirth. It is often a sign from Spirit not to take yourself so seriously. Sometimes it is a message that you can fool yourself, but you can't fool Spirit.

This is a sign for the physical material realm. The balance of male to female in a relationship. When you see this symbol - Spirit is trying to say something usually about the male/female bond or marital bond of the individual. Sometimes it refers to the sexual union.

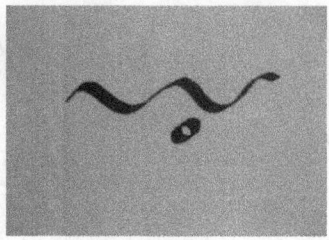

This is the sign for sorrow. Like energy flowing only it is usually side to side with the small circles under.

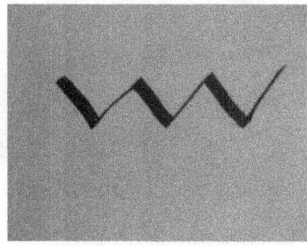

This is the sign for pain. It is like anger only side to side. Interesting correlation.

This is a sign of transcendance. If it is shown in regards to an individual, it is the sign of a person who has met the fleur d'leis challenges and is living Spirit on earth. The person bearing this symbol is neither male or female, they are a neutral being. They are in constant contact with Spirit. Learn from this person and treasure the contact. It also means "transcendance." As a symbol within a body of other symbols, it may be asking you to "rise above."

This is a sign that the water beings wish to speak to you or are speaking to you now.

This is a sign for prayer or meditation to Spirit. (Two hands in prayer.)

Balance - Also a symbol of male (left) and female (right). Also a symbol of fire (left) and water (right). The more equal the two sides, the greater the balance.

Imbalance - This is a symbol of imbalance it is a severing of the male to female and a severing of fire and water. A slash through any Pen'l Leina symbol is a severing. We all go through periods of imbalance - this symbol showing up should be our key to getting our physical, emotional and spiritual act back in order and to balance our fire/water elemental connection.

Male is overwhelming female creating imbalance. We are all unisex beings -both male and female. Both sides should ideally (most of the time) be equal. This symbol also means an overabundance of fire element which is weighed by a lack of water. (See <u>Spirit Speaks</u> aromatherapy section for elemental message.)
It is also an imbalance of Fire to Water. Too much fire.

Female is overwhelming male creating imbalance. Overabundance of the water elemental and lack of fire. (See Spirit Speaks aromatherapy section for elemental message.)

Like other languages, symbols have different meanings in different contexts (See Prime's message in Spirit Speaks) This is a symbol in the Pen'l Leina of someone who is only male in form. They have "killed" the female side and as a result are "dead" to Spirit. They will only live out this one last life and the spirit will not live on.

Someone who has "killed" the male side (See Prime's message in Spirit Speaks). This is an example of a person who has "killed" their masculine side and is therefor "dead" to Spirit. Their spirit will not incarnate further after this physical life. They are also sadly lacking in what makes a person whole.

Imbalance of earth to air. Also a sign of ego/id imbalance. Small top, the person's ego is small - esteem is really low, but the person is likely to abuse others in power and control issues (which is inflated) if they perceive the others have less power than they. They have a great deal to learn about themselves.

Imbalance of air to earth. Also a sign of ego/id imbalance. Large top, the ego is inflated.

Power and control issues deflated. (Others may be abusing them and to compensate - they are blowing their ego out of proportion.) They are "full of hot air." When you see someone like this. Be kind - don't judge too quickly. They have a great deal to learn about allowing others to have power and control over them.

Imbalance female to male. The feminine side is overpowering. Seek the teacher in Jupiter to be more at ease with the male side.

Imbalance male to female. The male side is overpowering. Seek the teacher in the moon to be more at ease with the feminine side.

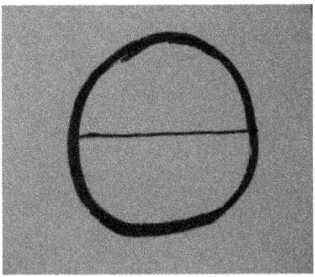

As we are both male and female, we are also elemental beings - the elements of air (top) and earth (bottom) are represented here. Both sides should be in balance for the health of the individual or the health of the planet. If the symbol is talking about the planet earth and it is high or low one way or another - the earth is imbalanced accordingly.

Subtle difference here between "not whole" and a division of fire (left) and water (right). Have to pay attention to the context of the message to decide which is which. Ask your pendulum if it is an elemental message.

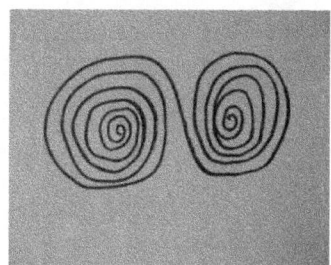

Perfectly balanced chakra. Six spirals clockwise, six spirals counterclockwise. All chakras have the ability to move energy in either direction in order to keep the body whole and healthy. Technically, it is male left, female right but with chakras that does not apply as much as tightening (doing) and loosening (undoing)

Chakra in need of healing. Send energy to the chakra.

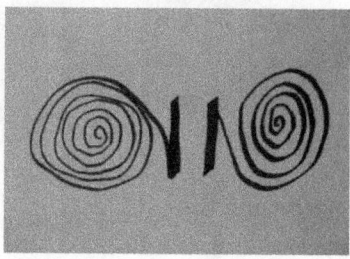

Energy to the chakra not being received or is blocked.

Healing energy to the chakra being received, keep working.

All four directional energies needed to heal the chakra (or may be just 1 or 2) Face the directions indicated and ask for guidance and assistance for the healing. The vortex beings will help too.

Polarity out of balance in chakra. Rebuild or recreate chakra with a spiral shell. Pull the energy through the shell and allow the perfect spiral to recreate it and move the energy back into the body.

Chakra is energy severed - either mend or rebuild with a spiral shell.

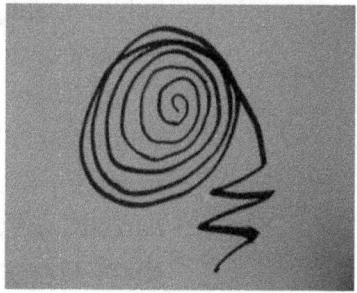

Anger, fear, worry or sorrow is being held in the chakra - Heal the source of the anger, fear, worry, sorrow and rebuild the chakra.

Directional Energy of the North wishes to speak to you. This is a great blessing and it is not very often they speak. Be respectful and listen carefully. Face that direction. When they ask to speak, they are visible in the sky in the direction. Look to the heavens. When you see them, say "May I see you?" and listen for their answer or watch carefully as they expose themselves to you. They may take the form of a face, animal or whatever form they wish to show to you. Stay open to the possibilities. Send healing and love in their direction as your gift for their openness to you and willingness to speak to you.

Directional Energy of the East wishes to speak to you. This is a great blessing and it is not very often they speak. Be respectful and listen carefully. Face that direction. When they ask to speak they are visible to you in the direction. Look to the heavens. When you see them, say "May I see you?" and listen for their answer or watch carefully as they expose themselves to you. The directional energy of the east is usually multi-formed, two sided in some fashion. Stay open to the possibilities. Send healing and love in their direction as your gift for their openness to you and willingness to speak to you.

Occidental Directional Energy - North and East wishes to speak to you. This would be a council of the Northern and Eastern directional energies and would be seen most likely as a two sided face or animal. Directional energies are always blowing with their mouths. The are the gods of the "winds" of older lore. the faces or images constantly change and evolve. It is a rare, rare gift to see the true face of this "god." Respect them and send healing and love in their direction as your gift for their openness to you and willingness to speak to you.

Directional Energy of the South wishes to speak to you. This is a great blessing and it is not very often they speak. Be respectful and listen carefully. Face that direction. When they ask to speak they are visible to you in the direction. Look to the heavens. When you see them say "May I see you" and listen for their answer and watch as they expose themselves to you. Stay open to the possibilities.

Directional Energy of the West wishes to speak to you. This is a great blessing and it is not very often they speak. Be respectful and listen carefully. Face that direction. When they ask to speak they are visible to you in that direction. Look to the heavens. When you see them say, "May I see you" and listen for their answer and watch as they expose themselves to you. Stay respectful and open to the possibilities.

Occidental Directional Energy - South and West wishes to speak to you. This would be a council of the Southern and Western directional energies and the appearance would be singular to the individual. This is a great blessing and it is not very often they speak. Be respectful and listen carefully. Face that direction. Look to the heavens and say hello.

Quadrants of Elemental affiliations.

Directional Energy Message - Something about the air elemental. It may be that the air elemental wishes to speak to you or that the person is primarily an air being. More symbols will have to be given to clarify.

This is an imbalance of air.

Directional Energy Message - Something about the water elemental. It may be that the water elemental wishes to speak to you or that the person is primarily a water being.

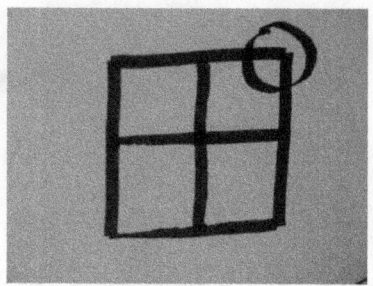

Directional Energy Message - Something about the fire elemental. It may be that the fire elements wish to speak to you or that the person is primarily a fire being.

Directional Energy Message - Something about the earth elements. It may be that the earth elements wish to speak to you or that the person is primarily an earth being.

Directional energy message. A balance of all elements. All elements involved including the 5th elements of plant, animal, gas, electricity. Depending on where the circle is placed - good indication of what is overweighing or outweighing the other elements. Try to be balanced elementally.

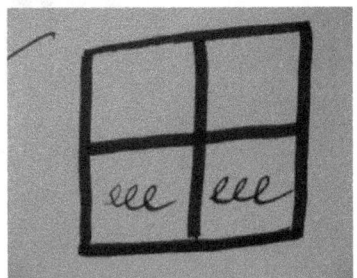

Example of lack of air and fire. Water and earth predominant. It may also be that the person you are working with is balanced elementally this way. We are all predominantly one or two elements. Ideally, we try to balance all elements within us. If we lack an element - example earth - we will need some aspect of that element in our daily lives in order to feel "whole." (See section in <u>Spirit Speaks</u> on aromatherapy.)

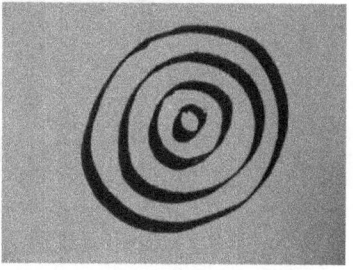

Aura - Note the layer - may show many layers.

Aura - Blowout in the auric layer - mend and seal.

Aura - Hole in Aura - Mend and Seal - Hole is shown by 3 parallel lines.

Wholeness can also represent male and female - the pendulums often use a circle to show male/female yin and yang difficulties. Sweeping away the male? No, it refers to a need to cleanse the male side.

Wholeness with the elemental energy sign on one side - this person is sending too much elemental energy to the feminine (right) or masculine (left) side of the body. Balance the elements on the blank side.

SECTION SIX
DIVINE HEALING

INTRODUCTION TO THE STONE LANGUAGE (THE PEN'L LEINA) HAND CHARTS
by Johan Adkins

The Pen'l Leina is important at this juncture of the writing because the teaching that was presented next relied upon these symbols. The next teaching by Stone People was the physical hand charts. They are presented in a number of formats - the whole physical hand and the sublayers so that the systems can be better seen and understood. The "systems" may not be traditional Western medical systems as the interrelation of body ailments lies along different paths than is traditionally accepted by "modern" medicine.

The whole point of the hand charts is to help the individual heal himself. There are two chakras located just below the collar bones that have been "sleeping" in modern man with the exception of the visionaries and mystics and legitimate healers. These chakras are known in the Pen'l Leina as the Hocaieah. (Ho-Ky-A-a). The color is forest/kelly green. As you work on self healing they begin to awaken and open up. The process of the Hocaieah opening is a self-purging of ego and all the spiritual baggage we have carried around all of our lives. The opening process may take weeks or months or years if the lessons are not heeded. It is the pre-process to the raising of the kundalini - the personal power that seats itself in the base of the spine and rises with great spiritual awareness and in the period of great testing.

When the Hocaieah fully opens - transformation truly begins. The body's polarity becomes dual and balanced. Both Hocaieah chakras need to be open for the Fleur d'leis process to begin fully. The Hocaieah is earned increment and by the time you have fought your dragons - worked on the spiritual/emotional and physical housekeeping you will <u>definitely</u> know something is happening.

At the same time the Hocaieah process is in full swing - the dream patterns and sleep patterns begin to drastically change. There is generally a period of intense "schooling" and quite frankly exhaustion. Data is being dumped and assimilated so fast that many undergoing this process quite frankly thought they would go insane. I recall having a visionary dream in which I was lying on a slab in a desert area. Many Kachina like figures were dancing around me in a circle. Several opened the top of my skull and as each danced by they tipped a basket full of knowledge inside my skull.

The passage of knowledge feels just like that. It is generally also a time when the skull feels as though it is about to burst - I found myself creating a visualization of a flexible "drum" plate on the top of my skull to allow for "expansion." Many Fleur d'leis experience problems along this line. They all feel some need to spread the skull in some fashion to keep the crown and transpersonal and third eye chakras open during this process. If you are in this same situation, a similar visualization will manifest the extra room you need for all of the information you will be receiving. One lady visualized hinges - another visualized a screen.

It is not unlikely that a kundalini experience will ensue when the Hocaieah is fully opened. The energy (which is earth energy/primal lifeforce) will rise from its seat in the tailbone or genital area and the body will be infused with kundalini or earth energy.

As you work on the physical areas of the body to heal yourself, relate these areas also to the Emotional and the Fleur d'leis charts. The key to help you find the answer is within one or all of these charts. If you wish to heal yourself, you must also help others heal themselves and extend healing and well being to the universe. All are one.

Organ Hand Charts
for Physical Readings

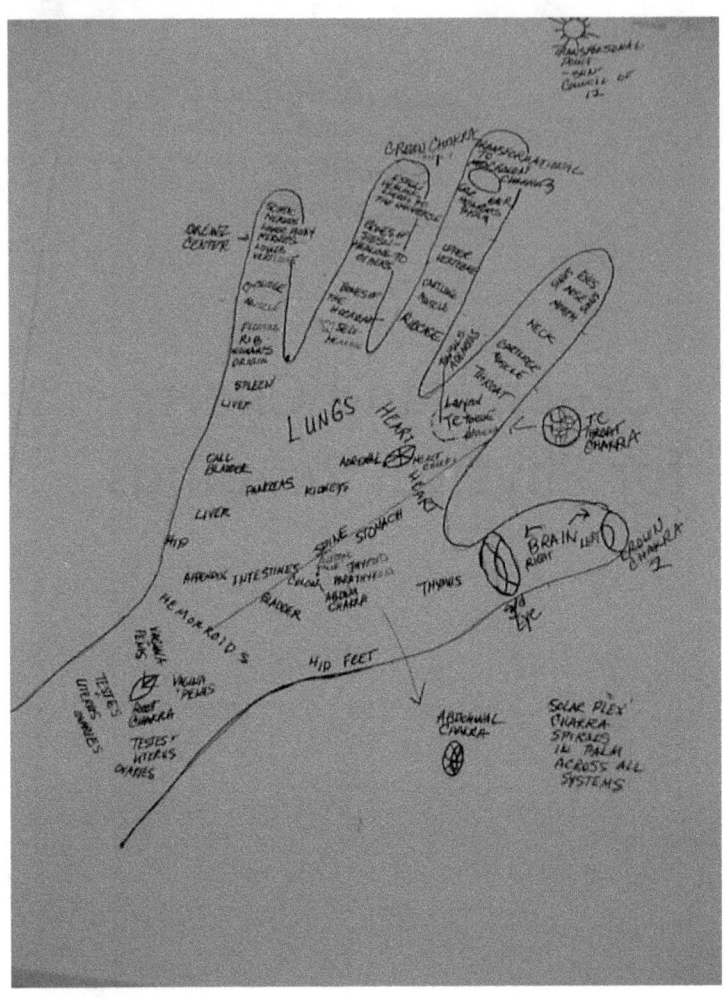

Physical Organ and Chakra Hand Chart

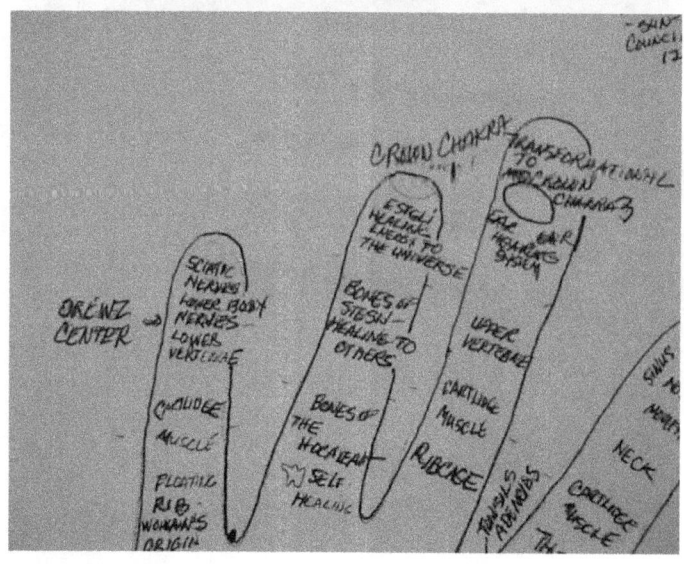

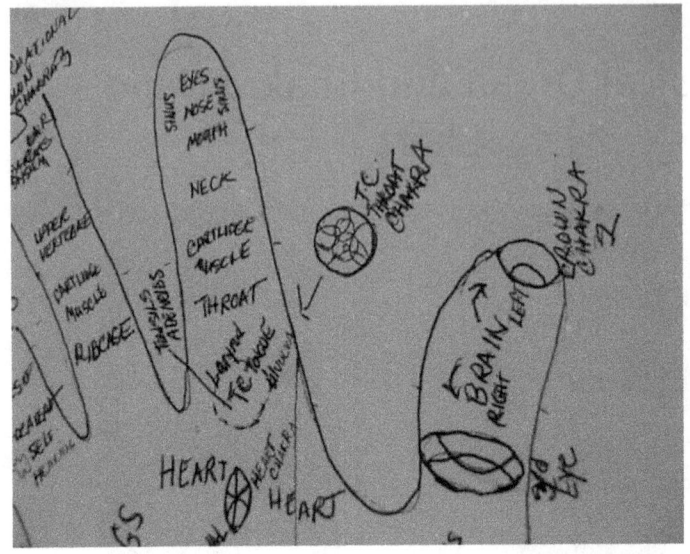

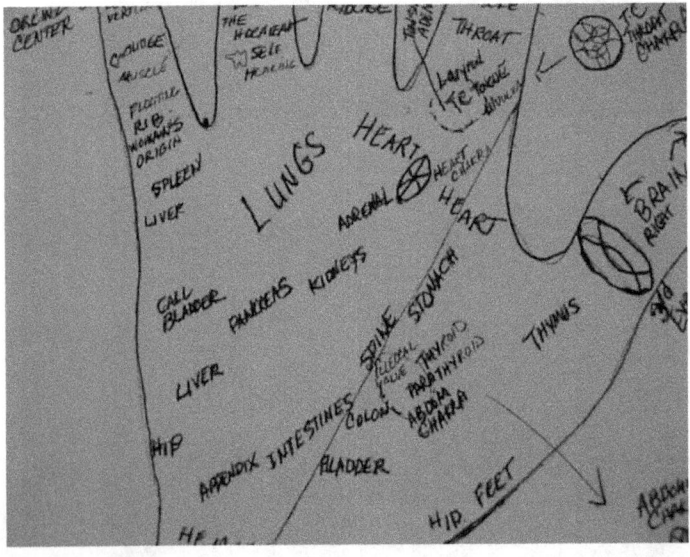

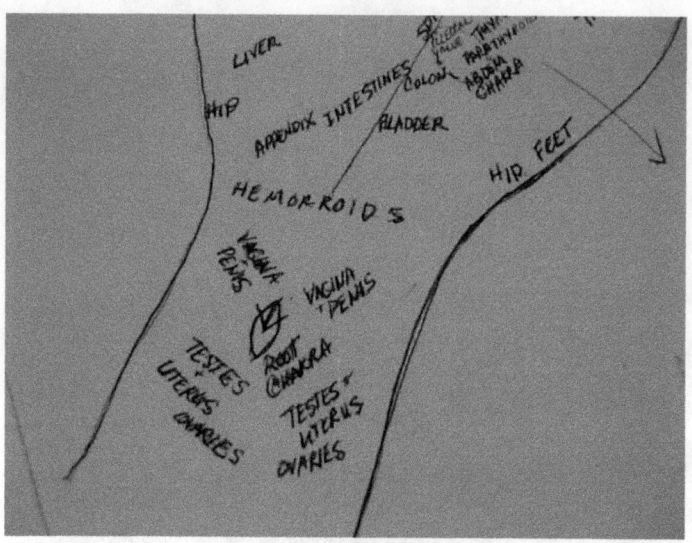

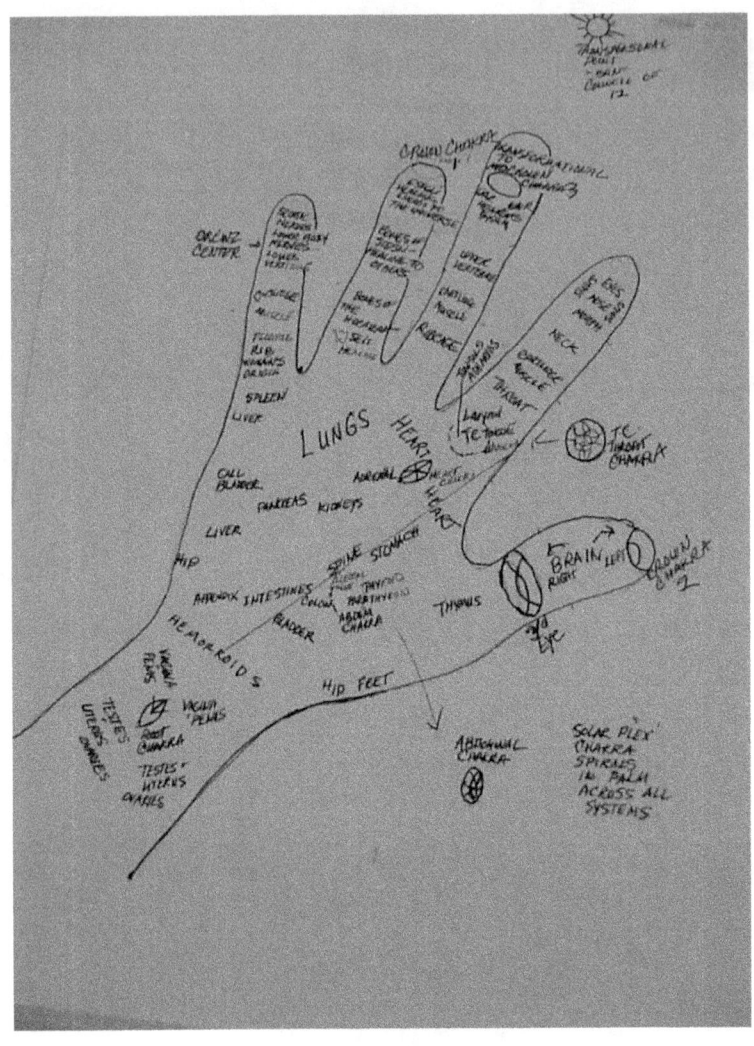

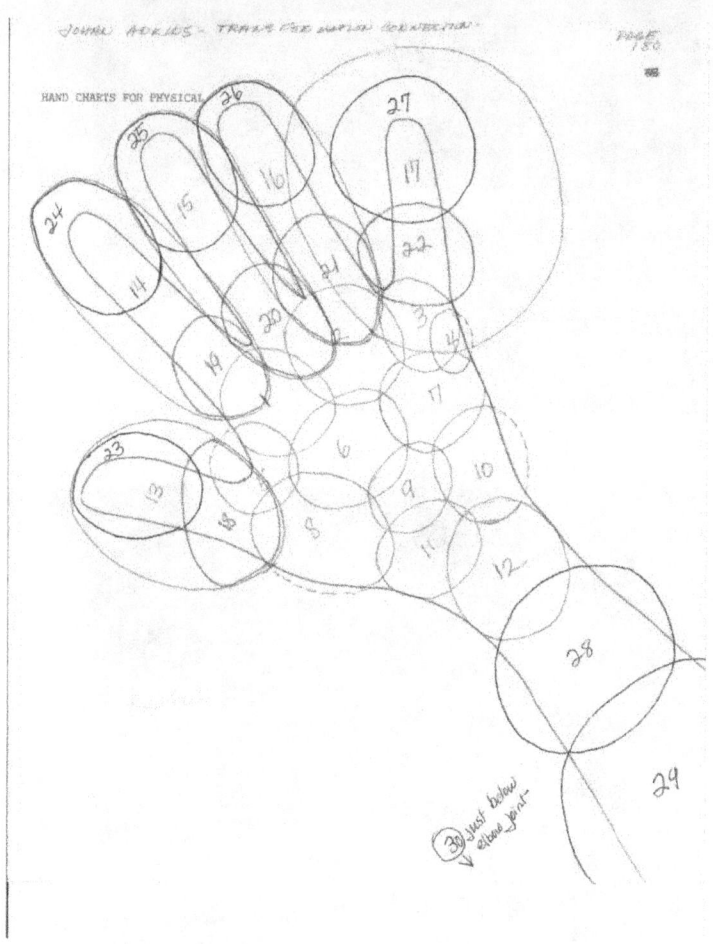

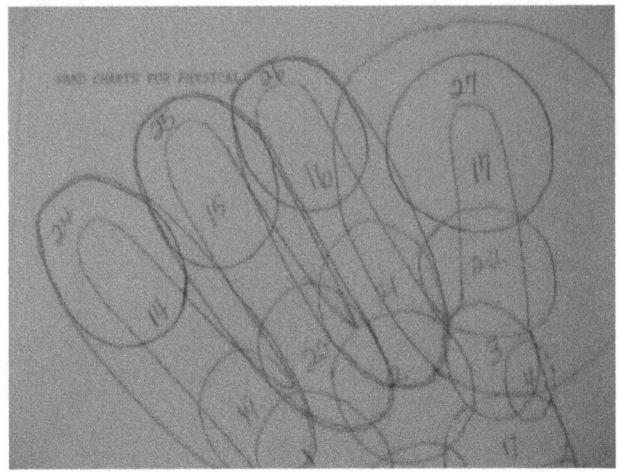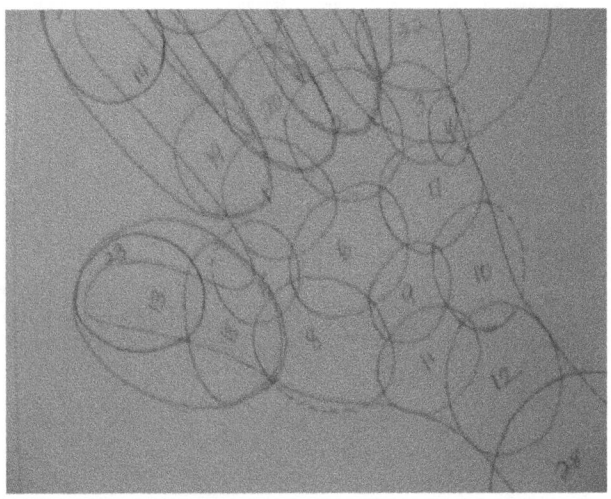

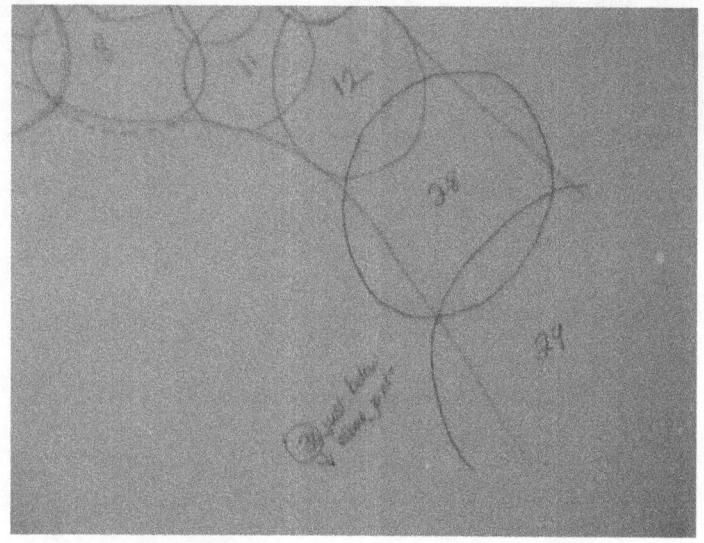

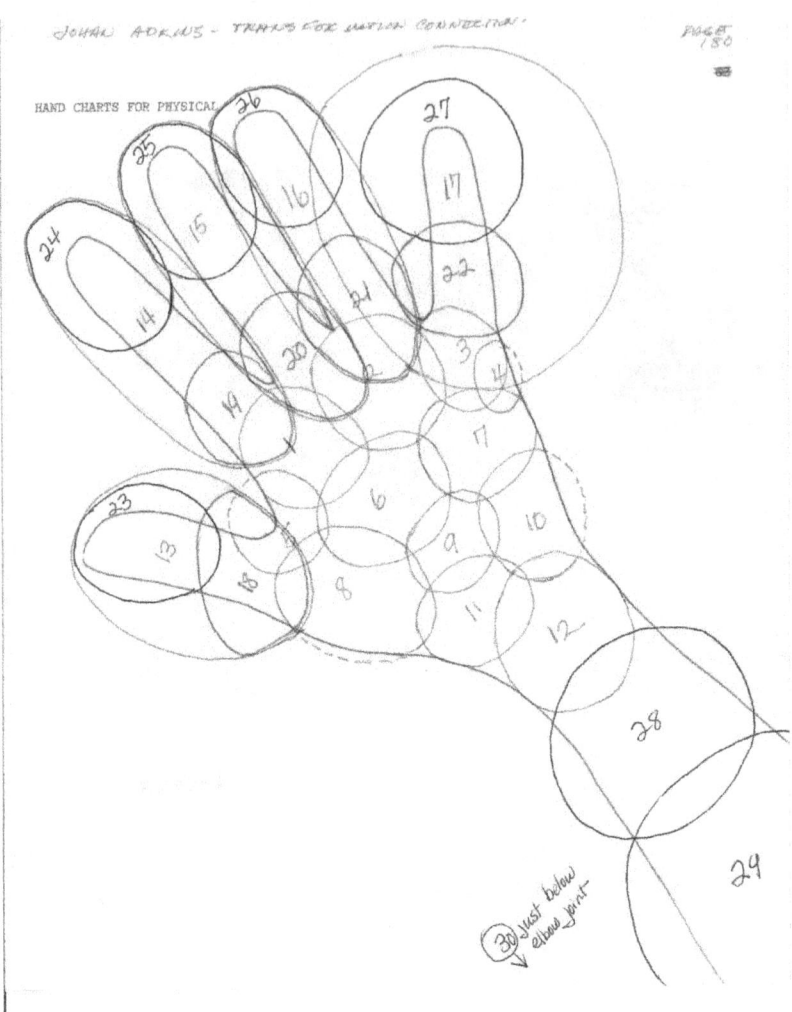

PHYSICAL HAND CHART FOR FLEUR D'LEIS TRANSFORMATION

1. This is the area of the right ventricle. As the heart is the seat of the loveforce a blockage in this area is a blockage of loveforce energy. The right side of the heart is the female aspects of love. Look for problems regarding either the feminine part of the individual or pain caused by love aspects with a female to help heal this area. Spiritually, it is much the same. Love must flow equally from both sides of the body. If damage results in this area, the emotional and spiritual issues of love are damaged and those issues must be healed for long term healing to take place. If fatty tissues clog this area it is because the person is too self-indulgent in the love aspect and is not extending love to others to break up the fatty deposits. A crystallization or constriction of the love aspect results in angina pain here - and lessons of love returned to others or given unconditionally must be learned to ease the constriction.

    The color here is pink (raspberry pink of a sunset) and the tone is LA. The visualization of the color and expression of the tone will help bring health to this area.

2. This is the area of the left ventricle and the same holds true as above but the aspect is the male part of the individual or pain caused by love aspects with a male.

   The color here is peridot green - clear and crystalline green and the tone is FA. The visualization of the color and the expression of the tone will help bring health to this area.

3. This is the area of the spleen. Within the spleen is a mechanism that cleanses the blood of toxins. Some of this knowledge passed here may not be medically "sound" with what is known in modern medicine. The spleen acts with the liver and the kidneys to balance the energies of power (domination and subordination issues) and anger/fear/worry issues. It is the spleen that begins the mechanism to cleanse the body of toxins that constrict the muscles. Toxins that build up in tissues that can lead to debilitating diseases if not resolved. This area also touches upon the hocaieah - the ability of the body to resolve health/emotional/spiritual issues to heal itself and exert healing to others. The spleen has important spiritual tasks as well - it is necessary to cleanse evil, corruption and residue and in order to do that job well needs wellspring in generous quantities. It acts as a

spiritual filter against attack. This area also affects the lungs if the corruption is not cleansed from the body a result may be emphysema or asthma or any corruption of the lung. When the lungs are compromised there is a lack of the air element to the body. This is due largely to action or attack upon the spleen and the spleen being ignored or not cured must eventually lead to compromise in the lungs.

The color of health here is kelly green - the green in a prism or rainbow with the sun shining through it. The tones are all tones in half scales in three octaves.

4. This area is also the spleen - but in closer connection to anger/fear/worry issues of the liver. A compromise in this area sets up chains of events that affect the liver, spine and kidneys. Kidney infections and inflamed liver are often spleen oriented problems. This area is a warning signal that the spleen is overloaded with negative/fear/worry issues and the next major organ to be affected will be the liver which can hold a great deal of the anger/fear/worry issues. When this area is highlighted it is a sign that the individual is not dealing with their own negativity and resolving the issues that need

to be addressed before it results in major liver damage.

Those who drink to excess generally show damage here (and also <u>perhaps</u> directly in the liver) because they are not addressing the source of the addiction. This area highlighted usually points to addiction in some form. Addiction to people, drugs or spirits (which are evil in excess) or spiritual addiction to a cult or religion that borders on fanaticism will show up here. Addiction is addiction whether to a person or a debilitating drug or liquor. This person is in need of AA counseling or private psychological counseling. It is very probable that they are involved in a very destructive relationship in any case whether liquor or drugs are also present or not.

The color of health here is bright sun yellow/white gold. The tones are minor tones between fa and sol.

5. This is the area of the heart that contains the core being of the individual. The whole area of the heart is a miniature of the entire aura of the individual - a check and balance of the whole entity including its place in the soulforce can be seen by the health of this area. The emotional chart refers to this area

as "self-esteem and self-love." But more to the point - it is the health of that system as a whole. Pain or discomfort in this area is an indication that on some level the self needs healing. It may be in other auric layers if the individual feels fine and what is recommended for healing is an auric cleansing. This area extends to the back of the hand as well...it is the twin heart to the left and right ventricle. By pinching this area a resulting "tinge" may be felt in the area that is compromised in the aura. Problems may be uncovered here and dealt with before they manifest in problems in the physical/emotional or spiritual body.

A soreness or scar or damage here can alert the system to do very generalized basic physical/emotional/spiritual clean up before bigger problems result. This area itself is often damaged and no amount of damage on the physical/material plane changes the spiritual aspect of this spot to pinpoint problems before they become bigger problems. If the area is sore and tender, cleanse the body inside and outside and purge the bowels. A fast is in order to discover and fine tune what may be going on in the other auric layers. Spirit will definitely help you uncover the source of problems showing up here if you ask. It is much easier and greatly advisable that problems seen here be resolved early before they manifest into bigger, less manageable problems.

The color of health here is pure white light. The tones are all tones and any tones - just sing and dance and be joyful! Sing songs of joy and the proper and perfect song will come to you!

6. This is the air aspect to the body and as such encompasses the entire lung function and the respiratory system. Again, modern science does not equate problems with the lungs with possible source problems elsewhere as in the spleen as discussed above. If this area is highlighted it is an elemental problem and may affect not only you, but the planet you live on - for air is scarce and it is compromised in some fashion - either by pollution of the lungs by cigarette, cigar, pipe (or other) smoking or by pollution.

This area is a large area with sub areas to pin-point more exactly what specifically is going on - but generally meditation or purse-lip breathing or calming and cleansing of the lungs is in order here. A meditation which will cleanse the lungs should include a meditation to cleanse the pollution around you (in a small area or as large as the earth itself.) To heal one, is to help heal the other. Adrenal insufficiency will result in compromised air. Abuse of the flight or fight syndrome will manifest problems in the lungs - most generally asthma or emphysema. This results because the body is trying to tell the individual to do something about their present situation. The physical signals ignored will result in debilitation of air in some fashion - either a feeling of smothering, strangulation, hyperventilation, or claustrophobia or in advanced stages collapsed lung or severe asthma or emphysema. This person really needs to determine what is constricting their air - their freedom - and make some changes - even drastic ones!

A fight or flight syndrome abused results in the body's inability to manufacture adrenalin. When adrenal messages are ignored for too long - the body stops producing it properly and begins to break down the lungs and will, in many cases affect the stomach and bowel as well. This is the reason that a sudden fright or vigorous exercise or excitement will sometimes stop an asthma attack - it takes more and more stimulation to get proper adrenal levels. It is best to discover where the problem is an eliminate it before it results in such drastic results! If the flight or fight situation does not apply to you, the adrenal is still compromised in some way and your problem may be emotional or spiritual.

This area also encompasses the stomach and the spine and kidneys and partially the pancreas - but all of these organs are set up here in area six because they perform the same function. All tell you when energy or power is being abused and if you ignore the signals of an acid stomach or kidney infections or pancreatism or colitis - you may be in for major organ "meltdown."

Other areas highlighted should help give you an idea of how to address the problems showing up here. It is well to note that power - personal power attached to universal power resides in the kidneys and if the area feels "heavy" you are either being attacked or someone is trying to attach themselves to you to use your power or energy. If that is not the case (or is not the whole case) perhaps the problem lies with you exerting too much of your personal power to do something. Heaviness indicates a power drain. If you push too hard for too long and over-stress the kidneys and do not address or work to lighten the burden, kidney failure can result. If you are doing energy work and feel the drain here - you are giving too much of yourself or too much is being taken and you should stop - and do serious evaluation of "power" issues. Ground, revitalize, regroup and re-center before you attempt to do anymore.

Make sure, if you are working to help another that the request of help came from them and they are receptive to receiving help from you. If you try to "manhandle" the healing by assuming control - they may be either blocking you or vampirizing you because you have not established the parameters of give and take. They must request help, receive it and give, in return a revitalization of energy back to you. It helps to lighten the burden by wearing a leather belt when doing energy work or if you suspect someone is attempting to drain you of energy or perhaps they are working against you and attacking in some fashion. A leather belt helps to hold in personal power.

The colors of health here are the colors of the rainbow. Picture yourself in a pyramid filled with rainbow light lit by the sun. One color will be predominant and just go with your instincts in this matter. The tones are all tones - again; a song will come to mind that has the tones necessary to help with the specific problem. Even if it is a silly song!

Just sing it or whistle it or play music and hum along!

7. This is the area of the liver where anger/fear/worry issues manifest physical liver ailments. Liver enlargement or a poor filtration system. Anger/fear/worry are the same energy dynamic and very little distinction is made between the three. Problems in this area or a highlight of this area indicates that the organ has been compromised and much is being held within that must be addressed before other major organs and body systems are toxified. Think of this area as a toxic chamber and begin to eliminate the toxins (with water and cranberry juice to help) but more to the point with eliminating what placed the anger/fear/worry there to begin with. This is a very strong indication that spiritual/emotional/physical housekeeping is in order.

The color of health here is maroon/pink lit from within by the sun or the moon. One will feel appropriate. The tones are minor tones along 3 octaves.

8. This area is very complicated and it basically boils down to the lower half of the body including the lower stomach, intestines,

uterus, hips, legs and feet, but it also includes the thymus, parathyroid and the thyroid.

It is the area in which the family aspects as relates to the individuals show up. A soreness or a problem in this area reflects that the individual is concerned with a family matter or themselves in relation to the family. It is more, however, it is the link between parent and child and husband and wife in terms of family cohesiveness, happiness and esteem.
Most blockages in the intestines are concerns for unresolved family issues - most thyroid imbalance is concerns for the place of the individual within the family or among their loved ones. Remember that the area of the feet is also the body systems in "blue-print" so any area that encompasses the feet encompasses the whole body. The area is dominant and important because the love aspect is extended here to family. If there is disfunction within the family - the love aspect needs to be healed for the individual to be fully healed and for that healing to extend to the universe - the family has to be as healed as possible.

Sometimes this area highlighted is a reminder that the individual cannot be everything to everybody and must relax their expectations or their "control" issues to allow the rest of the family to be themselves and follow their own individual spiritual path. This area is the area of control of others and constriction is an indication that the individual is trying to control too much. Blockage is an indication that the individual is trying to control too much and being blocked in their efforts by the physical body. Live and let live is the lesson here. Love without control. Loving unconditionally.

The color for health here is pale baby pink lit by the sun or the moon, whichever feels appropriate. The tones are lullabies and soft music. Think of music that makes you feel safe, secure and protected - the kinds of songs a parent will sing to a child. Sing to the child within you.

9. This area is more specifically the intestine, colon and bladder. Oddly enough problems specifically in these areas are indicators of the nurturing aspect being compromised in some fashion. Nurturing aspect can be many things and more times than not, it is a lack of self-nurturing. It is an indication that you may be giving too much to others and not taking care of yourself. It may be an indication that you are being abused

physically/emotionally or spiritually (either by yourself or others) and you are not asserting your needs or addressing the abuse.

It may, however, be a lack of receiving the nurturing you think you need from others. It generally does reflect on the individual's need to give nurturing. Generally, those most in need of nurturing, nurture others in hope of reciprocal nurturing. More times than not, however, this need goes unfulfilled because the need may be the problem.

Nurturing others is not a positive aspect unless the children are infants. A mature adult does not truly "need" a mother. They may need a friend, or an equal or a partner, but they do not need a mother. In contradiction, however, we all have periods of our lives in which we do wish for nurturing. The lesson here is to nurture yourself- become parent to your child and help your child within to grow out of the need for constant nurturing.

A large need here may be the lack of love in your life...the partial solution is to love yourself and extend love and support to others and ultimately to teach yourself the difference between mothering (smothering) and being a supportive person who requires support back.

The lesson here also is, if you are in an non-supportive, non-loving, non-affectionate relationship that is not meeting your basic needs, you are liable to have colitis, bladder infections or frequent urination or a constriction of urination. You need to re-evaluate your needs and make your needs known as an adult must do. Do not assume friends or family should know and inherently understand that you need something back for as much as you give - they do not know unless you state your needs. Quite frankly, something given only of value to you is not valued by the receiver. It is quite the opposite. It may become a burden upon the person "gifted" that can result in a feeling of entrapment or obligation or even resentment because you have obligated them without their permission or against their will. Re-evaluate your "gift" giving. Do you give in order to receive? What do you hope to receive back? Universal law states a healing for a healing. A gift for a gift.

It is not, as some would have you think, improper to "give" it is only "improper" to force a gift upon one who does not wish to be obligated to you, or is unwilling to give in return something of like value that you need. As an adult, you may have to deal with the consequences of those around you being unable to fulfill even the minimum you require to be happy and healthy and feel "nurtured."

This whole communication (stating your needs) may be terribly frightening as you may know the limitations of what others may give already. You cannot teach a non-giver to give _you_ what you need. Some can take everything you give without feeling any obligation whatsoever to return anything to you. They feel it is somehow "owed" to them. Can you handle living with this? You may have to make the decision to find more compatible mates or resolve to nurture yourself more and "give" less. When a relationship is equitable and mature - the need to nurture (mother) and be nurtured (mothered) will be relegated to occasional - rather than constant times.

A person with problems in this area is called the "give-away" person. Comanche medicine practices, for example, tell this person to work with a turkey feather and turkey "medicine" to learn the aspects of when it is proper to give and when giving is done for the wrong reasons. This is very sound mythology because the turkey "whispers" that this is a give-away situation and a choice is here. "Do you wish to give? Do you wish to receive? Can you give with a pure heart and can it be accepted with a pure heart? If nothing is to be repaid, do you still give freely? If the answer is no - do not give, but trade."

The healing colors here are the colors of the earth and fall. The oranges, pinks, yellows and shades of green and brown. The turkey is the animal teacher and the tone is yellow - by that we mean - high frequency tones. Carnelian is the stone teacher for give-away people.

10. This area is pretty tricky. It is, on the emotional chart, the nurturing aspects of anger/fear/worry. In the physical arena it represents the gall bladder, liver, hip, pancreas, hemorrhoids, and part of the intestine. In addition, it represents the appendix - which incidentally, is not a prehistoric throwback, it has a very specific spiritual function that we will explain here.

Who wants to nurture anger/fear/worry? Why would anyone do that? Generally, people do that because the issues are very unresolved and a twisted logic has replaced the need for nurturing. If the need for nurturing is not met and the individual does not transcend beyond the need for nurturing, than denial of nurturing (love aspect) results in anger/fear and worry. If pain was inflicted by a trusted one, or love twisted in some fashion that hurts the child or the child within, this aspect will sometimes show up. If the individual does not transcend the pain and the lesson that was taught to love in spite of abuse.

If denial goes on too long it twists further into a need to court anger/fear and worry to replace more basic needs. To give meaning to life - negativity and a jaundiced viewpoint of relationships, love and humanity fills the void of neediness. In very advanced stages, this is a person who has given themselves to evil by virtue of rejecting the love aspect. This is the typical martyr syndrome and nobody loves a martyr. Because nobody loves a martyr - the martyr becomes a tyrant and as a result many physical malfunctions can ensue. Appendicitis for one thing. The appendix is the last straw for a outlet for anger/fear/worry. It is a failsafe in that, if it were not able to be removed, the individual would surely die - their situation has evolved that far to extremes. When a "hot" appendix is removed, it contains pure toxic evil and removal of that evil gives the person a new chance to begin again - the last chance before they self-destruct and kill 1/2 of themselves or in some cases commit suicide. Much has been written in this book about killing the feminine or masculine part of the soulforce - please refer to Prime's message. This is the extreme of what will happen if this problem is not worked on and hopefully resolved.

This is a very sad aspect to see in someone, because it indicates a person who was initially trusting and needing nurturing and whose need has taken extreme bounds in the other direction which produces someone who demands attention - any attention - right or wrong and someone who will tend to become more and more tyrannical, selfish and demanding unless some serious re-evaluation is done.

A gall attack or gall bladder surgery is another attempt to rid the body physically of that which "galls" or is bothering the individual emotionally and spiritually. Gall stones are physical entrapments of the evil of anger/fear/worry. Kidney stones are the physical entrapments of evil of power misused or abused. Removal of all or passage out of the body is a new chance to resolve the issues and an indication that indeed the physical body is rebelling against this situation.

This is an aspect of too much fire - an elemental problem that burns away the energy and the vitality. Counseling is suggested and a re-evaluation of relationships is definitely in line. Try to get time to yourself - a separate vacation and please yourself - pamper yourself and try to re-evaluate what you really, truly want from those around you. It is probable that someone reaching this stage will not particularly like themselves - try to find things that are positive about you and "clean up your own house" before you attempt to change or alter others. Surround yourself with pinks and blues and cool ocean colors in meditation or prayer.

The ultimate healing color is bright blood red and the healing visualization requires the individual to see the blackness that they have incorporated within themselves and turn the blackness to healthy blood red which will help them to see the problems and heal them. As the problems are faced, dealt with and rejected for healthier and happier viewpoints - the red will fade and fade to hopefully eventually become bright raspberry pink and when the situation is healed fully, it will be baby pink. Avoid wearing blacks and maroons and deep reds and wear the colors of health. Red colors that tend to pinks are ok in the course of working through all of this - as you get better and better replace the reds with lighter pinks.

The healing tones are psalms or poetry. The music in language spoken aloud. Do you enjoy singing or writing? Start keeping a journal and let your anger/fear/worry go with the written word. Write down your feelings and frustrations and then burn them and let them go. The Lord's Prayer is healing here - not just as a prayer, but as a series of tones and intonations and the colors those intonations emit within the universe. It is probably time to re-evaluate your spirituality and get back into a supportive environment of some sort, not necessarily church, but a writing club, or chorus, acting, civic or social organization - something you enjoy and believe in. Stay away from "unhappy" or politically motivated clubs as these are people dealing with unresolved "control" issues - that is the last thing _you_ need. Join, but do not jump into an organization in "leader" status lest you re-create the tyranny you have in your family/friend circle. Sit back and listen and try to be a part of something larger than yourself. Give yourself in service to others - with no hope of repayment or return. Do something that comes from your heart with no strings attached.

11. This area is the area of the hip joints, legs, feet, bladder and part of the intestine and colon. Strange combination, but not so strange when you consider that in some form or another all of these things represent movement. Moving parts and moving toxins out of the body. As the feet are the blueprints for the organ systems just as much as the hands are - this area is very important to show how the body toxins are moving out of the system and where - precisely they are blocked or incorporated. Emotionally, it is also movement in some form or another and spiritually as well. If energy does not flow properly from the bottoms of the feet through the legs to the hip, bladder, colon and intestine - there is a blockage of earth energy and blockages in energy produce blockages in the intestine or blockages in blood to the lower extremities. If the area is incorporated, and by that it means that toxins are merged throughout the eliminatory organs - this area can be a hotbed of infection due to toxins being held too long within the bowels. If this area shows up as an area compromised, it is time for the individual to

fast and take natural measures to move the bowels out thoroughly. They should drink plenty of liquids and eat lipid fats to smooth the muscles in the lower extremities. Eat garlic and exercise the extremities.

12. This area incorporates the genitalia and the reproductive systems for both male and female and the message - from a physical standpoint is in some fashion regarding sex or reproduction. Other "signs" will have to be considered as this area is very complex and it is also a very touchy area to be talking to someone about. Suffice it to say that if the pendulum spends time in this area, there is some concern of the individual regarding either his sex life or reproductive status. The right side of the body shows the feminine organs and the left side of the body the male organs. A woman could conceivably be having problems in her male organs - which would be an indication that the body is not producing proper progesterone levels and the opposite is the same for the man. If he is having difficulty with the feminine organs - the body is not producing proper estrogen levels for the man. Men and women go through chemical "menopause." The male menopause is less publicized, but certainly as worrisome for him as for females undergoing this natural process. It is probable that the

males may need chemical readjustment just as much as the females. Prostrate problems will show up on the left hand just below where area 10 meets area 12. Be sure to ask the pendulum to be specific as to whether it is indicating a physical problem or emotional or spiritual one for this area. It is suggested that you ask the pendulum to "spell out" specifics in this area with pen'l leina communication, communication chart or cursive writing.

13. Numbers, 13, 14, 15, 16 and 17 are broad "overviews" for whole systems. Number 13 is the thumb area and it has a big job. The thumb area is the brain - left and right hemispheres (top joint), the nervous system as a whole (all) and the third eye chakra (base of the thumb.)

14. As a broad overview, the index finger is the area of the face, neck and throat and the cartilage and muscles in the neck. A lot of stress is held in these areas and if the pendulum indicates the whole finger - the odds are 90% that the individual is carrying his stress there. The lower part of the index finger is the throat and larynx area. If the pendulum circles here, it is an indication that the throat chakra is in some fashion compromised. The individual may either be

holding in from speaking his mind or if the individual talks incessantly - the throat chakra is too open and he needs to ground and center. The pendulum can specify. The eyes are located at the top of the index finger and the mouth just at the top joint. The neck is the area of the second joint and the throat and larynx is the third joint. The throat chakra and the tonsils and uvula are just below the third joint - also in the area of the heart. The throat and heart are very closely tied together.

15. As a broad overview - the middle finger is your connection to Spirit. The crown chakra is located at the very top of the middle finger and the ears are to either side of the top joint. The upper vertebrae are in the 2nd joint and the rib cage, cartilage and muscles are located in the 3rd joint. The connection of rib cage to lungs is just below the third joint.

16. As a broad overview - the ring finger is your connection to the healing aspects and your commitment to healing yourself and healing others. Self healing is vital to the fleur d'leis process and this area is a barometer of how you are doing. Heal yourself. Heal others. Heal the universe. Clean up your own house before you attempt to reform anyone else's house. In order to heal others, you must be healed of ego. Number 16 is the physical

house of ego and the physical test of ego. The Bones of Stesrn in the physical house does not have an especial meaning. It has meaning when you have achieved fleur d'leis status. Esglii also has meaning when you have achieved fleur d'leis status.

If you have not achieved fleur d'leis status and the third joint is being circled (not spiraled,) it simply means that you are in the processes of healing yourself. If it circles the 2nd joint, it means you are trying to do something to heal others or are at least in the process of learning about healing from others or teaching others about healing. In the top joint, it means that you are concerned about universal truths and are searching for some answers.

17. As a broad overview, the small finger has a large energy field. This is because it covers so many things. It is the physical home of the sciatic nerve and the nerves in the spinal cord (top joint.) It is also the lower vertebrae and the muscles, cartilage and cushioning tissue in the backbone (2nd joint.) This overview is also the feminine aspect of the individual and the "health" of the feminine (3rd joint).

18	This is an egg shape area at the base of the thumb (in the larger area of thumb-13.) The third eye chakra is located below the bending joint of the thumb and if that area is sore or the joint is achy, it is because the third eye chakra is compromised and needs to be opened. Massaging this area periodically helps to keep the nervous system and brain stimulated. Watch the body language of people when they need to engage their brain prior to some challenging task (a medical operation comes to mind) - they will rub this area! Remember this area in case of choking on tests or the inability to remember something, it helps! This area is also important because it is a microcosm of the male/female aspects of the individual as well as how well they have incorporated the melding of the lifeforce/loveforce energy. Soreness or numbness in some area of the thumb may be an indication of problems spiritually. Emotionally, soreness and/or numbness has a lot of baggage with stress and physically, it could lead to migraines or headaches or a feeling of being "disconnected."

19	This is the area of the 3rd joint of the index finger. This area is the area of the physical throat - teeth, uvula, tonsils, larynx, adenoids, tongue, etc. Just below the index finger "base" sitting over the heart is the throat chakra. The throat chakra is the most complicated chakra in the body. So much can and does go amiss in this area. The practice of tonsillectomies that used to be practiced in the 50's and 60's was ill conceived.

The tonsils are natural filters for toxins. They hold the negativity you speak OR the negativity you wish to speak but hold within. Think about what you do when you "choke on, or swallow" your words. Something is at the tip of your tongue and you have to swallow hard not to say it? You swallow it as far as the tonsils go and they take it from there. You harm yourself when you do not address harm, abuse, disregard and disrespect from others. You harm yourself when you utter words that harm another.

Those "swallowed words" manifest the negativity you create for yourself by not standing up for yourself. Conversely, if you are hurtful or harmful, the words you uttered that caused unfair pain to someone manifest toxins in the tonsils as well. It is for that reason it is unwise to remove them. If they have become so diseased that they pose a threat to the body - it is the negativity of the person's situation that is posing the threat. Address that issue and heal the body and forgive yourself and reaffirm your commitment to speaking your truth and not harming others.

Many people "cough" up small white or yellow nodules that have a vile smell. They cough up the negativity and toxins that would infect the tonsils. This is a sure sign that the individual is either remorseful for the harmful things they cannot say to another or is remorseful of someone else for the harmful things they say. They have issues that they are having a great deal of trouble "swallowing" and because these issues would create harm to others if spoken, they go unspoken. This is your body's way of forgiving you for these unspoken words and allowing you to "spit" them up rather than allow them to seat (for long) on the tonsils and cause further infection or inflammation. Sometimes, a gentle heart cannot speak out to protect themselves when others abuse their sweet and gentle nature - it is a great love aspect in some fashion to accept the pain rather than cause another pain, but when the throat begins to become inflamed or sore, it is a sure sign they better start standing up for themselves or perhaps someone close to them.

20. This is the area of the third joint of the middle finger. This is the area of the rib cage. The rib cage is symbolic (and actual) structure of our lives and areas that remain sore in the rib cage are indications that structure is lacking and a strong foundation is weak. Broken or cracked ribs are a structural defect and when this happens, it is a sign to regain a firmer "hold" on what is important. As the rib cage is very important to protect the softer major organs underneath, it is important to provide a strong "house" to protect yourself. The muscles and cartilage in the area of the rib cage is very intricate and a great deal of "motion" is afforded just the course of breathing in and out. The breast bone is the natural "breastplate." It is the area that protects the "seat of the soul - the heart. It is a sacred part to the body. Adornment of stone people here vibrate very specifically to the breastbone which transmits stone energy healing to the rest of the body. It is inadvisable to have this area tattooed. Symbols are sometimes not what they seem and the inks and dyes in this particular area interfere in the work that is naturally going on there.

21. This is the area of the 3rd joint of the ring finger. This is the physical area of the

hocaieah - the healing centers of the body and the gage in the body for the rising of the kundalini. When self-healing is actualized, the kundalini process begins a thorough housecleaning of the body on all levels - spiritual/emotional and physical. You can expect to feel <u>lousy</u> when your body is undergoing this process and you may doubt your sanity to boot. The physical changes in your body in the transformational process' are astronomical and the heightened awareness you will undergo will make the whole process seem endless. It has an end, either you will complete your fleur d'leis cleansing and spiritual housekeeping and pass the tests that Spirit demands of you - or you will not become fleur d'leis and the hocaieah will sleep. In either event, you will feel better and hopefully be stronger for the process. Those who "fight" the kundalini rising and the opening of the hocaieah actually fare much worse than those who work with their bodies a step at a time and take the necessary steps to self-healing.

If this area is circled, it indicates either than you are in a self-healing process or are approaching one. Expect to really become aware of your body and do not be overwhelmed with your physical problems. Work on healing the physical aspects that you feel are wrong with you, ONE AT A TIME

AND A STEP AT A TIME. You may not cure everything, but the test will be that you tried with a pure heart and if you get the energy flowing well, your body will heal itself over the long run. Sometimes this requires years of patient and constant work. You heal yourself to the ability you can, based upon the script you wrote for yourself. Your script may have called for you to have an illness that you have to learn to deal with.

22. This is the area of the 3rd joint of the small finger. This area is complicated. It is the area of the feminine part of the individual - male or female. It is an area that requires flexibility within a structure. It is an area that cannot become crystallized, or the individual will become emotionally detached and will loose more and more of their ability to reason from the heart and "think on their feet." It requires that emotional issues be looked at and weighed in the course of physical healing and when it circles there - it is an indication that the individual needs to look at the feminine aspects of themselves to help with their problems.

This is closely tied to communication. To converse, convince and cajole - you have to be able to react from "gut" or instinctive reactions - that is the feminine aspect as well.

A physical problem in this area indicates some problem in communication - a problem that may or may not be manifest in a physical communication problem. Check the area of the throat chakra and see what is going on. If the throat is closed or shutting down and this area is shutting down, physical problems of communication and the feminine "aspect" are affecting the body.

The other aspect that may be going on is that in some fashion, anger/fear or worry is manifesting into a problem. If the problem is resolved here, it does not have to incorporate the liver or the gall bladder. Because it shows up as a problem in the "feminine." It is an indication to talk out your problems with someone before they become more physically serious.

23   This is the area at the top of the thumb. Physically, it is the area of the brain and emotionally and spiritually, it is the area of family and family love. There are three "crown" chakras. At the top of the thumb is the 2nd crown chakra. This is the area that gauges and adjusts the loveforce in the individual. A lack of loveforce or an interrupted flow can cause headaches or migraines. In some cases an interruption of loveforce causes "panic" type reactions and a

feeling of being unloved or unlovable. Before you doubt the love of your family - try to get this connection flowing more freely.

Lifeforce and loveforce are necessary to sustain life in the individual. In transformational states those forces merge, but there are times when one or the other will be "transmitting" stronger frequencies. The goal of the transformation is to work with balanced loveforce and lifeforce and teach the individual to deal with all aspects of life and Spirit in adult and neutral fashion. To loose the ego and to love all things equally. To do no harm. A headache at the top or back of the head is an interruption of loveforce and an indication that the love aspect of life needs to be reviewed. Perhaps it is time for some emotional "housecleaning."

24   This is the area at the top of the index finger. This is a multi-purpose area that encompasses the face, eyes, nose, mouth (speaking), muscles and tissues in the face. It encompasses all sinus areas. Sometimes, in a physical message the "eyes" (at the top of the index finger) are simply circled to say, "look at, or see." The messages are often quite literal.

A nose is probably the sense of smell. Generally when there are problems in the sinus which may be indicated by a sweeping around or blocking motion with the pendulum, the smelling sense is affected. When the nose area is circled, it may be an indication that smudging or incense is needed to assist Spirit in the communication. Ask the pendulum if that is what is needed. Smudging and incense add protection to you as well as energy to Spirit as well as a physical offering and sign of respect. It may be as literal as to tell you to be aware of the sense of smell - or something that smells (gas for instance.)

Angelic presence is often heralded with a beautiful flower or "other" scent. The scent is something you cannot recreate on earth. It has a sense of purity and joy. That is an indication that angelic presence is in a room. A sudden and delightful scent that fills you with a sense of joy and well being. To be gifted with that scent is such a blessing. Please recognize it and greet and thank the presence that alerted itself to you! It is probably very important to speak to that Spirit - but they generally will not impose themselves upon you unless you speak to them and recognize them and ask them if they have a message for you or if you may help them in some way.

25. This is the top joint on the middle finger. This is the area of the ears and the hearing system. Again, "ears" can be a literal message to "listen." They may be trying to get through to you. The hearing system is our system of translating vibrations into tone. It is, however, much, much more complicated than that. The vibrations are also translating into color and sounds beyond our hearing range that help to direct the processes in the whole physical/material world we have created for ourselves. This is the process whereby Spirit becomes a physical manifest form. Remember, time and space do not truly exist. We live rather, holograms of physical existence created for our pleasure and delight and as teachers to us in earthly physical/material trial.

That is why it is very important to take care of our hearing. So much can be damaged from overly loud music or industrial noise or sudden gunfire. When the ears are damaged, the ability of Spirit to maintain our physical existence is greatly hindered. A person who is deaf or hard of hearing lives in a very isolated world as they will be the first to tell you. This is largely because they are cut off (never fully, or the form you see "dies") from sense vibrations, tones and colors that they do not even know is missing from their senses. The body tries to accommodate the universal tones in other ways, but it is very difficult to do this. The body is a miraculous organism. If the person is hearing impaired, it goes through a very convoluted series of re-routing the information. That is another reason the other "senses" are more acute. All "senses" help to create the reality of the physical/material world.

The crown chakra that translates lifeforce is at the top of the middle finger. The transpersonal point (sun - energy) "feeds" directly into this point to keep the physical body alive. When a person is sun depleted or does not periodically "recharge" in the sun or out of doors - they become depressed, lethargic and their immune systems and all systems start a "shut down" process similar to hibernation.

If the connection from this crown point (or the others really) to transpersonal point (sun) is severed for some reason, it is vital that the connection be reestablished or the entity may develop serious physical and emotional difficulties. Their will to live may be affected and suicidal tendencies or thoughts may begin to surface. Many emotionally disturbed patients have this problem. It is a catch 22. They are depressed and don't feel like getting "out" and if they do not get "out" it will progress into further depression and neurological symptoms.

If this area has been "severed" over a long period of time, the individual may either disassemble the feminine or male aspects in whole or in part or may physically "die." It is essential to humankind <u>and all animals</u> to have a good dosage of sunlight daily to stay healthy. When you have friends that are depressed insist on buying them a yellow balloon with a string and take them outside to walk it! Or some visualization of sun/gold/white light (or <u>any</u> light connection transpersonal to crown is needed and healing or self-healing is vital!! BUT PLEASE NOTE! Nothing is as healing as direct sun light and a reconnection to Mother Earth. Ask her to help as well!

26   This area is more significant in the emotional and spiritual chart as it is the extension of energy to heal Spirit and a commitment to do so there. If it shows up as a physical message prior to the person achieving fleur d'leis status - it is an indication that the person has some "soul-searching" to do regarding their

extension of energy to others. Possibly the person is misusing energy in some fashion in an attempt to manipulate others or get attention.

If the person has achieved fleur d'leis status and this area shows up as a circle -it is not a physical message relating to the body of the individual except in the vein that Spirit wishes the person to physically help them by extending energy to Spirit. Seek guidance and try to help. It is a plea for physical assistance of some kind.

27. This is a tricky area as this area in the emotional chart is the love of anger/fear/worry and manipulation of others with it. In the spiritual chart it is overcoming this manipulation aspect - which shows up as a spiral in the area.

If the person has not achieved fleur d'leis status and the area is circled in the physical chart it refers to the sciatic nerve, lower body nerves and lower vertebrae and the muscles and cartilage in the back. The sciatic is located at the tip of the little finger, the lower body nerves just above the top joint - the lower vertebrae and the muscles and cartilage are in the 2nd joint area. Sciatic pain generally vibrates down the hips and legs and the pain is a reminder that in some fashion, power and energy are being misused.

Lower back pain and back pain in general indicates a lack of flexibility and nerve pain in the back is a real signal to the individual that "flexing" of spiritual and physical and emotional muscles are needed. People can be totally devastated by back pain and they seek to "numb" the pain with pain pills. The pain is there to tell you to rethink what you are doing and your control issues. Back pain does precisely that - it will grind a person to a slow pace or a stop completely to allow the area bed rest and contemplation. It is a very extreme way that the body has to force you to relax, regroup, re-think and reorganize your life.

When a person is suffering from severe back pain, it is the body's last defense to force a change that is to the total health of the organism. People who get "laid-out" flat on their back for weeks will be the first to tell you that the pain they suffered changed their lives and outlook and reset their priorities. Operations will not help unless the person changes their lives and the origin of the problem. These forced job lay-offs due to severe back pain sometimes have drastic job results. Often, a job that is causing the problem becomes one that the body can no longer do. Back pain is our body/mind/spirit going on strike to change, sometimes drastically, the direction the person is taking in their lives.

If a person has received an injury to these areas remember what Spirit has told you; there are no accidents. A body in good balance will hear warnings that will prohibit injury in time. If a person is badly injured, it is either because he "scripted" this injury or illness, or the body is so imbalanced that spiritual direction and intervention was not possible. Some back injuries heal faster than others, but generally, the process is painful and life altering.

If this area shows up on a fleur d'leis, it is an indication that they are backsliding with control/power issues and need to rethink. Judge not lest ye be judged. If a fleur d'leis develops back pain or injuries, it is a rather serious set back spiritually and much rethinking needs to be done. A fleur d'leis earns their status because they manage to loose the ego. Ego loss doesn't require power issues to be addressed - all thoughts are valid, all points are valid and manipulation is no longer necessary. To prove power to another is no longer necessary. What may be happening is that somehow the fleur d'leis has forgotten that others who have a need to exert power over anything or anyone need to be forgiven and taught by example to honor all beings as worthy and sacred and divine as they themselves should be honored. Teach by living the example.

The exception to the rule regarding backache is if the body is misaligned and energy cannot flow properly the back will also ache. Seek an osteopathic or chiropractic adjustment of the back. The pendulum will tell you exactly where the adjustment is needed if it is needed and the problem will show up along the line of the spine as an "interruption in energy."

28 This area is the area of the sexuality and sexual preference shows up here. If the area spirals in this area it is an indication that there is latent male homosexual tendencies. If the area is circling and the individual is not fleur d'leis, it is an indication that something is amiss sexually, they are not being fulfilled sexually. Generally the male patterns show up in area 28, but keep in mind God Primes, message; the body may be female and the soulforce male and vice versa.

If the person is fleur d'leis and this area shows up circled. There is male (lifeforce) imbalance in some aspect that needs to be healed. The rest of the message should help the fleur d'leis discover in which area the male (symbol for lifeforce) needs to be healed.

29. The same holds true for this area as above, but it is the feminine (loveforce) and not the masculine area.

30. This is a symbol for many things. A circle in the area just below the elbow joint is a message of "whole thing," wholeness, earth, and overall lifeforce. Usually, in any given message all of these apply, however, sometimes one meaning more clearly stands out. Ask the pendulum if the description is "all," or the planet earth or "lifeforce."

Once earth has undergone fully her spiritual transformation, this area will be "lifeforce/loveforce." A "sign" that earth transformation has transpired is when the pendulum circles first one way and then the opposite way in this area, or a sideways 8 replaces the circle. The sideways 8, in penl leina is not only "infinity," it is the gauge of the balance of lifeforce/loveforce. If the eight is larger on one side or the other, it indicates one power is predominating right now, which can be very normal. The two powers are very "flexible."

A very distorted 8, however, is an indication that an imbalance in the two forces exists. If there is imbalance the 8 will show a "cancellation" or line between the two halves of the 8. If this situation arises, the earth, wholeness, all is imbalanced and the fleur d'leis needs to work very hard very quickly to help heal the situation. Imbalance in this area is a call to arms and the fleur d'leis should contact everyone they know to get to work healing <u>everything!</u>

Pen'l Leina Emotional Hand Chart

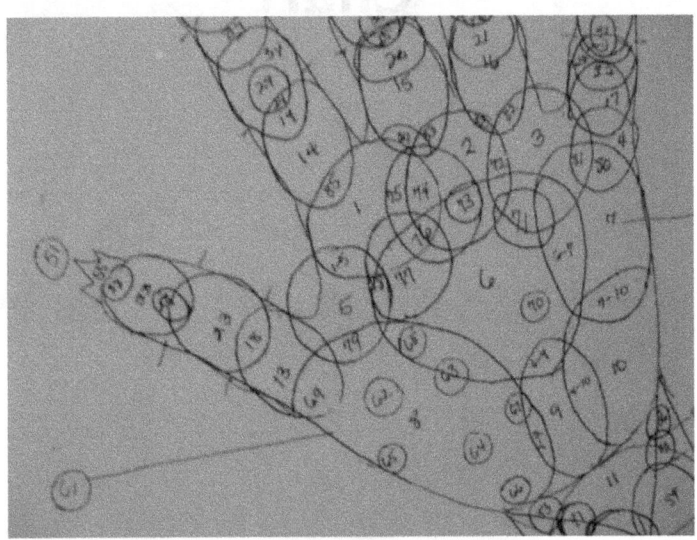

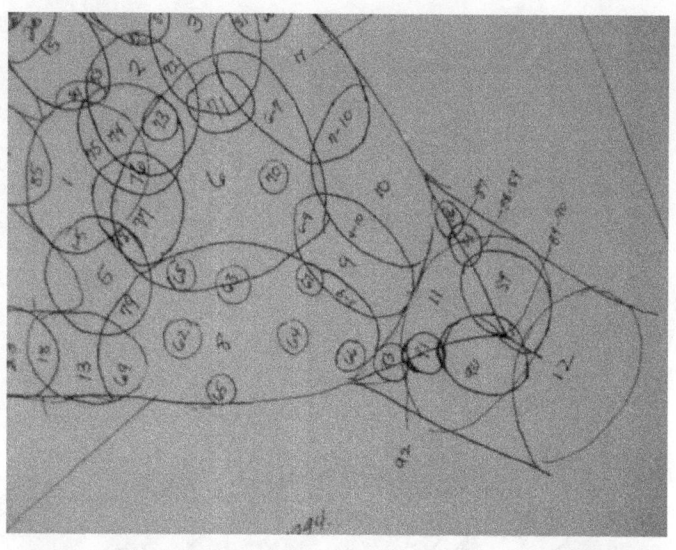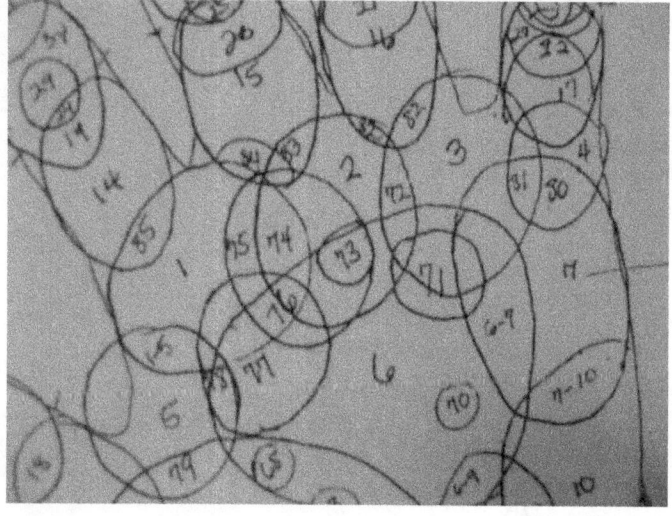

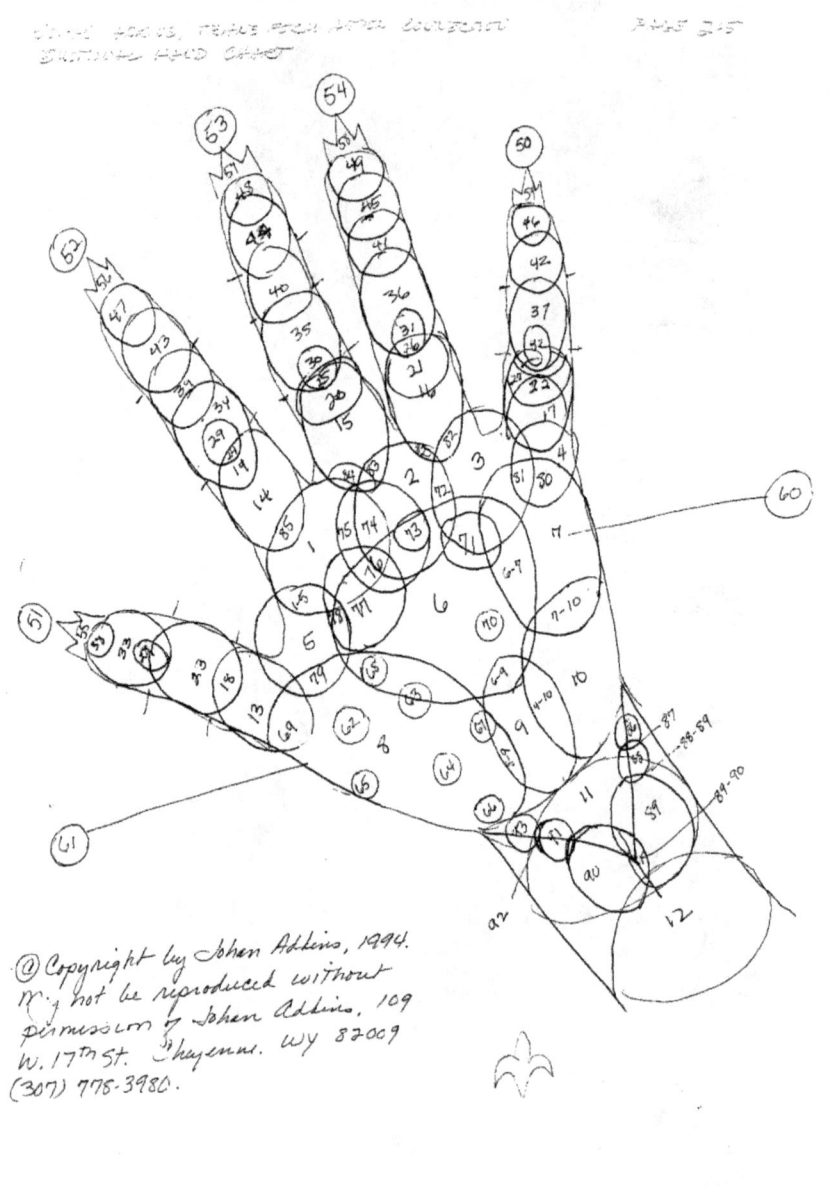

EMOTIONAL CHART - NUMERICAL CHART DATA

1	Communication
2-3	Emotional - heartfelt desire
4	Stress due to anger/fear/worry issues
5	Self-esteem and self-love
6	Energy
7	Anger/fear/worry
8	Family esteem - family love - concern for family
9	Nurturing aspect
10	Nurturing aspect of anger/fear/worry
11	Female/male aspect of self-balance and relationship balance
12	Energy of relationships - how balance are they between male and female aspects.
13	Stress in family relationships
14	Stress in communication

15   Stress due to emotions - love

16   Stress due to emotions - other

17   Stress due to anger/fear/worry issues and lack of physical attention to alleviate. Needs some physical action. Lack of physical exercise.

18   Stress due to family problems not being addressed. Some sort of action is needed to alleviate family problems.

19   Stress in communication is not being addressed. Some sort of action is needed to alleviate communication problems.

20   Stress due to emotions of love is not being addressed. Some sort of action is needed to alleviate love problems.

21   Stress due to emotions - other - not being addressed. Some sort of action is needed to alleviate problems.

22   Badly needs physical exercise.

23   Badly needs family counseling. Situation critical.

24   Badly needs communication counseling. Situation critical.

25   Badly needs counseling on love/emotion issues. Situation critical.

26   Badly needs counseling on emotional/other issues. Situation critical.

27   Badly needs counseling on anger/fear/worry issues. Situation critical and exercise vital.

28   Worry over family issues somewhat affecting family.

29   Worry over communication issues somewhat affecting individual.

30   Worry over emotional/love issues somewhat affecting the individual.

31   Worry over emotional/other issues somewhat affecting the individual.

32   Worry over anger/fear/worry issues somewhat affecting the individual.

33   Worry over intellectual issues somewhat affecting the individual.

34 Worry over how communication is perceived by others is somewhat affecting the individual.

35 Worry about how emotions/love is perceived by others is somewhat affecting the individual.

36 Worry about how emotions/other is perceived by others is somewhat affecting the individual.

37 Worry about how anger/fear/worry is perceived by others is somewhat affecting the individual.

38 Love of family is predominant to this person.

39 Love of communication. Likes to talk!

40 Love of emotions - loved ones. Will stir up emotions of loved ones to control the strings.

41 Love of emotions - others. Will stir up emotions of others to control the strings.

42 Love of anger/fear/worry. Will stir up anger/fear/worry to control the strings. Oftentimes these are people who are seeking an emotional outlet in the wrong way - by inspiring or inciting the extremes of

anger/fear/worry upon the emotions of others. These people often need an extreme reaction from others to feel or feed their own emotions fully. The heart must be healed and the love aspect of self must be healed. This is using the caring of others to abuse and the result is always the same - rejection. The person who employs this emotional tactic needs to question the need to arouse the anger/fear/worry or sometimes passion or violence of others in order to feed week emotional responses. Physically check the thyroid levels. Also a lack of adrenal function may be initiating the person to "feed" on the emotions of others to function fully.

43   Love of communication - mass groupings. Good for actors, actresses', politicians and preachers. Manipulative element of communication.

44   Love of emotion of loved ones- mass grouping. Mark of a spiritual leader (or cult leader.)

45   Love of emotions of others - mass grouping. Leader of politics or perhaps leader of left-wing groups. Not necessarily underlying the good qualities of others. User and abuser.

46   Love of anger/fear/worry mass groupings. May be journalist, elemental movement (doom and gloom - end of the world stuff) or serial killer or serial mystery writer. Likes to be afraid (or angry or worry) and likes to scare (or anger or worry) others.

47   Communication is uppermost to this person. May be journalist or TV or movie personality.

48   Love of emotions - loved ones is uppermost to this person. Will go to any length for emotion of love. This isn't necessarily positive or healthy for the individual or loved ones.

49   Love of emotions of others is uppermost to this person. Person "feeds" on emotions of others. Emotional vampire.

50   Person has transcended anger/fear/worry issues and is on the way toward balance.

51   Person has transcended family issues and is on the way toward balance.

52   Person has transcended communication issues and is on the way towards balance.

53   Person has transcended emotional/love issues and is on the way towards balance.

54 Person has transcended emotional/other issues and is on the way towards balance.

55 Person has been given divine love for service to family or family groups. Balance achieved.

56 Person has been given divine love for service to communication or mass communication. Balance achieved.

57 Person has been given divine love for service <u>to</u> the emotional needs of loved ones. Balance achieved.

58 Person has been given divine love for service to the emotional needs of others. Balance achieved.

59 Person has been given divine love for service to alleviate the anger/fear/worry of others. Balance achieved.

60 Something or someone outside of self causing anger/fear/worry. May be work related or spiritually related.

61 Something or someone outside of family is casing stress to the family. May be relations to extended family or friends.

62   Concerns about money and balancing finances are somewhat affecting the individual and the family.

63   Concerns about savings, funds and investments are somewhat affecting the individual and the family.

64   Concerns about installment loans, real estate loans and/or taxes are somewhat affecting the individual and the family.

65   Concerns about lending systems are somewhat affecting the individual and the family.

66   Concerns about lending to others are somewhat affecting the individual and the family.

67   Concerns about the children are somewhat affecting the individual and the family.

68   Concerns about the individual's leisure is somewhat affecting the individual.

69   Concerns about the individuals spiritual leisure time is affecting the individual.

70   Concerns about the individual's diet is affecting the individual.

71   Concerns about the heart and/or emotions is affecting the individual.

72   Concerns about heart valves, murmurs and/or fatty cholesterol buildup is affecting the individual.

73   Concerns about heart problems or emotional problems is affecting the individual. If the problem is not manifest physically, it is manifest in concern about others leaving them, or a problem with commitment issues. All emotional concerns could result in physical manifestations of heart problems if not faced and addressed.

74   Concerns about heart attack or heart lesions are affecting the individual. Person has suffered emotional heart-ache that could (or will) result in heart attacks if not faced and addressed.

75   Concerns about heart melanoma or severe heart imbalance is affecting the individual. This person's heart has been broken in some fashion and it is probable that they are having physical heart symptoms or have already suffered physical problems in the heart or circulatory system.

76	Concerns about heart lesions on the left ventricle are affecting the individual. If the problem is manifest and healing but concern is still affecting the individual - the emotional baggage has not been jettisoned and the emotional issues need to be faced and addressed.

77	Concerns about knee injury is affecting the individual. If the person is concerned about the physical knee - they are not facing the issues of humiliation or humility on the emotional plane. They are resisting humbling themselves in some fashion.

78	Concerns about knee surgery or knee recovery is affecting the individual. If physical damage has actually resulted and the resultant emotional issues of humility and humble "bending" are not addressed, then anger/fear/worry issues occupy the mind of the individual. The individual will tend to "baby" the injury instead of facing and addressing the issues that cause the worry to begin with.

79	Concerns about family's acceptance of individual's spirituality is affecting the individual.

80   Concerns about overall stress due to anger/fear/worry is affecting the individual.

81 &
82   Concerns about emotional stress due to anger/fear/worry is affecting the individual.

83 &
84   Concerns about emotional stress due to heart or emotional issues is affecting the individual.

85   Concerns about stress due to communication issues is affecting the individual.

86   Concerns about female members of the family are affecting the individual.

87   Concerns about communication between female members of the family, work or social systems are affecting the individual.

88   Concerns about the emotional health and well beings of a specific female is affecting the individual. This may be self-concern if the individual is in body female or concerns about the feminine aspect of the male.

89   Concerns about the feminine reproductive system is affecting the individual.

89 &
90   Concerns about communicating about concerns about the reproductive systems or the inability to sexually perform or the ability to get pregnant are affecting the individual.

90   Concerns about the male reproductive system is affecting the individual.

91   Concerns about a specific male is affecting the individual.

92   Concerns about communication between male members of the family, work or social systems are affecting the individual.

93   Concerns about the emotional health and well being of a specific male is affecting the individual. This may be self-concern if the individual is in body male or concerns about the male aspect of the female.

PEN'L LEINA AND ELEMENTAL SPIRITUAL HAND CHART FOR FLEUR D'LEIS

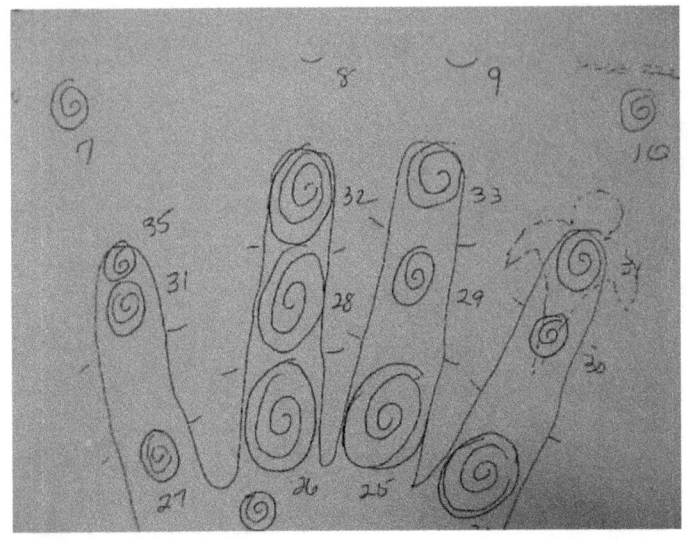

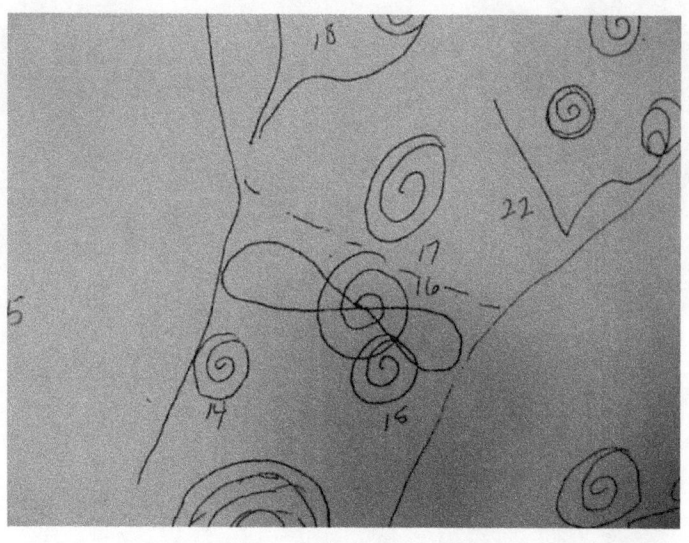
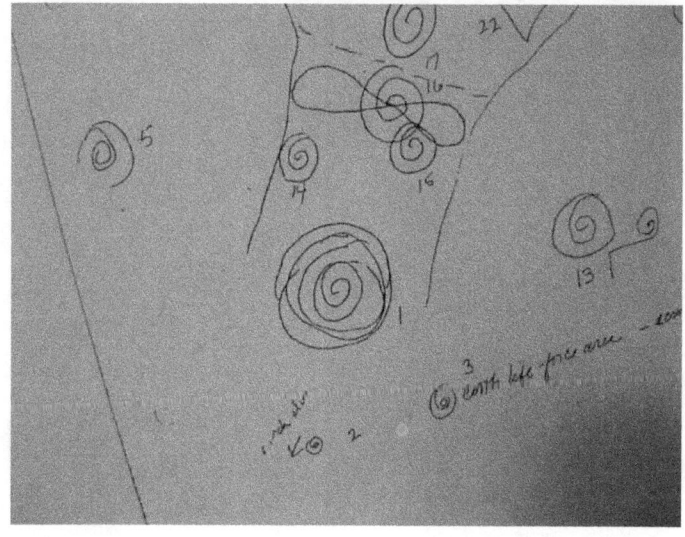

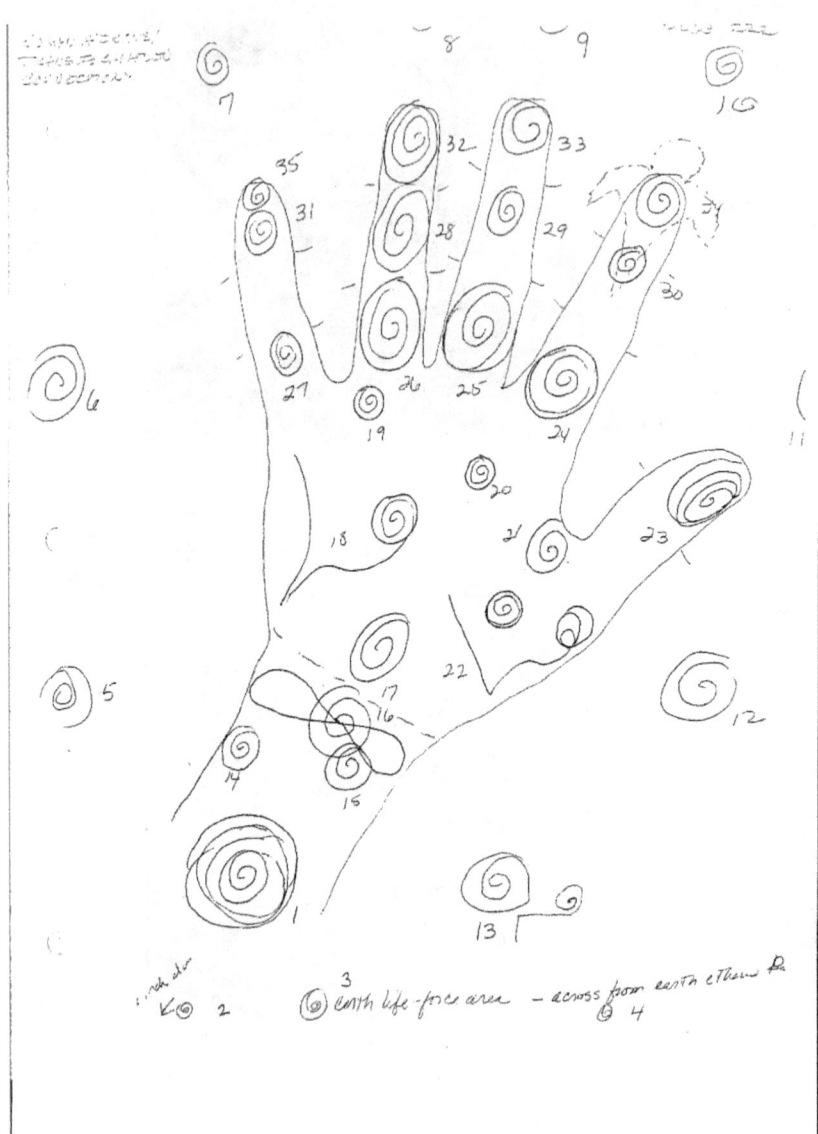

SPIRITUAL CHART

Spiritual patterns are shown as spirals and the pendulum will be indicating spiritual traits with a spiral movement. This is how to tell the difference between a spiritual and an emotional message. If you see spiral movement you are being given a FLEUR D'LEIS message. The spiral movement can be either clockwise or counterclockwise. In the fleur d'leis, energy flows both ways.

1. Latent homosexual energies - male.
2. Latent homosexual energies - female.
3. Lifeforce is strong. Lifeforce is open to becoming pregnant or if male open to getting female pregnant.
4. New lifeforce is near. Balance to get pregnant.
5. Lifeforce is balanced - fleur d'leis is near.
6. Lifeforce is imbalanced.
7. Lifeforce is stressed beyond healthy levels - may be leaving the physical body if not balanced as a whole.
8. Lifeforce is largely balanced but sun energy is needed.
9. Lifeforce is surrendering balance to imbalance. Imbalance will sever physical lifeforce if balance is not achieved all the way around.

10   Lifeforce is serenity. This person meditates serenity, peace and balance. They are fleur d'leis.

11   Lifeforce is trying to tend to balance, but balance/imbalance pattern is leading to imbalance. Person needs help moving negativity away and dealing with balance/imbalance. If this person asks for aura cleansing, they will transcend the balance/imbalance pattern provided they begin to meditate peace, serenity and balance and do their own spiritual housecleaning and housekeeping after that. Pyramid energy needs to be taught.

12   Lifeforce is nearing death of the physical form. Balance energy to prepare for returning to the soulforce.

13   Lifeforce is near fleur d'leis transformation, but balance/imbalance energy is not understood and needs more work.

14   Lifeforce is in transformation process. Balance is predominant over imbalance. Needs more work to fully transform. Meditate peace, serenity and balance and practice maintaining balance.

15   Lifeforce is nearing transformation. Balance is prevailing. Practice peace, serenity and

balance and teach it to others.
Balance/imbalance is better understood.
Serenity, peace, balance must be maintained to fully transform. This would be a good time for a fast and body cleansing.

16   Lifeforce transformation balanced. Fleur d'leis is earned. Individual must ask for transformation. Fleur d'leis energy is a gift from the divine. It offers the individual overall healing lifeforce derived from balanced energies from the universe. Fleur d'leis energies remain for life. As long as the individual seeks serenity/peace/balance, the energies will be available to enhance many aspects of the individual's lifeforce. The nature of fleur d'leis is balance. The individual needs to seek balance in all aspects of their lives. Fleur d'leis is a cosmic gift and a cosmic responsibility to utilize the energy to heal not only the self but others and not only others but the universe.

Each person is capable of achieving fleur d'leis. Fleur d'leis means Flower of Peace - literally, the Flower of Life, lifeforce. Hereinafter a symbol of peace and brotherhood. Fleur d'leis are the Peacemakers...and that title is well regarded throughout the universe. All planetary beings; rocks, plants, evolved animals and humans may derive healing energies from a person healing with fleur d'leis energy. The ability to work closely with planetary energy requires that the fleur d'leis individual remain in and retain balance. Fleur d'leis energies are usually never taken away, however the degree the individual is able to help is directly tied to the balance of the individual.

Fleur d'leis as a whole is equalized energy. The individual's energy polarity is dual and as a result any energy source may receive and/or lend energy to/from the individual. This is not the case with everyone who has not achieved fleur d'leis status. A fleur d'leis energy will "roll" both clockwise and counterclockwise in a spiral pattern on each side of their bodies over the palm. "Normal" energy will "roll" either - in towards the body across the palms or out - away from the body across the palms in circular patterns on an individual who is not fleur d'leis. Anyone or anything seeking help from a fleur d'leis must request the help and the request must be granted or denied.

Fleur d'leis individuals are also granted dimensional and interdimensional insight. That is to say they can communicate directly with Spirit and the spiritual realms. They have constant divine guidance if they ask for it. With permission, Spirit may enter the body of the fleur d'leis to assist in healing tasks or to speak to the fleur d'leis and in some cases others who need direct communication. If you are fleur d'leis and represent yourself "commercially" as a "channel" for Spirit to gain wealth, fame or notoriety, that is an abuse of the fleur d'leis status and will likely cause embarrassment. If there is something that must be said to the individual you are attempting to help - they will tell you to impart the information. Fleur d'leis must learn discernment. Do not impart what you hear without permission. No information will be denied to you if you have the maturity to deal with it to the highest good of the universe. You will receive information that is confidential in order to aid you to help in the best possible way.

Most of the work a fleur d'leis does is in the dream realm for the most part and is largely dimensional and interdimensional in that they are actively participating in healing endeavors with Spiritual guidance. Very important work is done in the physical realm. Thought is manifest form to any they wish to heal. All they have to do is "Think and wish the healing" and, if balanced and the healing is to the highest good, the healing shall be accomplished in the other dimensions <u>AND</u> on the physical material realm if it is meant to be.

The work the fleur d'leis does is very important to the physical beings, planets and planetary beings. This work balances the energies of planetary beings, planets and Spiritual beings that request or require help because they are out of balance.

The way each fleur d'leis individual does this work may differ with the individual, but the work each fleur d'leis person does towards balance or restoring the balance is vital to the survival of life in the universe. What the fleur d'leis person understands that many others do not is that the planets and planetary systems are alive and greatly interdependent upon each other for continued survival. One person out of balance affects planetary balance.

People on earth are a planetary power -each person's energy is capable of great balance or great imbalance which exponentially travels to and affects the universe. As a planetary power, <u>each</u> person has a responsibility to themselves, the earth, the planetary beings (on their planet as well as other planets) and the planetary systems to seek serenity/peace/balance and healing - not only for themselves but extended to <u>any</u> who need balance and a restoration of energies. Each person directing energy to planets (or indeed the whole universal structure) with a heart of serenity, love, healing, peace, joy, brotherhood and wholeness, reinvents the universe and re-establishes the perfect balance structure.

Some systems have to be imbalance to maintain the structure. A system balanced that should be imbalanced creates an incorrect energy necessary to sustain a dual polarity system (or simply a yin/yang relationship.) Fleur d'leis can safely work with both balance and imbalance to right the universal polarity structure and power grids.

Imbalance is not evil or bad - it is a poor word for the opposite of balance. The true object of the fleur d'leis is to help the universe maintain a neutral structure with the "balanced" state at one end of the neutral healing structure and the "imbalanced" state at the other end of the neutral healing structure.

Great systems out of the delicate yin/yang structure cause rifts in the fabric of space and great imbalance could mean annihilation. Annihilation not only of the planets and the lives who inhabit those planets, but of Spirit itself - the end of life forever. The universe is also a living organism. One small tiny solar system containing the planets above which is grossly out of balance is like a virus in a cell. The virus can be completely eliminated rather then allow the imbalance to spread to the rest of the cell **OR** it can be healed by the fleur d'leis and other energies.

As a living organism, the universe will seek to restore health to the whole. It will choose <u>life</u> by a destruction of what the universe can only deem is a corruption of goodness and an overall healthy condition. That is why it is very important to understand the role of a fleur d'leis. <u>One</u> fleur d'leis **working** (not just giving lip service but working with diligent effort and a loving heart) can restore the delicate balance not only to themselves, but others and not only to others but to planets, solar systems and the whole universe.

The method of healing oneself is the same as healing a planet. The method of healing a planet is the same as healing the entire universe. ONE fleur d'leis can heal the whole universe. Fleur d'leis working together can accomplish phenomenal healing. The general universal "rule" is, "A healing for a healing." If you respond to a request for healing, you may ask for a reciprocal healing when your need is great. It is considered "bad manners" to accept healing without asking if there is something you can do for them. Many universal energies are very needy, but do not ask for help unless you specifically ask them what you may do to help them. Please, remember this. They need the fleur d'leis energy to help them too. Very often, wellspring father, God Prime and Lord God and all the rest of the universal entities and energies could use your reciprocal help!!

Within the vast universes are Sentinels. Sentinel beings are group beings - one mind, group intellect and individual traits within a group. They are a group energy (Michael's Blue or Electric Blue energy,) who, like leukocytes in a cell are true neutral powers that seek only to restore and correct the universal energy by re-balancing (albeit balance or imbalance as discussed above.)

At one time, the Sentinels did not necessarily care overly for tiny lifeforms that crawl around within the diseased portion of the universe. They have the unhappy task of doing what must be done to help restore the balance/imbalance to a perfect structure. If the Sentinel contacts a fleur d'leis to help restore balance - indeed, the need is great, for his great power is requiring fleur d'leis healing.

Sentinels will now work with the transformed ones in union to reestablish the correct energy patterns. It is important to understand, however, that the Sentinel are primarily responsible to restore balance to the entire universe and sometimes they are very, very far away and cannot respond instantly to the fleur d'leis' requests. If that is the case, your spirit guides will inform you that he is either "on his way" or they may offer alternative help if Sentinel power is not necessary. In any case, a fleur d'leis may request to speak to the Sentinel through the vortex systems even if he is "far away." A request can be made through the vortex to speak to any Spiritual being. They may or may not choose to speak to you. That is their choice. A request is made, a request is granted or denied. Generally, a great effort will be made if you are fleur d'leis to respond to your requests. The party you wish to "call" may be contacted through the vortex "telephone" network (with the permission of the vortex to act as an intermediary. Please refer to the chapter on vortex travel and communication.)

There was a time that Sentinels could not place emphasis on human or planetary lifeforms above the overall planetary lifeform - that time is definitely past and a new mandate from the Council of Sentinels requires that the Sentinel ask for and work with fleur d'leis before entities or beings or indeed vast systems are annihilated. They are to give fleur d'leis all opportunity to save themselves and their planetary systems. The Sentinel can be counted upon to respond to requests from the fleur d'leis for help in restoring a neutral status.

The Sentinel is the dragon of the universe and its preferred form is that of a dragon in the skies. Physically, when he is around, he can be seen in the physical/material realm. Listen and he will guide you to the part of the sky in which he is in. He appears as a dragon "cloud" and the form definitely maintains its basic shape as it moves through the skies. His "secret" identity will be given to those who communicate directly with him and work with him.

Fleur d'leis are the universal warriors. They are potentially interdimensional and dimensional travelers who are blessed with Spiritual guidance every step of the way. **BUT** fleur d'leis must maintain balance to be effective healers. **HOWEVER** if they are <u>very</u> imbalanced they may be subject to confusing information from manifest evil, corruption or residual corruption from evil. The physical/material realm may manifest evil by evil deeds and thoughts and giving power to negativity, corruption or evil. Evil is tricky - and **often** masks itself as goodness and light and is not above misrepresenting itself as <u>anything or anybody.</u> Evil indeed, may speak enough "truth" that it is very difficult to determine to whom you are speaking.

If the fleur d'leis knows they are in a state of imbalance - it is important to balance before speaking to any Spiritual guides and follow "gut" reactions and feelings. If a being speaks of negativity or feels "wrong," generally, there will be a feeling of "creepiness" or a fleur d'leis will actually feel a weight on the back or shoulders. In this case, the procedure for removing negativity should be implemented and the fleur d'leis is being corrupted upon. When negativity speaks - the fleur d'leis should just stop the conversation and resume it after the corruption is dealt with and balance is restored. It may be a time to do a aura cleansing and meditate to ground and center the energies for "serenity, peace, brotherhood, wholeness, healing and strength.

It is well for the fleur d'leis to state aloud that they will not hear nor they speak to negativity "evil" or corruption within or without. Speak only to beings of a "pure heart." Ask the universal powers who can help you to help you rid yourself of what is attempting to influence you or inhabit you.

KNOW THIS. If a fleur d'leis is actually being corrupted upon - nothing can harm you permanently. Fleur d'leis are blessed with wellspring cleansing. Wellspring can heal threefold or it can condemn and kill that which attacks them with intent to harm. It is for this reason that fleur d'leis do not have to fear "evil." They are protected by the universe from any form of corruption. They may take on **any** negativity or corruption in a balanced state and defeat it. No "evil" is a match for wellspring blessing and fleur d'leis status. "Evil" is not stronger in any way than goodness and neutrality.

One fleur d'leis method of healing is to take "on" the wrongness within and heal the individual fleur d'leis rather than have others, (who may not have the benefit of direct wellspring healing) suffer unduly. To take on karma of others is inadvisable and cosmically immature; however, if a pure heart is corrupted upon by negativity and requests help - the fleur d'leis may open or extend their energies to capture the corruption and eradicate it - much easier than exorcising it from another.

Fleur d'leis require mature spirituality because they are "open" channels to the energies of the entire universe. It is vital to be able to discern "wrongness" and correct the wrongness. This may entail a wellspring cleansing of the wrongness - or calling upon other energies - such as the Sentinel - to rid the fleur d'leis of negative entities or energies that may attempt to influence. Fleur d'leis status does not come to those who cannot eventually discern the difference and deal maturely with <u>all</u> energies.

If a fleur d'leis makes a choice to do the bidding or work <u>with</u> negativity or corruption - this is the only case when the gift may be taken for the good of the fleur d'leis as well as the good of the entire universe. Fleur d'leis energy may not serve "evil" knowingly without very, very strict guidance from the balance or neutral Spiritual realm.

17. This is a movement toward initial testing (or retesting if fleur d'leis status has already

been granted.) It may be the assignment of an important task. It is the sign of "work in process." When this sign shows up cleanse, purify and de-toxify the body.

18 This is a test of the loveforce aspect regarding friends and family. There are two distinct energies in the universe - loveforce and lifeforce. Loveforce testing involves the love aspect in some form. Fleur d'leis must pass the loveforce testing in order to fully transcend into the higher spiritual realms.

19 This is a test of how loyal your heart is to Spirit. This is a period of testing to see if the individual is true to themselves and their Spiritual commitments. Spirit sees and hears everything and knows a true and pure heart. You have a pure heart or you would not be undergoing these Spiritual tests for the fleur d'leis. Your Spiritual commitment can be to any true and loyal principle - religion, creed or dogma aside - it does not matter. What matters is that your spirituality come from within - what you hold to be true for you. It matters that you "walk your talk." It does not matter that you preach or espouse your beliefs to others. That is not necessary. Each person - each entity has their own spiritual paths and all paths must be honored that are of a pure heart. Fleur d'leis are gifted with

"non-judgement" or they will never achieve fleur d'leis status. Non-judgement does not mean, however, that any harmful or hurtful action is to be condoned. "Do no harm" is a motto of the fleur d'leis. "Accept no harm" is just as viable. Spiritual tests are not always earth-moving. More often then not they are very simple tests in day to day life. Very often angelic presence will interface in the physical/material world to watch you or see how you respond to a plea for help, for instance. Sometimes the test *is* very important for you to respond to for a substantial healing for the universe...sometimes, it is as simple as watering your plants when you notice they are thirsty - or listening to the trees.

20 This is a test of how loyal your heart is to the love aspect.

21 This is a test of the love aspect between the physical and the spiritual realm.

22 This is a test of the love aspect between the object of carnal affection and the physical and spiritual realm. It is also a test of "self-esteem" and self-value. This is one of the toughest tests of the fleur d'leis. It may involve changing marital or love relationships to a more equal basis so that

relationships do not imbalance the individual. An individual in a "caretaker" mode is not balanced. Balance requires an adult/neutral stance - standing up for what is important to balance the needs of everyone - including the fleur d'leis.

This period of time generally brings about a lot of evaluation and re-evaluation of all the relationships. Many relationships are energy draining and not productive for anyone - least of all the individual who is being drained. This period may be difficult for family members to adjust to - because it is the task of the fleur d'leis to return the responsibility to their family members for their own karmic and cosmic paths. This is the ultimate test of the universal "adult."

23   This is earned increment for the fleur d'leis in the area of the family. Exerting healing to family members and having family accept and seek the wisdom and healing of the fleur d'leis gives this "gift." This will show up only after fleur d'leis is achieved.

24   This is earned increment for the fleur d'leis in the area of teaching and speaking to others about healing and about specifically spiritual fleur d'leis training. This symbol on the hand is the "gift" of teacher and wise woman or

wise person designation. This will show up only after fleur d'leis is achieved.

25 This is earned increment for the fleur d'leis in the area of spiritual adjustment. That is to say that the fleur d'leis has recognized and accepted the concept of soulforce oneness and has been working actively with Spirit and the higher self. The energy is extended to Spirit in the dimension of one and two and the fleur d'leis is actively working. This is the gift of the spiritual "doer" and is achieved only after fleur d'leis status is achieved.

26 This is earned increment for the fleur d'leis in the area of self-healing and extending the healing beyond self. It is a blessing upon the Hocaieah that permanently gifts the fleur d'leis with balanced polarity. It is a sign that self-healing as a continuing process has earned the fleur d'leis the blessings of eternal balance by Spirit. When this gift is "won," the balance extends to the families of the fleur d'leis into perpetuity. It is a protection of the loved ones against imbalance and spiritual guidance for them.

27 This is earned increment for the fleur d'leis in the area of flexibility and is an indication that the fleur d'leis has, in some measure actively recognized the presence of evil in the

physical/material realm, met evil and corruption and defeated it in battle. This "gift" is generally a sign for a female fleur d'leis because it is in the area of the floating rib - but can definitely show up on a male that has proven flexibility in recognizing evil where it exists even in the guise of good. The reason it will generally show up on a female is that it is closely tied to the emotions of the feminine side. When this shows up on a male, it is a double blessing because it shows a male very tuned into his feminine side. Generally, females will "feel" corruption and have a better handle in the -1, 1 and 2 dimension to "sense" the presence of evil. Men are usually not as sensitive in this area. It is earned increment usually only after fleur d'leis status is achieved, but not always.

28   This is earned increment for the fleur d'leis only because it involves the area that is known as the bones of stesrn. This is technically best explained as working with the full healing of the hocaieah in conjunction with other fleur d'leis to re-create or restructure bones or chakra structures on another fleur d'leis. The bones of stesrn are spiritual "implants" that replace lost bones or bones that have, in some physical/material fashion been damaged broken or are in a state of deterioration that will cause the

individual pain (or is causing the individual pain.) In order for this increment to be earned, the fleur d'leis must remove a bone and replace it with a spiritual bone of stesrn. The individual must believe and accept the replacement in order to feel the relief that can be theirs with an "operation" of this sort. This earned increment is also given if fleur d'leis work together to restructure compromised chakras on another fleur d'leis. The chakras are rebuilt with the help of the shell people. They are "wound" out of the body and captured in the shell and rewound, recreated from the perfect structure of the spiral shell back into the body. This can only be done by fleur d'leis for other fleur d'leis.

29. This is earned increment for fleur d'leis only and it involves remaining steadfast and strong to create a structure for continued work within the home or office. It involves a commitment to creating a sacred place within the home in order to continue to do the universal and healing work. This space may be any size, but it involves a permanent commitment to a sacred area - a sanctuary that is blessed by Spirit.

This falls in the area of family acceptance. Many people, who may give "lip service to universal healing" worry so about family acceptance of the work they must do that they resist "coming out of the closet" by providing a space in the home for the "tools of their healing trade." When this gift is earned, it is earned because they asserted the needs of the universe above the acceptance of family and possibly were forced to explain or "fade the heat" for what might appear bizarre to others. For example, if a pyramidal structure was built in the middle of the family room with stones, divining rods and herbs within - it might cause concern with family members who may not be so spiritually inclined. This is not a small gift nor is it taken lightly because it represents an individual commitment to this work regardless of what others may think or how they may judge.

30 This is earned increment for fleur d'leis and potential fleur d'leis because it represents the gift of defending personal or universal healing and the transformational process to others. It is given when a person "stands up" for their own beliefs regarding physical/emotional and spiritual "housecleaning" in the fleur d'leis universal healing process. It is given when an individual "talks their walk and walks their talk." It is given when an individual defends or asserts their rights to pursue their own paths. It may be given for a very small thing.

Or, in spousal harmony it could be a very large thing; for instance, a wife that telling her husband that she reserves the right to a period of meditation to heal herself (especially if the husband is wont to condemn or attempts to dissuade or forbid the practice.)

It shows a verbal and concrete commitment to self-healing. It is individual "defense" of the right to spirituality - whatever the spirituality is. It is the gift given for assertive behavior and not accepting the judgement or limitations of others because the individual "knows" what they must do for self-healing or spiritual transformation. This again, is not a small "gift" in the society of Earth. It is well understood that the individual takes a "chance" of rejection when they assert their individual rights to their own spiritual path.

31 & 35   This is earned increment for fleur d'leis or potential fleur d'leis who have overcome a personal attachment to being manipulated or manipulating themselves or others with of anger/fear/worry. This person is gifted with a reward for recognizing that they were, perhaps, initiating extremes of responses just to get a reaction or causing trouble for trouble's sake. It may also have been gifted

because the individual would not accept manipulation by someone who gets attention with anger/fear or worry. For instance, not accepting responsibility or feeling guilt or remorse when "mother" lays a guilt trip on you to get her way.

In the emotional chart this area is the area of someone who has a love for anger/fear worry and enjoys being angry/afraid/worried. To overcome or recognize this flaw and attempt to heal oneself of this trait is very, very commendable. It is sometimes given because the individual has recognized that their attachment to being afraid, for example (watching scary movies or negative gory, horror films) is not an acceptable "thrill" to get the adrenalin flowing. It also may be that the person had a need to anger/cause fear or cause worry and no longer needs to get "attention" in such a negative and harmful manner. It is one of the signs of being a universal adult and a great recognition of a hard lesson.

32   This is earned increment for fleur d'leis or potential fleur d'leis who have extended, love, healing and energy to Spirit to heal Spirit. It is a reward for extending "estgii" -spiritual loveforce or spiritual healing force, to the

universe. It is a very remarkable step to understand that Spirit needs the manifestation of healing and energy occasionally and that as a loving, healing person, you have the power to provide that healing to them. It may be granted for universal healing, but more likely it is granted for the mind shift that Spirit can benefit from your healing them! It means that a request came from Spirit for a need they had of you and you listened and responded!

33   This is earned increment for fleur d'leis or potential fleur d'leis because they did not give into emotional blackmail. A lesson of personal accountability and responsibility had to be asserted in some fashion.

This may have involved a "tough love" situation with a child. It may also have been given because the fleur d'leis did not accept personal blame (or "explain away") what was clearly someone else's karma to deal with or accept. To shield people from their karma out of a misguided sense of mothering or protection is harmful to the individual because it sets up a universal set of circumstances that will require the lesson to be learned in a harsher manner. As parents, we do not wish to have our children learn "too harsh" a lesson, too soon. But if the parent continues to shield the child from learning the natural consequences for unacceptable behavior or social disfunction - the lessons for the child will only get harder and harder and may have dire consequences in the future.

The gifts are sometimes given for tiny, little "tests" of will. Each "test" is unique and the individual will never know which situations are designated spiritual tests and trial. The above example is given to show the dynamics of one situation in which an individual may be sorely tested. When tests involve our families - that is the hardest test of all.

34   This is earned increment that fleur d'leis status was granted, a request by Spirit was made to "hear" an acceptance of the fleur d'leis and the individual responded accepting the responsibility that goes along with fleur d'leis status with a full understanding of what it means to be a fleur d'leis. Over this spiral will be the fleur d'leis symbol. It will look like a bird sitting on the index finger tip! This is the blessing of the fleur d'leis and a sign that the person will be undergoing transformational processes in the future. It is a sign too, that the kundalini has risen and

the individual is given wise woman or wise person status.

35 This is earned increment because the individual has transcended fear - the individual has transcended spiritual or cultural upbringing that preyed on fear/worry anger aspects to a more loving and accepting philosophy that sees the truth running in a vein throughout all. This individual has transcended traditional upbringing or cultural/spiritual taboos about looking beyond the "accepted" to a totally humane and individual transformational spirituality. Sometimes this sign is literally a "trial by fire." They may have had to undergo mass rejection by friends, family or church or cult in order to follow their own personal spiritual truths.

The Dance of the Universe

Spirit delights in music - tones and vibrations and movement. Music, song and dance are the healers of the highest and purest order. The universe is music - in a very simple and pure way. Dolphins and whales heal with vibration and tone. One of the most precious gifts we can give Spirit is to dance and/or sing the healing. When we loose ourselves in the music and rhythm and vibration of dance or song - we can feel the treasure of universal ecstasy and pure joy. Spirit joins with us in the dance. Please invite them and visualize them dancing with you. It is a gift to us and to them.

This dance can be done to any record that is close to your heart. It lends itself especially well to Native American beats.

> Within the pyramid - face East and do standing bird movement (flying arms)
> This invites the air, wind beings and winged people.
>
> Face north - invite the four legged with the 1 & 2 movement (feet apart, feet together) no arm movement.

Face west - invite the earth and fire elements with the up and down knee movement.

Face south - invite the soulforce pool, water beings and elementals with the balance movement. Incorporate all or any movements and just enjoy the dance. Use the healing movement for all - healing to all. Fire movement to honor the fire dancers.

Ask your animal guides or teachers to teach you their movements and dance.

Spirit's Closing Blessing

Dance the universe.
Dance the healing.
Be sure to thank Spirit for joining you in the dance!!
Learn well from Everything and Everybody.
Look to the Pure Heart.
The Inner Heart Light Core is the Key to recognizing
        fellow transformational beings.
Find Your visual Guide.
Listen
Show reverence and respect
Be a Teacher
Be a Student
Work with simplicity - Color, Tone, Vibration
Be Open and Balanced
Love Yourself
Love Each Other.

BLESSINGS
MY
CHILDREN

the Soulforce Pool

MESSAGE FROM THE AUTHOR –
JOHAN ADKINS

Blessings to You!

My message is this:
Simplify, unify, purify.
Love, peace, brotherhood, healing, strength and JOY!!
Sing, dance, laugh and be silly.

I would dearly love to hear from you and would like to be able to respond to each one of you who writes to me. Please write to the publishing company, Bon Nuit Publishing, 1740 H Dell Range Blvd.#142, Cheyenne, Wyoming 82009 or go to the blog on the website at http://www.johanadkins.com or you can email me at bonnuitpublishing@johanadkins.com.

If you do not receive a personal or written response, know that if you requested energy or healing from myself or the network, it is forthcoming and please make yourself receptive to it.

Good luck in your spiritual adventure!!

Johan Adkins

www.ingramcontent.com/pod-product-compliance
Lightning Source LLC
Chambersburg PA
CBHW070713160426
43192CB00009B/1176